D1790179

Perspectives on Sino-American Strategic Nuclear Issues

Initiatives in Strategic Studies: Issues and Policies
James J. Wirtz
General Editor

Jeffrey A. Larsen
T.V. Paul
Brad Roberts
James M. Smith
Series Editors

INITIATIVES IN STRATEGIC STUDIES provides a bridge between the use of force or diplomacy and the achievement of political objectives. This series focuses on the topical and timeless issues relating to strategy, including the nexus of political, diplomatic, psychological, economic, cultural, historic, and military affairs. It provides a link between the scholarly and policy communities by serving as the recognized forum for conceptually sophisticated analyses of timely and important strategic issues.

Nuclear Transformation: The New U.S. Nuclear Doctrine
Edited by James J. Wirtz and Jeffrey A. Larsen

Proliferation of Weapons of Mass Destruction in the Middle East: Directions and Policy Options in the New Century
Edited by James A. Russell

The Last Battle of the Cold War: The Deployment and Negotiated Elimination of Intermediate Range Nuclear Forces in Europe
Maynard W. Glitman

Critical Issues Facing the Middle East: Security, Politics and Economics
Edited by James A. Russell

Militarization and War
Julian Schofield

Global Politics of Defense Reform
Edited by Thomas Bruneau and Harold Trinkunas

Perspectives on Sino-American Strategic Nuclear Issues
Edited by Christopher P. Twomey

Perspectives on Sino-American Strategic Nuclear Issues

Edited by Christopher P. Twomey

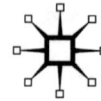

PERSPECTIVES ON SINO-AMERICAN STRATEGIC NUCLEAR ISSUES
Copyright © Christopher P. Twomey, 2008.

All rights reserved.

First published in 2008 by
PALGRAVE MACMILLAN™
175 Fifth Avenue, New York, N.Y. 10010 and
Houndmills, Basingstoke, Hampshire, England RG21 6XS
Companies and representatives throughout the world.

PALGRAVE MACMILLAN is the global academic imprint of the Palgrave Macmillan division of St. Martin's Press, LLC and of Palgrave Macmillan Ltd. Macmillan® is a registered trademark in the United States, United Kingdom and other countries. Palgrave is a registered trademark in the European Union and other countries.

ISBN-13: 978–0–230–60660–9
ISBN-10: 0–230–60660–1

Library of Congress Cataloging-in-Publication Data

   Perspectives on Sino-American strategic nuclear issues / edited by Christopher P. Twomey.
     p. cm.—(Initiatives in strategic studies)
   Includes bibliographical references and index.
     ISBN 0–230–60660–1
     1. Nuclear weapons—Government policy—21st century. 2. East Asia—Strategic aspects. 3. China—Strategic aspects. 4. China—Military policy—21st century. 5. United States—Military policy—21st century. 6. China—Foreign relations—United States. 7. United States—Foreign relations—China. I. Twomey, Christopher P. II. Title. III. Series.

UA10.P46 2007
355.02'170951—dc22
                                                2007047142

A catalogue record for this book is available from the British Library.

Design by Newgen Imaging Systems (P) Ltd., Chennai, India.

First edition: July 2008

10 9 8 7 6 5 4 3 2 1

Printed in the United States of America.

Table of Contents

List of Tables   vii

Acknowledgments   ix

Section I: Theoretic Perspectives on Dangers in Sino-American Strategic Relations

1. Introduction: Dangers and Prospects in Sino-American Strategic Nuclear Relations   3
   Christopher P. Twomey

2. Lessons of the Cuban Missile Crisis for Nuclear Crisis Management and Their Implications for U.S.-Chinese Relations   13
   David A. Welch

Section II: Comparing National Views on Strategic Context, National Security Priorities, and Doctrines

3. The U.S.-China Strategic Relationship   41
   Michael May

4. The Changing Strategic Context of Nuclear Weapons and Implications for the New Nuclear World Order   57
   Major General Pan Zhenqiang (Retired)

5. Confronting Gathering Threats: U.S. Strategic Policy   73
   Michael Nacht

6. China's Nuclear Weapon Policy 87
   Jia Qingguo

7. U.S. Nuclear Posture Review and Beyond: Implications for Sino-American Relations 93
   James J. Wirtz

8. Chinese Nuclear Policy and the Future of Minimum Deterrence 111
   Yao Yunzhu

SECTION III: REGIONAL CHALLENGES AND THREAT REDUCTION POLICIES

9. East Asia's Nuclear Future 127
   Yang Yi

10. Sino-Indian Strategic Relations 137
    Shen Dingli

11. The Challenge of a Nuclear North Korea 153
    Scott Snyder

12. Chinese Arms Control and Nonproliferation Policy 173
    Gu Guoliang

13. Arms Control and Sino-U.S. Strategic Stability 185
    Brad Roberts

14. Comparing Perspectives: Dangers to Avoid, Prospects to Develop 201
    Christopher P. Twomey

List of Contributors 211

Index 215

List of Tables

2.1 Generic Challenges of Nuclear
    Crisis Management   21
2.2 Illustrative Cuban Missile Crisis
    Management Pathologies (United States)   22
2.3 Illustrative Cuban Missile Crisis
    Management Pathologies (USSR)   23
2.4 Potential Crisis Management
    Pathologies: Hypothetical Future
    Taiwan Strait Crisis (United States)   28
2.5 Political Crisis Management Challenges:
    Hypothetical Future Taiwan Strait Crisis (PRC)   29
11.1 Estimates of North Korea's Possible
    Nuclear Stockpile   159

Acknowledgments

The United States and China share many interests in the twenty-first century. They are also the two most important great powers in Asia today, and this raises the potential for competition between them. Should such competition occur, nuclear issues will serve as a backdrop for all other security areas. This book squarely examines those issues. If Sino-American security competition in Asia intensifies—by no means likely, and certainly an outcome detrimental to both sides—it will behoove all sides to understand the nature of the nuclear and strategic dynamics between them.

At the broadest level, a deeper understanding of each side's threat perceptions can reduce misperceptions about the sources of security policy in the other capital. More narrowly, increasing our understanding of crisis dynamics, red lines, and potential for escalation can lead to stability in the unfortunate instance of any militarized crisis between the two.

The Advanced Systems and Concepts Office at the U.S. Defense Threat Reduction Agency presciently supported this book financially. That office's support of the broader project from which these chapters emanate—the U.S.-China Strategic Dialogue—has produced not only this volume but also funded annual conferences between the authors and other analysts and scholars on this topic, which is entering its fourth year. The contributions of Dr. Michael Wheeler, Dr. Kerry Kartchner, Michael Urena, and in particular, David Hamon of that office have been irreplaceable.

Any suchbook also depends on the contributions of numerous others in the editorial process. The editor would like to express appreciation for the work of Dr. Jeffery Larsen, and he is indebted to Kali Shelor for her diligence in bringing the manuscript to closure and compiling a through index. Dr. Peter Lavoy and Professor James Wirtz provided sound guidance from the earliest conception of the manuscript and through to its final structuring. Toby Wahl at Palgrave Macmillan recognized the importance of the topic at an early date. All their contributions have helped to improve the final manuscript significantly.

It is the editor's sincerest hope that the issues raised in this book will decline in importance over time, and that the prospects for cooperation assessed in some of the chapters will overwhelm the dangers highlighted in others. If this book increases our understanding of these issues in even a small way on their way to obsolescence, then its contribution would be beyond the highest aspirations of the editor.

Monterey, California, 2007

Section I
Theoretic Perspectives on Dangers in Sino-American Strategic Relations

1

DANGERS AND PROSPECTS IN SINO-AMERICAN STRATEGIC NUCLEAR RELATIONS

Christopher P. Twomey

Sino-American nuclear relations have the appearance of a deep, abiding stability. There is no overt arms race between the People's Republic of China and the United States, and since 1998 they have maintained an agreement not to target their nuclear weapons at each other. The two sides cooperate on important counterproliferation policies, such as the Six-Party Talks that address the North Korean nuclear program. Their militaries also have participated in a number of joint exercises in the past year.
 This Panglossian view, however, conceals great potential for a more problematic relationship. Even restricting one's focus to strategic matters, there are grounds for concern: both China and the United States are in the midst of extensive modernization of their strategic forces. As their forces shift in quantity and quality, fundamental vulnerabilities may threaten the survivability of their strategic arsenals. Furthermore, possible substantive conflicts of interest over Taiwan, North Korea, Japan, or other parts of East Asia make the basic diplomatic relationship between the two great powers potentially contentious. Shifts in strategic dynamics beyond the bilateral relationship complicate what might have appeared to be a simple Sino-American strategic calculus. For these three reasons, a deep understanding of the nature of the strategic nuclear relationship between Beijing and Washington is critical.

This volume brings a unique perspective to this set of issues. Its contributors, analysts and scholars from both China and the United States, have long been involved in strategic issues in their respective countries. The authors hail from the People's Liberation Army (both active and retired), universities from both countries, and policy-focused think tanks. The volume is structured around paired, national perspectives on contemporary nuclear issues, including perceptions of strategic context, national security priorities, doctrines, perceptions of regional threats, and strategies to address these dangers.

This chapter briefly surveys the overall importance of Sino-American nuclear issues and some of the recent changes in the global strategic situation. It begins with a discussion of the dangers posed by strategic nuclear weapons in Sino-American relations before highlighting other substantive issues that bear on the nuclear relationship (Taiwan, Japan, etc.). It then discusses the shift in the global nuclear environment since the end of the cold war and concludes with a roadmap of the rest of the volume.

DANGERS IN SINO-AMERICAN NUCLEAR AFFAIRS

Despite the contemporary attention commanded by the Middle East and terrorism, the nuclear relationship between the United States and China is one of the most important international security issues today. Chinese military spending has increased, on average, 15 percent a year over the past decade. Its nuclear arsenal is being modernized and will soon include road-mobile missiles capable of being launched within minutes of warning, a viable nuclear-missile-carrying submarine force, and likely multiple-warhead-bearing missiles. Chinese conventional missiles have achieved increased accuracy in recent years, and it seems likely that the same can be said of its nuclear-armed missiles. China has recently conducted two successful tests against satellites: one was a laser illumination of an American intelligence satellite and the other a kinetic destruction of a Chinese weather satellite.[1] In its most recent annual report on Chinese military power, the U.S. Department of Defense has for the first time emphasized a number of destabilizing trends in Chinese nuclear force posture and doctrine.[2]

On its part, the United States is qualitatively upgrading its existing arsenal even as its overall numbers shrink. Under the provisions of the Moscow Treaty, the United States is gradually drawing its arsenal down to no more than 2,200 deployed strategic warheads by 2012.

Nevertheless, it is also engaged in a number of modernization efforts, leading some analysts to conclude, "ambitious plans have emerged to design, develop, and deploy a new generation of nuclear warheads and to acquire new ballistic missiles, submarines, and bombers."[3] Certainly, the United States has updated its submarine launched ballistic missiles (to the Trident II D-5 model) and upgraded the warheads on its Minuteman III land-based missiles. Further, Washington is planning to develop a conventional arsenal capable of engaging in strategic missions and is deploying a missile defense system with increasing numbers of interceptors. As highlighted in one recent, prominent analysis, this modernization program can be construed as giving Washington unprecedented offensive options, even against a large Russian force.[4] The Chinese strategic arsenal is an order of magnitude smaller than Moscow's and has a much less diverse pattern of deployment, both of which deepen its potential vulnerability.

As described by Lieber and Press, this situation can present two broad problems.[5] First, there are potential dangers if a crisis was to break out and China feared for the security of its own arsenal. These scholars warn of dangers if Beijing "feel[s] pressure[d] to alert its small intercontinental ballistic missile (ICBM) force either to signal China's resolve or to (slightly) reduce the vulnerability of its arsenal." To facilitate quick response in a crisis, thereby reducing its arsenal's vulnerability, China might mate its warheads with its missiles or pre-delegate the authority to launch China's arsenal.[6] Another strategy would be to surge its poorly trained, poorly controlled SSBN (nuclear-powered submarine carrying ballistic missiles) to sea. All of these raise important command and control problems for Beijing that have not, as far as outsiders know, been thoroughly addressed in Beijing.[7] Other possible Chinese responses are also problematic: fuelling liquid-fueled missiles increases their readiness for a brief period, but it opens a larger window of vulnerability shortly thereafter when the fuel must be removed and the missiles serviced.

A second set of dangers stems from the potential responses China might choose to take to rectify the nuclear imbalance. While the modernization discussed above is significant, it is far from an all-out mobilization program. Such a response might include substantial quantitative buildups, development and implementation of a launch-on-warning doctrine, or deployment of more significant long-range attack SSN capabilities. All of these programs run counter to American interests, and in each case it is likely that U.S. policymakers would respond to a perceived provocation, leading to a more tightly coupled arms race between the two countries.[8]

The existing Chinese modernization program already poses a number of important problems. While data is exceedingly scarce, it seems that Beijing will move toward a land force of ballistic missiles armed with multiple warheads. In the cold war, such a force was regarded as relatively destabilizing due to the high exchange ratio of defender warheads destroyed per attacker warheads expended, thus providing the incentive for a first strike.[9] Further, the accuracy improvements of China's strategic arsenal—regardless of whether they were originally developed for shorter range, conventional forces for Taiwan scenarios—also enhance its utility in a counterforce strike that might be used in an attempt at crisis limitation.[10] The acute vulnerability of China's arsenal to date has led to the ability of the United States to possess escalation dominance at every single step of an escalatory ladder in possible Taiwan scenarios, reducing the prospect of inadvertent escalation.[11] As China's modernization program continues, dangerous uncertainties regarding crisis behavior could emerge as both Washington and Beijing jockey for position in an intense conventional fight.

To be clear, the parallel modernization programs are not tightly coupled in a way that might accurately be described as an arms race today. However, there are signs that the relatively benign Sino-American strategic relationship is changing. Already, some analysts have concluded that American modernization efforts have been made primarily with the Chinese in mind: "we believe that America's drive for nuclear primacy is primarily driven by concerns about future relations with China, rather than Russia."[12] As shown in several chapters in this volume, Chinese analysts noted with deep concern the leaked portions of the 2001 Nuclear Posture Review that pertained to China and a Taiwan scenario. It is clear that China's modernization of its long-range forces is being done with the United States in mind: facing either India or Russia (nor its nonnuclear armed potential rival Japan) requires an ICBM-based force. Nevertheless, the interaction between the Sino-American competition and these other factors is a theme that other authors address in chapters 9 and 10 of this volume.

Future Chinese and U.S. weapons development programs suggest an increased coupling in military modernization efforts on both sides of the Pacific. China's recent moves in the anti-space realm have deep implications for the United States. Cuing data for the national missile defense system comes primarily from the Defense Support Program satellite constellation today and will be from the Space Based Infrared System network in the future. Both these satellite systems are in geostationary orbits[13] and so are far out of range of the tested Chinese antisatellite (ASAT) systems. Rather, the Chinese ASAT tests would be relevant against intelligence systems of higher resolution that are useful for identifying missile silos (as well as conventional forces). China's ASAT program could be an attempt to enhance their ability to blind American assets used to target China's strategic arsenal (although the ASAT capability would also have substantial utility in the context of conventional conflicts). On the other hand, few target sets require the U.S. Strategic Command's global strike capabilities other than those in China.[14]

Thus, the potential of each side's conventional and strategic modernization programs to threaten the others' strategic forces is substantial. This raises the prospect for a tightly coupled nuclear arms race, one in which each side's action leads to a rapid and explicitly responsive reaction by the other. Such arms races can accelerate rapidly and intensely. These dangers are particularly grave in the context of underlying political competition between the two sides; the next section surveys some of the most pronounced dangers in that regard.

POTENTIAL SUBSTANTIVE DANGERS IN SINO-AMERICAN RELATIONS

While it is hard to imagine a conflict of interest that might escalate to violence between the United States and Russia (the second largest nuclear power in the world today), such areas are abundant in Sino-American relations. North Korea was the site of the last major war between the two Pacific powers, and that country remains deeply unstable today (despite ongoing multilateral diplomacy). If—due to conflict over Pyongyang's nuclear program or due to state collapse—there is a military conflict on the Korean Peninsula, it is likely that Chinese and American military forces will be operating in close proximity using wartime rules of engagement. It is unclear how each side would view the prospect of the other's forces being deployed in North Korea.

Taiwan is an even more contested issue. For some analysts, it represents a direct and fundamental conflict of interests between the two countries: the United States may have an interest in its continued separation from the mainland, and China clearly asserts an interest in reunification. Others see Taiwan as an important area of overlapping interest, with the avoidance of military conflict being high on each side's prioritization of interests. Yet, even for such optimistic analysts, Taipei is a third actor with its own evolving political system and increasingly vibrant nationalism that poses substantial dangers to bilateral Sino-American stability. Both Beijing and Washington often express a degree of confidence that the (nonnuclear) balance in the Taiwan Strait favors their own side. One side has to be wrong, and this suggests that dangerous dynamics might emerge in the context of a conventional conflict that causes unexpected defeat on one side. The use of nuclear threats or weapons as a wildcard to remedy failures of conventional forces is exceedingly worrisome and has already been alluded to by Chinese military leaders.[15]

The United States has a longstanding mutual security treaty with Japan—a country with territorial disputes and nationalist passions aimed at China. The ebbs and flows of Japanese domestic politics notwithstanding, there has been a steady move by Japan toward an increasingly assertive role on regional and global security issues.[16] Even without exogenous conflicts of interest, this could be a dangerous situation as the two sides' conventional forces increasingly stretch their reach and build up their capabilities. The recent erosion of the nuclear taboo in Japanese domestic debates bodes poorly for strategic stability between the two Asian powers as well.

Finally, the South China Sea, Central Asia, Indochina, and potentially South Asia are other areas that maintain possible seeds for Sino-American friction. In each case, the United States has strong, although often dynamic, relations with various regional players. China is likely to contest these relationships as Beijing's power continues to grow.[17]

Clearly, conventional conflict does not appear imminent over any of these issues. But all are contentious, and all depend on the complex interaction of domestic politics of a third—or fourth, or even fifth—polity (again, a theme of several chapters in this volume). Conflict, were it to break out in any of these circumstances, would certainly begin with only conventional forces. Yet, the dynamics of escalation are not well understood, particularly in the context of highly destructive conventional war between nuclear-armed great powers. Thus, it is critical to understand the nuclear backdrop to the Sino-American relationship.

Changes in the Global Nuclear Environment

Since the end of the cold war, traditional concerns about nuclear deterrence among established powers have not disappeared but rather have grown more complex. This too emphasizes the importance of deepening our understanding of Sino-American dynamics in this arena. Three changes are briefly highlighted here: proliferation, nuclear multipolarity, and qualitative changes away from purely offensive nuclear forces.

Beyond the modernization of the Chinese and American nuclear arsenals discussed above, the stabilization of the Russian drawdown, the North Korean nuclear test, and increasingly robust force deployments in South Asia have increased the number of players in the new strategic environment. (Any future nuclear developments in Japan would only further complicate this picture.) All of these factors affect the balance in Northeast Asia. The proliferation spiral in South Asia has paused, but such a status is unlikely to be permanent. Iran's program continues to move forward and, if successful, would link strategic interaction in South Asia and the Middle East. Further, the development of viable South Asian arsenals has done nothing to stabilize conventional conflicts there, contrary to the expectations of proliferation optimists.[18]

The reactions to North Korean proliferation are just beginning, but they have already led to a marked shift in Japanese views on missile defense systems, overturning decades of opposition to exporting military technology and integrated joint operations with the United States. Of course, factors that are both indigenous and external to Japan will determine the long-run effect of these changing views and whether they shall presage a true shift in Japanese policy in this regard. At the very least, the United States has already been obliged to reassert the efficacy of its extended deterrent commitment to Japan.[19]

This proliferation adds complexity to the nuclear arena today and promises continued change. Soon, nuclear relations will be conceived of not in bilateral terms for most conflict scenarios, but rather nuclear multipolarity will be the central analytic framework. For a nation considering nuclear use, not only will it have to evaluate its ability to control escalation within a particular bilateral conflict but also consider its ability to face additional adversaries later. In the end, states will have to size their arsenals such that they can deter multiple actors sequentially or engage in warfighting in several directions. This will put upward pressure on arsenal sizes and complicate any tacit or explicit arms control. During crises, states will have to be concerned about their vulnerability to multiple actors. For instance, medium-ranged systems moved to face one adversary may create vulnerabilities to threat from a second adversary. Similarly, surging submarines in a time of crisis against one adversary creates a longer period of lower readiness after a crisis against other rivals (who have not similarly stressed their strategic systems to confront a crisis). All of these factors are new to the twenty-first century.

Finally, strategic nuclear dynamics in the cold war were rather simple—only offensive nuclear forces faced each other. For several reasons, primarily due to developments on the U.S. side, that is no longer the case. Progress toward achieving the objectives outlined in the Nuclear Posture Review, especially the emergence of conventional global strike capabilities and missile defense, have enriched U.S. strategic capabilities substantially. Russian research in ballistic missile defense is also ongoing. Space is a critical arena for many aspects of the strategic equation: warning, targeting, control of missile defense, and so on. The Chinese ASAT test emphasized to all sides that space is not a sanctuary.

Thus, today, rather than considering the relative sizes of two similarly structured arsenals, or the potential for each of two sides to dominate different levels of escalation with similar nuclear weapons, the situation is much more complex. Offensive nuclear forces must be evaluated in the context of defensive capabilities as well as comparing arsenal size. Attacks on nuclear forces with accurate, long-range conventional forces will erode the clarity of the "nuclear threshold." Satellites today are a critical piece of military infrastructure for nuclear forces, other strategic forces, and of course for high-end U.S. conventional capabilities. Military conflict in space will increase tension for rapid escalation. Lines between strategic and conventional conflict have blurred, and assessing the balance in the former realm has become much more complex.

The implications of these changes are tremendous for strategic dynamics among established powers, emerging nuclear weapons states, and client states dependent on the extended deterrence of the great powers for their security. More actors interact in an increasingly complex environment, and the trend in quantity and complexity is rising. This backdrop alone, aside from the specific points raised above regarding China and the United States, demands additional attention to the nuclear relationship between Beijing and Washington.

SUMMARY OF THE VOLUME'S CONTENTS

The book is divided into three sections to enrich our understanding of these dynamics. In the first section, this chapter has outlined the dangers of the contemporary nuclear environment compared to the previous eras, and the next chapter raises specific concerns regarding crisis management and stability that might pertain to Sino-American relations. The second section turns to a series of paired studies of Chinese and American approaches to their strategic relationship, national security priorities, and nuclear doctrines. The final section addresses different perceptions of regional threats and includes paired chapters on strategic approaches to address these dangers. The last chapter concludes and summarizes the key findings of all these chapters and draws together the lessons from the different perspectives in them.

Notes

1. Vago Muradian, "China Attempted to Blind U.S. Satellites with Laser," *Defense News*, September 22, 2006; Joseph Kahn, "China Confirms Test of Anti-Satellite Weapon," *New York Times*, January 23, 2007.
2. Office of the Secretary of Defense, "Military Power of the People's Republic of China: Annual Report to Congress" (Washington, DC: Department of Defense, 2006).
3. Robert S. Norris and Hans M. Kristensen, "U.S. Nuclear Forces," *The Atomic Bulletin* 63, no. 1 (2007).
4. Keir A. Lieber and Daryl G. Press, "The End of Mad? The Nuclear Dimension of U.S. Primacy," *International Security* 30, no. 4 (2006).
5. Keir A. Lieber and Daryl G. Press, "U.S. Nuclear Primacy and the Future of the Chinese Deterrent," *China Security*, no. 5 (2007). Lieber and Press also note the potential for one positive result from the perspective of U.S. policymakers: coercive power that would come from dominating the nuclear escalatory ladder.
6. Both the quote and the two points listed here are from Ibid., 67.
7. Typically, Chinese assurances on the command and control issue, and on unauthorized launch more generally, boil down to an emphasis on the military's fealty to the political leadership of the Chinese Communist Party and highlighting that the warheads are stored separately from the launch vehicles. The latter point would be changed in the scenarios suggested above, and the former is called into question by such scholarship as Andrew Scobell, "China's Evolving Civil-Military Relations: Creeping *Guojiahua*," *Armed Forces & Society* 31, no. 5 (2005).
8. That is, a situation in which each side's action provokes a rapid and directly focused response.
9. William C. Potter, "Coping with MIRV in a Mad World," *The Journal of Conflict Resolution* 22, no. 4 (1978).
10. Given the overall size of the arsenal, it is unlikely that an "escalation dominance" strategy could be pursued with this small force.

11. Herman Kahn, *On Escalation: Metaphors and Scenarios* (New York: Praeger, 1965).
12. Lieber and Press, "U.S. Nuclear Primacy."
13. The latter will include some elliptical orbits.
14. Standoff cruise missile can reach the vast majority of time-sensitive targets globally, requiring only the offshore deployment of a submarine or nearby deployment of a heavy bomber. In contrast, a number of Chinese targets could be usefully targeted by a conventional, deeply penetrating missile: e.g., space launch facilities, etc.
15. The context of statements by both Maj. General Zhu Chenghu and Lt. General Xiong Guankai make clear that escalation from a Taiwan scenario underlay their nuclear saber rattling. See Office of the Secretary of Defense, "Military Power of the People's Republic of China: Annual Report to Congress" (Washington, DC: Department of Defense, 2006).
16. David Arase, "Japan, the Active State? Security Policy After 9/11," *Asian Survey* 47, no. 4 (2007).
17. For instance, see the Chinese role in securing the Shanghai Cooperation Organization's criticism of the U.S.'s role in Central Asia in 2005.
18. Regarding the lack of a stabilizing role for nuclear weapons in recent conventional conflicts, see Peter R. Lavoy, "Pakistan's Nuclear Posture: Security and Survivability" (**Washington, DC**: Nonproliferation Policy Education Center, 2007). For the most famous statement of optimism regarding proliferation, see Kenneth Waltz's contributions in Scott Douglas Sagan and Kenneth Neal Waltz, *The Spread of Nuclear Weapons: A Debate Renewed*, 2nd ed. (New York: Norton, 2003).
19. Thom Shanker and Norimitsu Onishi, "Japan Assures Rice That It Has No Nuclear Intentions," *New York Times*, October 19, 2006.

2

LESSONS OF THE CUBAN MISSILE CRISIS FOR NUCLEAR CRISIS MANAGEMENT AND THEIR IMPLICATIONS FOR U.S.-CHINESE RELATIONS

David A. Welch

> I don't think the Cuban missile crisis was unique. The Bay of Pigs, Berlin in '61, Cuba, later events in the Middle East, in Libya, and so on—all exhibit the truth of what I'll call "McNamara's Law," which states, "It is impossible to predict with a high degree of confidence what the effects of the use of military force will be because of the risks of accident, miscalculation, misperception, and inadvertence." In my opinion, this law ought to be inscribed above all the doorways in the White House and the Pentagon, and it is the overwhelming lesson of the Cuban missile crisis. "Managing" crises is the wrong term; you don't "manage" them because you can't "manage" them.
> —Robert S. McNamara[1]

In December 2006, Chinese President Hu Jintao called for the building of a strong, modern navy. Hu declared that Chinese territory included "a large sea area," and stressed that a powerful navy was "of vital importance in defending state interests and safeguarding national sovereignty and security."[2] Hu no doubt had in mind China's persistent territorial disputes with its neighbors over the Spratlys and Paracels, and with Japan over the Senkaku/Diaoyutai Islands; but by far and away China's most pressing "territorial" dispute is over the status of Taiwan. Beijing evidently thinks its hand would be strengthened in a possible future confrontation with Taipei and Washington if it wielded greater maritime power.

A belief in the utility of military force for the pursuit of diplomatic objectives would hardly be exceptional; indeed, many would consider it commonsensical. Still, relatively few policymakers are sensitive to the dangers of a misplaced faith in military tools. Students of crisis and war will know that statesmen stumble into disaster more frequently as a result of overconfidence than of skittishness, of too much rather than too little faith in the utility of force. How can policymakers guard against this danger? How can they arrive at an appropriately nuanced understanding?

One way—perhaps an unavoidable way, certainly an intuitive way, and potentially a very valuable way—is to learn from history. But drawing valid "lessons" from past events is a difficult business.[3] History rarely repeats itself exactly, and situations that are similar in certain important respects are usually dissimilar in others. It is even difficult to identify similarities and dissimilarities, and to distinguish the relevant features of past events from the irrelevant ones, because these are judgment calls that are susceptible to a wide range of perceptual biases. It may be true, as George Santayana once put it, that "[t]hose who cannot remember the past are condemned to repeat it," but remembering the past is certainly no guarantee against error.

Since it is natural and inevitable that people *do* and *will* draw lessons from history, it is important for us to try to discipline the enterprise as much as possible while bearing in mind its inherent difficulties and dangers. The first task is to identify appropriate antecedents. What prior events share the crucial features of the current or future situation that we seek to understand? What is it that they share? How do they differ? Do the differences render the comparison meaningless or misleading?

The second task is to explore the antecedents. Why did things work out well or badly? How could they have worked out better? What mistakes or pathologies were evident that we have good reason to suspect might be problematic once again? What is our "good reason" for suspecting this?

The final task is to draw the appropriate parallels. How do the crucial dynamics map from the past to the present or the future? What adjustments must we make as we try to recontextualize what we have abstracted from prior events? What opportunities can we see? What perils and pitfalls should we particularly seek to avoid?

In this chapter I attempt to illustrate these three tasks by making the case that the Cuban missile crisis holds valuable lessons for nuclear crisis management in general, and for a future hypothetical Taiwan Strait crisis in particular. I will also suggest that Robert McNamara is entirely correct: crisis "management" is a misleading and inappropriate term because it connotes a degree of control that leaders cannot reasonably expect to enjoy. We do not "manage" nuclear crises so much as weather them. We can weather them well, or weather them ill. This, I submit, is the most important lesson of all.

ARE NUCLEAR CRISES DISTINCTIVE?

Any time two nuclear-armed countries confront each other there is a possibility of escalation to nuclear war. This would certainly be true of a U.S.-Chinese confrontation in the Straits of Taiwan, widely considered one of the most dangerous flashpoints in the world precisely because of this risk. Most observers agree that the event most likely to trigger a serious U.S.-Chinese crisis would be a Taiwanese unilateral declaration of independence (UDI). Both the People's Republic of China (PRC) and the United States of America are strategic nuclear powers, and while there are gross asymmetries in their nuclear capabilities, in a serious shooting war each side would be capable of inflicting enormous destruction on the other.

The possibility of a crisis escalating to strategic nuclear war is what makes it a "nuclear crisis," and many analysts would insist that nuclear crises differ in kind from nonnuclear crises for one crucial reason: namely, both sides have little difficulty imagining in advance the worst possible outcome. Joseph Nye has characterized this as the functional equivalent of possessing a crystal ball, and what he calls the "Crystal Ball Effect" is supposed to induce great caution, particularly under conditions of Mutual Assured Destruction (MAD).[4] It is easy to imagine, for instance, that European leaders in the summer of 1914 would have exerted much greater effort to avoid a general war if they had genuine second strike nuclear capability and if they knew that everyone else also had this capability. It is primarily the induced caution of the Crystal Ball Effect that leads "Proliferation Optimists" to argue that a world full of nuclear powers could conceivably be both safer and more peaceful.[5]

Whether nuclear crises differ in kind or in degree is a debatable point. Any sane leader will know that war involves destruction, and the capacity to inflict destruction varies on a sliding scale. MAD is merely the limiting case where, for all intents and purposes, the shadow of the future disappears. Whether Proliferation Optimists are correct about the pacifist implications of the Crystal Ball Effect is also a matter of debate and turns crucially on whether leaders exhibit the kind and degree of rationality, and can maintain the integrity of the chain of command and control, that Optimists assume.[6] The arguments on both sides of the issue tend to be heavily deductive, precisely because there are so few empirical cases of serious nuclear crises.

Exactly how many cases are there? Nuclear-armed superpowers have only engaged in organized, energetic direct combat once: in 1969, when the Soviet Union and the PRC fought a series of sharp skirmishes along the Ussuri and Amur rivers in the course of an ongoing border dispute.[7] China's nuclear capability at the time was relatively meager, however, and it is doubtful that a condition of MAD obtained.[8] The same can be said of the conflict between newly nuclear India and Pakistan in the Kargil region of Kashmir in 1999. The 1973 Middle East crisis certainly occurred under a condition of MAD, but did not involve direct hostilities between the United States and the Soviet Union, who engaged in little more than ineffective signaling.[9] The Correlates of War Project's Militarized Interstate Disputes dataset includes only twenty-nine fatal or possibly fatal events involving the use of force with nuclear-armed countries on opposite sides of the issue, most of which were relatively minor incidents easily taken in stride, such as the 2000 Hainan Island EP-3 incident.[10]

The Cuban missile crisis of 1962 was the only nuclear crisis in which the participants themselves perceived a serious and immediate danger of strategic thermonuclear war. Had such a war occurred, it almost certainly would have resulted in the destruction of the Soviet Union as a functioning society. Notwithstanding the United States' enormous advantage in deliverable nuclear weapons at the time, tens of millions of Americans would probably have died as well. There is general agreement that the episode represented the closest the world has ever come to World War III. It is also, for this reason, the most closely studied and best understood cold war event. For these reasons, and in the interest of space, I will confine my analysis to this pivotal, archetypal event—for if it is impossible to draw valid general lessons from this episode, it is doubtful that we could draw them from any.

The Genesis and "Management" of the Cuban Missile Crisis

It is important to note that the Cuban missile crisis was a crisis that no one expected or wanted.[11] The Kennedy Administration did not anticipate it because no one could imagine that Soviet premier Nikita Khrushchev would be so foolish as to attempt a covert deployment of strategic nuclear weapons in a traditional American sphere of interest, let alone in America's backyard. For his part, Nikita Khrushchev did not anticipate it because he believed, in part through wishful thinking, that he could deploy operational strategic nuclear weapons in Cuba without the United States discovering them, whereupon it would be too late (so he felt) for the United States to object. Moreover, he was confident that the world, if not the Kennedy Administration, would appreciate the symmetry he perceived between a deployment of Soviet strategic nuclear missiles to Cuba and the deployment of American strategic nuclear weapons to Turkey.[12] It is now apparent that these misperceptions and misjudgments had a variety of causes—so many, in fact, that we might well be tempted to describe them as overdetermined. They were the product of incompatible and incommensurable historical frames, rampant mirror imaging, the error on both sides of assuming the transparency and defensiveness of one's own motives, and mutual demonization. The result was that both sides interpreted defensively motivated actions as hostile, eliciting responses that each interpreted as aggressive, opportunistic challenges, generating an escalating spiral of hostility. President Kennedy's ostentatious display of U.S. military might in the Caribbean provoked precisely what it was intended to deter: a major Soviet military deployment in Cuba. Khrushchev's desperate attempt to shore up his strategic nuclear inferiority, and to safeguard Cuba from the American invasion that he (wrongly) considered inevitable, led him to grasp at the straw of a secret nuclear deployment, which came perilously close to triggering American military action precisely of the kind his gambit was meant to prevent. Ham-fisted attempts at mutual deterrence, in other words, backfired. It is important to recognize that nuclear weapons did not prevent a crisis in this case: to the contrary, they precipitated it. There would have been no Cuban missile crisis in the absence of strategic nuclear weapons.

Perhaps the most striking feature of the Cuban missile crisis is the contrast between the quality of Kennedy's and Khrushchev's decision-making prior to and during the event. While each was guilty of a long list of errors in perception, judgment, and inference that led them into the most dangerous confrontation of the nuclear age, they performed remarkably well in extricating themselves from a predicament of their own making. The successful peaceful resolution of the crisis was made possible by four crucial factors: (1) an ability to deliberate privately, out of the public spotlight and relatively immune from political or bureaucratic pressures; (2) an absence of externally imposed time pressures; (3) a gradually increasing appreciation by both sides of the dangers of accident, inadvertence, and breakdowns in command and control; and (4) the entirely fortuitous fact that during the public phase of the crisis, misperceptions broke in the right direction—that is, they inclined both sides toward settlement rather than rigidity.[13] At the denouement, the "management" of the Cuban missile crisis was as much a task of Kennedy and Khrushchev managing their own militaries and preventing things from spinning out of control as it was a task of bargaining or persuading each other to settle. The world owes an enormous debt of gratitude to these two leaders for their ability to learn the dangers of nuclear crisis management on the fly—lessons they were able to learn in large part because of the shock of stumbling into the crisis, which exposed the misplaced self-confidence and wishful thinking that got them there in the first place.

Crisis "Management" Tasks

The first and most important task for managing any crisis is, of course, anticipating it, and, if possible, forestalling it. As we now know well, this was a task at which both Kennedy and Khrushchev performed poorly. Once in a crisis, however—for whatever reason—a leader must accomplish six additional tasks:

1. Diagnosing the problem (deciphering the adversary's motives and intentions, for the purpose of identifying possibly acceptable peaceful outcomes);
2. Identifying options (that is, plausible means for the attainment of national objectives that do not run undue risks of catastrophic escalation);
3. Evaluating options (determining which of the available options offers the best chance of securing national goals without undue risk);
4. Making the right choices (preferably those that avoid war without sacrificing core objectives);

5. Trying to keep matters from spinning out of control during the crisis;
6. Implementing a durable settlement once a solution is found.

Since crises are dynamic events with unpredictable turns and twists, policymakers must constantly monitor, update, and occasionally quite radically revise their judgments. Hence these tasks do not represent a simple and linear to-do list. The first four may be iterated at any decision point and are equally important in the precrisis phase, where policymakers seek to anticipate their protagonists' behavior and forestall anything untoward (primarily through deterrent signals or other forms of communication); in the acute crisis phase, where policymakers must choose a response (which may well require bargaining with the adversary); and in the postcrisis phase, where policymakers attempt to step back from the brink and put in place measures intended to prevent a recurrence (see figure 2.1).

In attempting to accomplish these tasks, a leader faces at least three sets of challenges. The first set comprises *cultural* obstacles to crisis management, such as culturally specific values, norms, styles of decision-making or action, and culturally specific concepts that shape goals, perceptions, modes of interaction, and acceptable outcomes

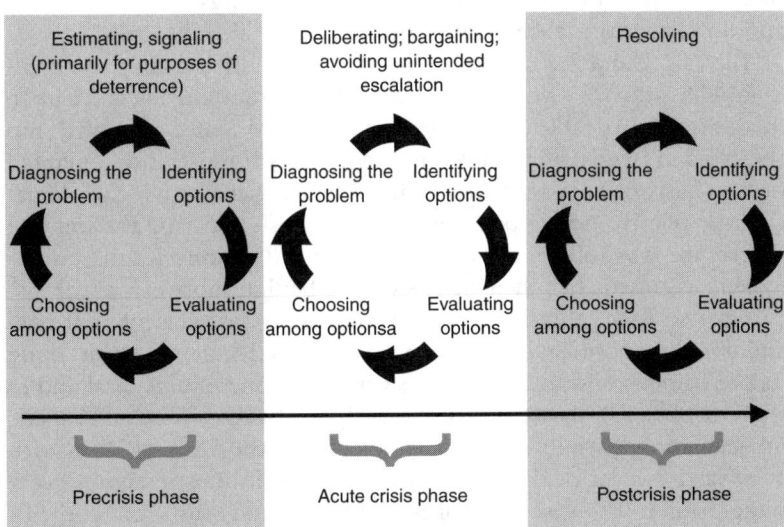

Figure 2.1 Crisis phases and management tasks

(many of which will be largely unintelligible to adversaries who do not share cultural lenses and who will be tempted to dismiss or discount culturally relative values). The second set consists of *psychological* challenges that include typically human and idiosyncratic limits on the ability to absorb and process information, or to make appropriate choices. These limits are both *cognitive*—having to do with the ways in which normal human beings simplify, edit, and process information to make sense of a confusing and ambiguous world—and *motivational*, a category of challenges rooted in the natural aversion people have to stress and to the psychological pain of having to admit error or accept responsibility for costly mistakes.[14] Finally, the third set comprises *organizational* challenges. These include pathologies in the collection, processing, or exploitation of information that stem from the sheer number of players involved in crisis management, how they function as organizations, and how they interact with each other. Organizational culture, organizational structure and complexity, and organizational routines (e.g., Standard Operating Procedures, or SOPs) all represent potential obstacles to information flows.

At the risk of some oversimplification, we might usefully identify particular important generic subtypes of these challenges that confront decision-makers at various phases of any serious international crisis (see table 2.1). In tables 2.2 and 2.3 respectively, I offer simplified summaries of the corresponding shortcomings of the American and Soviet performance during the Cuban missile crisis itself.

Tables 2.2 and 2.3 capture quite starkly the difference in the quality of U.S. and Soviet decision-making prior to and during the Cuban missile crisis. As table 2.2 suggests, the United States stumbled into the crisis in large part because the Kennedy Administration operated on the basis of an essentially "realist" world view, in which calculations of relative power predominated and assumed that the logic of deterrence was more or less universally valid.[15] American decision-makers assumed that their defensive and benign motives were transparent and that others could not fail to appreciate the international and domestic political importance to the United States of maintaining its preeminent position in the Western Hemisphere in general and in the Caribbean in particular. The largely unchallenged belief that the Soviet Union "would not dare" to challenge the United States with a forward nuclear deployment informed American estimates at every stage prior to the discovery of Soviet missiles in Cuba and contributed to the underestimation of the concomitant risk.[16] Interestingly, given the prevailing American image of Soviets as conniving and

Table 2.1 Generic Challenges of Nuclear Crisis Management

Task	Cultural challenges	Psychological challenges	Organizational challenges
Precrisis			
Anticipating, estimating, signaling	• Transcending parochial strategic concepts	• Avoiding mirror imaging (lack of empathy) • Avoiding overconfidence (lack of circumspection) • Noticing relevant signals	• Collecting information • Processing information • Moving information through the system
Crisis			
Deliberating, bargaining	• Transcending parochial styles of decision making, communication, and negotiation	• Searching for options and information adequately • Evaluating options adequately • Avoiding Groupthink/premature closure • Avoiding cognitive traps • Managing stress	• Communicating internally • Communicating externally • Managing competing bureaucratic interests • Finding adequate expertise • Maintaining central control
Avoiding unintended escalation	• Coping with escalatory tendencies in strategic culture • Maintaining civilian control	• Avoiding mirror imaging • Avoiding overconfidence • Correctly estimating adversary's resolve • Being aware of command, control, communications, and intelligence (C^3I) challenges • Avoiding premature judgment that war is inevitable or has started	• Accidents • Breakdowns in command, control, and communication (C^3) • Modifying or interdicting escalatory SOPs
Postcrisis			
Resolving	• Maintaining "face" • Demonstrating adequate concern for adversary's face	• Gratifying need for self-esteem • Gratifying need for social approval	• Providing adequate implementation capacity • Maintaining adequate implementation oversight

Table 2.2 Illustrative Cuban Missile Crisis Management Pathologies (United States)

Task	Cultural pathologies	Psychological errors	Organizational shortcomings
Precrisis			
Anticipating, estimating, signaling	• Overly deductive approach to foreign policymaking • Dogmatic hyperrealism • Rational deterrence orthodoxy • Uncritical use of U.S. strategic vocabulary (e.g., "offensive missiles") and stock U.S. threat phraseology (e.g., "the gravest issues would arise")	• "The Soviets must know that we would not tolerate missiles in Cuba" • "The USSR would never deploy nuclear weapons on another country's soil" • "U.S. Jupiter missiles in Turkey are defensive; Soviet missiles in Cuba would be offensive" • Failure to see Bolshakov channel as part of Khrushchev's broader campaign of secrecy and deception	• Inadequate signals intelligence (SIGINT) • Overwhelming volume of low-quality human intelligence (HUMINT) • Late collection of photo intelligence (PHOTINT) • Discovery too late for timely signaling of unwillingness to tolerate deployment
Crisis			
Deliberating, bargaining	Pathologies successfully avoided	• Misreading sequence of Khrushchev's Oct. 25 and Oct. 26 letters • Misreading Feklisov (a.k.a Fomin) initiative	• Delays in encoding, transmitting, and decoding cables
Avoiding unintended escalation	Pathologies successfully avoided	Pathologies successfully avoided	• Siberian U-2 incident • Vandenburg Titan launch • Malmstrom Minuteman incident • Moorestown radar incident • Antisubmarine warfare (ASW) operations
Postcrisis			
Resolving	Pathologies successfully avoided	Pathologies successfully avoided	Pathologies successfully avoided

Table 2.3 Illustrative Cuban Missile Crisis Management Pathologies (USSR)

Phase	Cultural pathologies	Psychological errors	Organizational vulnerabilities
Precrisis			
Anticipating, estimating, signaling	• Unwillingness to challenge authority • Hypersensitivity to maintaining secrecy and compartmentalization	• Khrushchev's wishful thinking • Khrushchev's penchant for gambling • Khrushchev's lack of tolerance for dissent • Khrushchev's failure to empathize	• Failure to leverage expertise • Absence of analytical intelligence capability (preoccupation with operations) • Poor quality of HUMINT assets • Lack of SIGINT and PHOTINT capability. • Overcompartmentalization of information.
Crisis			
Deliberating, bargaining	Pathologies successfully avoided	• Hypervigilance leads to impulsive and conflicting offers • Stress-induced performance degradation (Khrushchev was easily rattled; failed to process incoming information carefully)	• Delays in encoding, transmitting, and decoding cables • Overcompartmentalization (Dobrynin, Zorin caught off guard) • Freelancing (Feklisov)
Avoiding unintended escalation	Pathologies successfully avoided	• Submarine incident	• Ambiguous TNW standing orders • Oct. 27 U-2 shootdown
Postcrisis			
Resolving	• Paternalism toward Cuba	Pathologies successfully avoided	Pathologies successfully avoided

untrustworthy, the American estimates were also significantly affected by their inability to imagine that Khrushchev would misrepresent his true intentions through the only good-quality back channel contact between the White House and the Kremlin, the GRU's Georgi Bolshakov.[17] American attempts to deter a Soviet deployment in the period immediately prior to the crisis (i.e., July–September 1962) were feeble, ambiguous, overly diplomatic, and hence not well designed to be understood correctly by an adversary prone to blunt, graphic nuclear deterrent threats.

The quality of American decision-making during the private (October 15–22) and public (October 22–28) phases of the crisis was much better. President Kennedy managed to avoid or circumvent a number of the generic challenges, in large part because of his realization that he had performed badly in attempting to forestall a Soviet adventure. Kennedy gave Khrushchev as much time as possible to reflect soberly on the seriousness of the situation and to internalize the lessons of their mutual failures to avoid a crisis in the first place. He did his best to keep his military on a tight rein and to resist pressures for premature escalation or irrevocable military action. He made some effort at least (if perhaps less than the greatest possible effort) to enable Khrushchev to back down gracefully without too much loss of face. And, perhaps most significantly, he laid the groundwork for a quick exit that he believed Khrushchev would very likely seize so as to resolve the crisis peacefully in case matters seemed to be coming to a head and military action seemed imminent: Kennedy was prepared if necessary to accept a *public* trade-off of U.S. Jupiter nuclear missiles in Turkey for Soviet nuclear missiles in Cuba (a trade that he ultimately did make, though on the basis of a private rather than a public understanding with Khrushchev).

Kennedy did not and could not, of course, prevent a number of very dangerous and completely unintended actions on the part of his own military establishment that carried significant risks of inadvertent conflict and subsequent escalation with the Soviet Union. These included, for example, the following rather sobering events:

- An American U-2 returning from a routine air-sampling mission—a mission that should have been canceled, in view of the ongoing crisis—strayed over Siberia, in response to which the Soviets scrambled MiG interceptors. Owing to the heightened American alert, the American F-102A interceptors that in return scrambled from Galena Air Force Base to escort the pilot back into American

airspace were carrying live nuclear Falcon antiaircraft missiles.
- The Strategic Air Command launched a Titan ICBM from Vandenberg Air Force Base on October 26, in accordance with its preplanned flight test schedule. This particular missile was not carrying a nuclear warhead, but the other ICBMs at Vandenberg were, owing to the heightened alert. Fortunately, the Soviets never detected the launch, or they might have misinterpreted it as a first strike.
- Crews at a Minuteman ICBM complex at Malmstrom Air Force Base in Montana, eager to comply with their order to go to heightened alert, jerry-rigged their finicky launch control system, bypassing normal safeguards.
- On the morning of October 28, just before Khrushchev announced his agreement to withdraw Soviet missiles from Cuba, radar operators at Moorestown, N.J., reported a missile launch from Cuba. A training tape had mistakenly been feeding into the Moorestown monitors.[18]

The Soviets also faced a similarly daunting set of challenges to crisis management. Khrushchev's performance in the precrisis period cannot be described as anything other than appalling, reflecting intense wishful thinking, a shocking failure to engage and leverage his Americanologists, and a premature commitment to a highly risky course of action, the dangers of which he either did not recognize or managed to repress. Although there were those in the Soviet foreign policy establishment who had a more realistic understanding of the risks Khrushchev was taking in attempting to sneak strategic nuclear weapons into Cuba, it appears that norms of deference or fears of repercussions led them to self-censor or soft-pedal their objections. Had Khrushchev been appropriately circumspect and fully informed, it is difficult to imagine that he would have proceeded with his gambit.[19] But he was, as Fyodor Burlatsky would later put it, *azartny'*—a "risky person"—and his attempt to sneak nuclear missiles into Cuba was, in a sense, entirely in character.[20]

Fortunately, though willing to take risks when the dangers of escalation seemed low, Khrushchev was extremely risk averse in the face of imminent danger and, interestingly, willing to reverse course when his own recklessness got him into trouble. During and after the crisis, he displayed an acute sensitivity to the dangers of unintended escalation, and in the denouement he evinced a healthy circumspection that led him not to overestimate his own efficacy. The

October 27 shoot down of an American U-2 over Cuba—against standing orders—seems to have been a particularly sobering event. One can only speculate how Khrushchev might have reacted had he known that at the climax of the crisis one of his own submarine commanders, relentlessly harassed by U.S. antisubmarine forces and operating under crushing heat and dwindling oxygen, had concluded that war had probably already broken out and ordered his nuclear torpedo readied to be fired.[21] In most respects Khrushchev navigated the crisis well, proving willing and able to conclude and implement a mutually satisfactory resolution with the United States. The only significant blemish on his crisis resolution efforts was his insensitive and paternalistic treatment of Fidel Castro, which very nearly resulted in the undoing of the agreement he worked out so delicately with Kennedy under the most difficult and most dangerous conditions imaginable.[22]

Lessons of the Cuban Missile Crisis for U.S.-Chinese Relations

One case doth not a generalization make, but it would not be difficult, locating the Cuban missile crisis in a broader comparative context, to justify the following crisis-"management" maxims:

- Try to cultivate empathy (that is, to put yourself in your adversary's shoes).
- Treat the adversary with respect, not disdain.
- Focus on identifying mutually satisfactory outcomes.
- Do not overestimate the utility of military signaling; it can provoke as well as deter, and can easily be misread.
- In a crisis, maintain communication and try to avoid irrevocable acts as long as possible.
- Assume that everyone is fallible, yourself included.
- If smaller countries are implicated in the crisis, do not dismiss their needs and concerns. They can catalyze Great-Power conflict.

A leader following these maxims will not likely overestimate his or her degree of control, and will therefore be less likely to charge blithely forward unduly confident of success.

How might these maxims inform the "management" of a hypothetical future crisis between the United States and the People's Republic of China over a Taiwanese UDI? At this point, the analysis unavoidably becomes rather speculative. Much would depend upon the precise chain of events leading to a serious U.S.-Chinese nuclear crisis, and perhaps also upon the personalities on both sides attempting to handle it. But if the generic challenges identified in table 2.1 have any validity, and if the lessons of the Cuban missile crisis I draw from tables 2.2 and 2.3 travel, then the kinds of challenges for the United States that I flag in table 2.4, and for the PRC in table 2.5, would appear to be particularly acute and worthy of careful consideration in advance.[23]

It might be helpful to preface my remaining remarks with the following general observations. First, Americans tend not to understand the Chinese attachment to the "One-China" principle. Taiwan is not now, and has not been for a very long time, governed by the mainland. In fact, historically speaking, Taiwan can only be said to have been part of an integrated China for a relatively short period of time (from the late seventeenth to the late nineteenth century). Since the Second World War, Taiwan has been a self-governing entity de facto, a sovereign state in everything but name. Americans assume that mainland Chinese realize this, as no doubt they do. But what Americans do not appreciate is that the facts on the ground have no implications whatsoever, from a mainland perspective, for the PRC's legal, moral, or symbolic claim. For the PRC, the One China principle is sacrosanct. The attachment to it is intensely emotional and entirely heartfelt. Americans often interpret it as tactical and insincere—from an American perspective, what could one possibly hope to attain by insisting upon something so transparently belied by practice? Americans therefore have a natural tendency to explain away, or to reframe as instrumental, Chinese claims on Taiwan and Chinese threats to respond forcefully to a Taiwanese UDI. Whereas Americans tend to think that what is true of the world de facto naturally determines what is true of the world de jure, the PRC manages instead to think of the two categories as entirely unrelated—indeed, indefinitely so, as Beijing attaches no timetable to, and has articulated no deadlines for, the submission of Taiwan to mainland rule.

Compounding this misunderstanding is the American penchant to approach the world from a realist/rational-deterrence theory perspective. On this view, the PRC ought to be expected, when confronted with the challenge of responding to a hypothetical Taiwanese UDI, to evaluate the global balance of power and craft a response commensurate with a realistically modest estimate of Beijing's capability vis-à-vis the United States. Beijing is at least a decade away from being able

Table 2.4 Potential Crisis Management Pathologies: Hypothetical Future Taiwan Strait Crisis (United States)

Task	Cultural pathologies	Psychological pressures and errors	Organizational vulnerabilities
Precrisis			
Anticipating, estimating, signaling	• Overestimating balance of power/rational deterrence considerations • Underestimating salience of emotion/identity considerations in Chinese policy	• Reading Chinese signals as bluffs or as intended for domestic benefit	• Overreliance on technical intelligence collection • "Safe" estimates
Crisis			
Deliberating, bargaining	• Overplaying unipolarity hand • Failing to appreciate inflammatory nature of side-payment offers • Approaching crisis as a zero-sum game	• Inappropriate historical analogies (e.g., Munich, Korea) • Failing to conduct a thorough examination of options because of the pressure of restricted time	• Difficulty of maintaining secrecy to buy adequate time to deliberate • Difficulty of maintaining secrecy to conduct quiet diplomacy
Avoiding unintended escalation	Pathologies probably avoidable owing to robust military deference to civilian authority and highly reliable integrated communication environment	• Underestimating Chinese resolve • Overestimating centrality and coordination of Chinese military actions	• Complexity and common-mode failures • Blowback
Postcrisis			
Resolving	• Overvaluing "credibility" • Undervaluing mutual face-saving outcomes	• President does not want to be "the one who lost Taiwan" • Overidentification with Taiwan	• Difficulties in coordinating implementation with Taiwan, PRC

Table 2.5 Potential Crisis Management Challenges: Hypothetical Future Taiwan Strait Crisis (PRC)

Task	Cultural challenges	Psychological challenges	Organizational challenges
Precrisis			
Anticipating, estimating, signaling	• Underestimating power/rational deterrence considerations in U.S. calculus • Underestimating U.S. sympathy for Taiwanese self-government • Failing to note trade-offs between "One-China" fundamentalism and other implicated values	• Avoiding wishful thinking (e.g., that USA will back down because PRC cares more about Taiwan). • Failing to attempt to empathize with U.S. perspective because of dismissive beliefs about U.S. "arrogance" and "presumption"	• Ensuring leadership receives bad intelligence news as well as good intelligence news
Crisis			
Deliberating, bargaining	• Avoiding premature commitment to a particular outcome	• Avoiding inappropriate historical analogies (e.g., Korea, Vietnam) • Failing to conduct a thorough examination of costs and benefits of all options because of tunnel vision and emotional stridency • Avoiding simple "demand" bargaining mode	• Ensuring inputs from all stakeholders in deliberations • Ensuring discrepant information flows up to decision-makers
Avoiding unintended escalation	• Ensuring non-escalatory defaults in the event of a loss of communications integrity	• Underestimating U.S. resolve	• Maintaining coordination between branches/units and political developments
Postcrisis			
Resolving	• Underestimating U.S. concern with credibility and face	• Leadership does not want to be "the ones who lost Taiwan"	• Coordinating implementation with Taiwan, USA

to pose a credible military threat to Taiwan, and much further away from being able realistically to expect to prevail locally against the United States in a shooting war in the Taiwan Strait.[24] According to the predictable American calculus, in other words, Washington enjoys escalation dominance[25] and can expect the mainland to back down in the event of a serious confrontation. Having said that, of course, I should note that Washington has no interest in Taiwan triggering a serious crisis and has a strong interest in maintaining the currently ambiguous status quo whereby a de facto self-governing Taiwan pays lip service to the One China principle. Thus Washington and Beijing find themselves on the same side of a deterrence sub-game designed to dissuade Taiwanese leaders from a UDI.

Should a serious crisis erupt, there is little doubt that the United States would feel compelled to stand up for Taiwan. A powerful cocktail of incentives would rapidly come into play. First, Taiwan is a democracy and the United States, as the self-appointed beacon and champion of democracy in the world, would feel compelled on identity grounds to come to its aid. Second, the realist/rational-deterrence lens through which American policymakers approach the world, turbocharged by potent allergies to "appeasement," "Munich," "Korea," and "the loss of China" itself, would inevitably lead them to believe that the very honor and future of America lay in standing up to mainland encroachments on Taiwan. American leaders would also conclude that a failure to deliver on America's moral and legal commitments to Taiwanese self-government would also undermine U.S. credibility, a consideration to which postwar U.S. policymakers have been particularly intensely sensitive at all times. Third, Taiwan's importance to the United States and to the world economy as a vibrant capitalist society would incline American decision-makers to react forcefully to any dramatic attempt to alter the status quo. Finally, American domestic politics would virtually force any U.S. administration to come to the aid of a relatively small, beleaguered liberal democratic Taiwan being bullied by a larger communist mainland. For all of these reasons, the United States would have little choice but to come to Taiwan's aid, with military force if necessary. Not least significantly, American policymakers would be forced to craft a response in an information-rich environment of nearly instantaneous communications that would make it almost impossible to deliberate at leisure in private, or to conduct careful secret diplomacy with Beijing of the kind that proved so crucial to a peaceful resolution of the Cuban missile crisis. While American policymakers might not have to worry as much as President Kennedy about breakdowns in command and control or inadvertent military escalation stemming from inadequate C^3I—owing to the Revolution in Military Affairs and the U.S. military's unprecedented battlefield management capabilities—they might not be able to anticipate, and might well be vulnerable to, unforeseeable risks of blowback or aggressive information warfare operations. Nor might Washington be able to rein in a reckless government in Taiwan that anticipates a final reckoning with Beijing and presumes (probably correctly, in my view) unquestioning American support. The net effect of these dangers is a significant likelihood that American policymakers would overestimate the efficacy of their extended deterrent threats.

What errors might lead the PRC to fatal miscalculations? Perhaps the most obvious is the likelihood that China would expect Washington to back down in a serious confrontation. This particular error has its roots in the perfectly normal human tendency to assume that others see the world the way one does oneself—that is, a classic projection error. There is no doubt that mainland Chinese sincerely believes in the One China principle and have a powerful emotional attachment to it. But this inclines Chinese policymakers and analysts to assume that the American attachment to Taiwanese self-determination is significantly weaker. Viscerally aware of their own emotional attachment to Taiwan, mainland Chinese cannot, and therefore do not, appreciate the strength of the American attachment. Convinced that the United States makes choices in the world based upon a cold-blooded calculation of relative interest, Beijing tends to assume that Washington would back down if push came to shove because Taiwan is "more important" to China than it is to the United States.

Reinforcing this assumption is the common Chinese view that, for cultural reasons, China cares much more than does the United States about avoiding "loss of face," something a Taiwanese UDI would immediately threaten. The belief that Asian cultures care more intensely about "face" than do Western cultures fundamentally reflects the ease with which this particular concern can be expressed in an Asian linguistic and sociological context. But Americans care intensely about loss of face as well—they merely use the language of *credibility* to express it. Anyone who has any doubts about the American concern with avoiding loss of face need only reflect on the willingness of the United States to prosecute the Vietnam war for eight years, at enormous human and material cost, despite the general awareness among American leaders that the war could not be won militarily, for the overwhelming purpose of demonstrating a willingness to meet stated commitments,[26] or on the tragic and hopeless attempt of the George W. Bush Administration to prevail in its ill-advised conquest of Iraq simply because it had articulated a set of (unattainable) geostrategic and sociopolitical goals.[27]

Finally, fissures within the Chinese foreign and defense policy establishments could complicate any PRC response to a Taiwanese UDI. There is some evidence to suggest that in earlier Taiwan Strait crises, and in China's longstanding territorial dispute with the Philippines and Vietnam over the Spratly and Paracel Islands in the South China Sea (particularly the 1995 Mischief Reef incident), the People's Liberation Army may have taken liberties in responding to perceived foreign encroachments with a degree of belligerence not sanctioned by civilian authorities in Beijing.[28]

Conclusion

As the foregoing analysis suggests, there are important differences between the context of Cuban missile crisis in 1962 and any present or future context in which a hypothetical U.S.-Chinese Taiwan Strait crisis might take place.[29] Those that I have touched upon include differences in military technology, communications technology, the speed and volume of information flows, and the abilities of governments to deliberate out of the public eye. I have suggested these are likely to ameliorate some generic challenges of crisis management while exacerbating others. Differences that I have not dwelt upon, owing to space constraints, include the fact that a future U.S.-Chinese nuclear crisis would occur against the backdrop of a much longer history of "nuclear learning," including learning about nuclear crisis and the importance of confidence and security-building measures (CSBMs).[30] It is encouraging to reflect on the efforts of Americans and Chinese to cultivate greater levels of mutual understanding through both official and unofficial channels in order to reduce uncertainty and lay the foundations for avoiding if possible, and more readily handling if not, future serious challenges.

I have also not considered in detail the question of crisis stability, which of course is an important issue as well. The United States need have no fears about the vulnerability of its nuclear forces to Chinese attack, but the reverse may not be true. Interestingly, Chinese nuclear modernization and recent efforts to enhance the survivability of Chinese nuclear forces do not appear to reflect any panic or desperation in this regard, but it would be cause for concern if, during a serious crisis, Chinese military or civilian leaders perceived that a nuclear confrontation was inevitable and felt pressure "to use or to lose" their strategic nuclear arsenal. This renders all the more important the active promotion of CSBMs and as much advance coordinated planning as possible on how to handle a Taiwanese UDI that minimizes the danger of a resort to arms.

Despite the differences in contexts, however, I would submit that there is one enduring, overwhelming lesson from the Cuban missile crisis that makes it a valid antecedent, and hence a historical source of profound insight, for any serious nuclear crisis. As Clausewitz argued more than 200 years ago, war is, to some extent, inherently unpredictable. Once the threshold of the use of force has been crossed, it is impossible for leaders to be completely certain of where it will lead or where it will stop.[31] Under conditions that approach Mutual Assured Destruction, this must and should give leaders great pause; they cannot and should not assume that they will remain masters of a nuclear confrontation. Kennedy and Khrushchev, fortunately, came to appreciate this all too well. One can only hope that future U.S. and Chinese leaders will learn from their example.

Notes

The author would like to acknowledge the helpful comments and suggestions of James Blight, Jacques Hymans, Robert Patman, the participants at the U.S.-China Strategic Dialogue, Honolulu, HI, November 6–7, 2006, and two anonymous reviewers. Any errors are the responsibility of the author alone.

1. James G. Blight and David A. Welch, *On the Brink: Americans and Soviets Reexamine the Cuban Missile Crisis*, 2nd ed. (New York: Noonday, 1990), 100.
2. "Chinese President Calls for Strengthened, Modernized Navy," *People's Daily Online (English)*, December 27, 2006.
3. For further discussion, see Robert Jervis, "The Future of World Politics: Will It Resemble the Past?," *International Security* 16, no. 3 (1991/92); Yuen Foong Khong, *Analogies at War: Korea, Munich, Dien Bien Phu, and the Vietnam Decisions of 1965* (Princeton, NJ: Princeton University Press, 1992); Richard E. Neustadt and Ernest R. May, *Thinking in Time: The Uses of History for Decision-Makers* (New York: Free Press, 1986); David A. Welch, *Painful Choices: A Theory of Foreign Policy Change* (Princeton, NJ: Princeton University Press, 2005), 10–14.
4. Joseph S. Nye, "Old War and Future Wars: Causation and Prevention," in *The Origin and Prevention of Major Wars*, ed. Robert I. Rotberg and Theodore K. Rabb (Cambridge: Cambridge University Press, 1989), 11.

5. Bruce Berkowitz, "Proliferation, Deterrence, and the Likelihood of War," *Journal of Conflict Resolution* 29, no. 1 (1985); Bruce Bueno de Mesquita and William H. Riker, "An Assessment of the Merits of Selective Nuclear Proliferation," *Journal of Conflict Resolution* 26, no. 2 (1982); John J. Mearsheimer, "Back to the Future: Instability in Europe After the Cold War," *International Security* 15, no. 1 (1990); John J. Mearsheimer, "The Case for a Ukrainian Nuclear Deterrent," *Foreign Affairs* 72, no. 3 (1993); Kenneth N. Waltz, "Nuclear Myths and Political Realities," *American Political Science Review* 84, no. 3 (1990); Kenneth N. Waltz, "The Origin of War in Neorealist Theory," *Journal of Interdisciplinary History* 18, no. 4 (1988); Kenneth N. Waltz, *The Spread of Nuclear Weapons: More May Be Better*, Adelphi Paper (London: International Institute for Strategic Studies, 1981); Kenneth N. Waltz, "Toward Nuclear Peace," in *The Use of Force: Military Power and International Politics*, ed. Robert J. Art and Kenneth N. Waltz (Lanham, MD: University Press of America, 1993).
6. For the "Proliferation Pessimist" position, see Bruce Blair, *The Logic of Accidental Nuclear War* (Washington, DC: Brookings, 1993); James G. Blight and David A. Welch, "Risking 'the Destruction of Nations': Lessons of the Cuban Missile Crisis for New and Aspiring Nuclear States," *Security Studies* 4, no. 4 (1995); Lewis Dunn, *Containing Nuclear Proliferation*, Adelphi Paper No. 263 (London: International Institute for Strategic Studies, 1991); Lewis Dunn, *Controlling the Bomb: Nuclear Proliferation in the 1980s* (New Haven: Yale University Press, 1982); Peter D. Feaver, "Proliferation Optimism and Theories of Nuclear Operations," *Security Studies* 2, no. 3/4 (1993); Scott D. Sagan, "The Perils of Proliferation: Organization Theory, Deterrence, and the Spread of Nuclear Weapons," *International Security* 18, no. 4 (1994); Leonard Spector, *New Nuclear Nations* (New York: Vintage, 1985); Leonard Spector, *Nuclear Proliferation Today* (New York: Vintage, 1984). Cf. David J. Karl, "Proliferation Pessimism and Emerging Nuclear Powers," *International Security* 21, no. 3 (1996–1997); Scott D. Sagan and Kenneth N. Waltz, *The Spread of Nuclear Weapons: A Debate* (New York: Norton, 1995).
7. The Damaksky Island skirmishes. The two countries engaged in small-scale conflict along their frontier several times in the 1960s, 1970s, and 1980s.
8. Moreover, the conflict did not meet the 1,000-battle-death criterion for inclusion in Small and Singer's Correlates of War Interstate War dataset. (Interestingly, version 3.0 of the dataset makes a single exception for this criterion: the 1982 Falklands War, with 910 battle deaths.)
9. Richard Ned Lebow and Janice Gross Stein, *We All Lost the Cold War* (Princeton, NJ: Princeton University Press, 1994), 226–288.
10. Faten Ghosn, Glenn Palmer, and Stuart Bremer, "The Mid3 Data Set, 1993–2001: Procedures, Coding Rules, and Description," *Conflict*

Management and Peace Science 21, no. 2 (2004); Daniel M. Jones, Stuart A. Bremer, and J. David Singer, "Militarized Interstate Disputes, 1816–1992: Rationale, Coding Rules, and Empirical Patterns," *Conflict Management and Peace Science* 15, no. 2 (1996). The latest version of the MIDS dataset is available online at http://correlatesofwar.org/COW2%20 Data/MIDs/MID310.html. Accessed on February 14, 2008.

11. Don Munton and David A. Welch, *The Cuban Missile Crisis: A Concise History* (New York: Oxford University Press, 2007). Many of the themes I emphasize in this chapter are explained and contextualized in greater detail in this work, but draw broadly upon the extensive "Critical Oral History" of the Cuban missile crisis and for the period from 1987 to 2002, supplemented by the findings of scholars who have recently exploited the erstwhile secret archives in the United States, Russia, and elsewhere: Bruce J. Allyn, James G. Blight, and David A. Welch, "Essence of Revision: Moscow, Havana, and the Cuban Missile Crisis," *International Security* 14, no. 3 (1989/90); Bruce J. Allyn, James G. Blight, and David A. Welch, eds., *Back to the Brink: Proceedings of the Moscow Conference on the Cuban Missile Crisis, January 27–28, 1989* (Lanham, MD: University Press of America, 1992); James G. Blight, *The Shattered Crystal Ball: Fear and Learning in the Cuban Missile Crisis* (Savage, MD: Rowman & Littlefield, 1990); James G. Blight, Bruce J. Allyn, and David A. Welch, *Cuba on the Brink: Castro, the Missile Crisis, and the Soviet Collapse*, rev. and enl. ed. (Lanham, MD: Rowman & Littlefield, 2002); James G. Blight, David Lewis, and David A. Welch, eds., *Cuba between the Superpowers: The Antigua Conference on the Cuban Missile Crisis* (Providence, RI: Center for Foreign Policy Development, Thomas J. Watson Jr. Institute for International Studies, Brown University, 1991); Blight and Welch, *On the Brink*; James G. Blight and David A. Welch, eds., *Intelligence and the Cuban Missile Crisis* (London: Frank Cass, 1998); Dino A. Brugioni, *Eyeball to Eyeball: The inside Story of the Cuban Missile Crisis*, ed. Robert F. McCort (New York: Random House, 1991); Laurence Chang and Peter Kornbluh, eds., *The Cuban Missile Crisis, 1962: A National Security Archive Documents Reader*, rev. ed. (New York: The New Press, 1998); Aleksandr Fursenko and Timothy Naftali, *'One Hell of a Gamble': Khrushchev, Castro and Kennedy, 1958–1964* (New York: Norton, 1997); Aleksandr Fursenko and Timothy Naftali, "Using KGB Documents: The Scali-Feklisov Channel in the Cuban Missile Crisis," *Cold War International History Project Bulletin*, no. 5 (1995); Raymond Garthoff, "Documenting the Cuban Missile Crisis," *Diplomatic History* 24, no. 4 (2000); Raymond L. Garthoff, *Reflections on the Cuban Missile Crisis*, rev. ed. (Washington, DC: Brookings, 1989); Gen. Anatoli I. Gribkov and William Y. Smith, *Operation Anadyr: U.S. And Soviet Generals Recount the Cuban Missile Crisis* (Chicago: Edition Q, 1994); James G. Hershberg, "New Evidence on the Cuban Missile Crisis: More Documents from the Russian Archives," *Cold War International History*

Project Bulletin, no. 8–9 (1996/97); Ernest R. May and Philip Zelikow, *The Kennedy Tapes: Inside the White House During the Cuban Missile Crisis* (Cambridge, MA: Harvard University Press, 1997); Mary S. McAuliffe, ed., *CIA Documents on the Cuban Missile Crisis* (Washington, DC: Central Intelligence Agency History Staff, 1992).

12. We must also give due regard for Khrushchev's evident wishful thinking that the deployment would succeed, driven in large part by his anxieties over Soviet nuclear inferiority and his fears of American hostility to the Cuban Revolution. On the U.S. deployment of Jupiter missiles to Turkey, see especially Philip Nash, *The Other Missiles of October: Eisenhower, Kennedy, and the Jupiters, 1957–1963* (Chapel Hill: University of North Carolina Press, 1997).

13. For example, Kennedy feared that the unauthorized shooting down of an American U-2 over Cuba on October 27 was a deliberate escalation on Khrushchev's part, while Khrushchev was convinced that Kennedy's request for airtime on October 29 indicated that he would announce a U.S. invasion of Cuba. Each, in other words, mistakenly overestimated the other's resolve. See Fursenko and Naftali, *'One Hell of a Gamble'*, 280; Lebow and Stein, *We All Lost the Cold War*, 139.

14. Janice Gross Stein and David A. Welch, "Rational and Psychological Approaches to the Study of International Conflict: Comparative Strengths and Weaknesses," in *Decision-Making on War and Peace: The Cognitive-Rational Debate*, ed. Nehemia Geva and Alex Mintz (Boulder, CO: Lynne Rienner, 1997).

15. See Benjamin Frankel, ed., *Realism: Restatements and Renewal* (London: Frank Cass, 1996); Robert G. Gilpin, "The Richness of the Tradition of Political Realism," in *Neorealism and Its Critics*, ed. Robert O. Keohane (New York: Columbia University Press, 1986).

16. Raymond L. Garthoff, "US Intelligence in the Cuban Missile Crisis," in *Intelligence and the Cuban Missile Crisis*, ed. James G. Blight and David A. Welch (London: Frank Cass, 1998).

17. The GRU, or *Glavnoye Razvedovatel'noye Upravlenie* (Main Intelligence Directorate), was the branch of the Soviet military responsible for intelligence.

18. Scott D. Sagan, *The Limits of Safety: Organizations, Accidents, and Nuclear Weapons* (Princeton, NJ: Princeton University Press, 1993), 81–90, 137.

19. Aleksandr Fursenko and Timothy Naftali, "Soviet Intelligence and the Cuban Missile Crisis," in *Intelligence and the Cuban Missile Crisis*, ed. James G. Blight and David A. Welch (London: Frank Cass, 1998); William Taubman, *Khrushchev: The Man and His Era* (New York: Norton, 2003).

20. Blight and Welch, *On the Brink*, 235.

21. In this incident, allegedly, the submarine's second in command and deputy political officer talked the commander down. Svetlana Savranskaya, "Recollections of Vadim Orlov (USSR Submarine B-59): We Will

Sink Them All, but We Will Not Disgrace Our Navy," (National Security Archive, http://www.gwu.edu/~nsarchiv/nsa/cuba_mis_cri/020000%20Recollections %20of%20Vadim%20Orlov.pdf: 2002). Accessed on February 14, 2008.
22. Blight, Allyn, and Welch, *Cuba on the Brink*, 358–366; Fursenko and Naftali, *'One Hell of a Gamble'*, 290–315.
23. The analysis that follows draws liberally upon a variety of works, the most important of which include Thomas J. Christensen, "The Contemporary Security Dilemma: Deterring a Taiwan Conflict," *Washington Quarterly* 25, no. 4 (2002); Thomas J. Christensen, "Posing Problems without Catching Up: China's Rise and Challenges for U.S. Security Policy," *International Security* 25, no. 4 (2001); Bernard D. Cole, *Taiwan's Security: History and Prospects* (London: Routledge, 2006); Edward Friedman, "Chinese Nationalism, Taiwan Autonomy and the Prospects of a Larger War," *Journal of Contemporary China* 6, no. 14 (1997); Stephen P. Gilbert, "East Asian-Pacific Security: An Assessment," *Comparative Strategy* 19, no. 4 (2000); A. James Gregor, "East Asian Stability and the Defense of the Republic of China on Taiwan," *Comparative Strategy* 16, no. 4 (1997); David L. Shambaugh, ed., *Power Shift: China and Asia's New Dynamics* (Berkeley: University of California Press, 2005); Chih-yu Shih, "Psychological Security and National Security: The Taiwan Factor in China's U.S. Policy," *The Journal of Social, Political and Economic Studies* 16, no. 4 (1991); Xinbo Wu, "To Be an Enlightened Superpower," *Washington Quarterly* 24, no. 3 (2001); Philip Yang, "From Strategic Competitor to Security Collaborator? New U.S.-China Tri-Level Strategic Relations and Taiwan Security in a Post-9/11 World," *Issues & Studies* 39, no. 4 (2003). For a historical perspective, see H. W. Brands, Jr., "Testing Massive Retaliation: Credibility and Crisis Management in the Taiwan Strait," *International Security* 12, no. 4 (1988).
24. Cf. Jianxiang Bi, "Uncertain Courses: Theater Missile Defense and Cross-Strait Competition," *Journal of Strategic Studies* 25, no. 3 (2002); Christopher M. Farricker, "Chinese Military Modernization and the Future of Taiwan" (M.A. thesis, Naval Postgraduate School, 2003); A. F. Klimenko, "The Evolution of China's Military Policy and Military Doctrine," *Military Thought* 14, no. 2 (2005); C. Dennison Lane, Mark Weisenbloom, and Dimon Liu, eds., *Chinese Military Modernization* (Washington, DC.: AEI Press, 1996); Tai Wei Lim, "Implications of the People's Liberation Army's Technocratization for U.S. Power in East Asia," *Asian Affairs* 31, no. 1 (2004); Michael McDevitt, "The Security Situation across the Taiwan Strait: Challenges and Opportunities," *Journal of Contemporary China* 13, no. 40 (2004); Mark A. Stokes, *China's Strategic Modernization: Implications for the United States* (Carlisle Barracks, PA: Strategic Studies Institute, U.S. Army War College, 1999); Vincent Wei-Cheng Wang, "China's Information

Warfare Discourse: Implications for Asymmetric Conflict in the Taiwan Strait," *Issues & Studies* 39, no. 2 (2003); Adam Ward, "China and America: Trouble Ahead?," *Survival* 45, no. 3 (2003); Peter Kien-hong Yu, "Modernizing China's Military: A Dialectical Critique," *Issues & Studies* 40, no. 2 (2004).

25. I.e., the ability to prevail militarily at any level of violence.
26. Fredrik Logevall, *Choosing War: The Lost Chance for Peace and the Escalation of War in Vietnam* (Berkeley: University of California Press, 1999), 388–389.
27. Gary J. Dorrien, *Imperial Designs: Neoconservatism and the New Pax Americana* (New York: Routledge, 2004).
28. On differences between U.S. and Chinese civil-military relations, see especially Peter D. Feaver, Takako Hikotani, and Shaun Narine, "Civilian Control and Civil-Military Gaps in the United States, Japan, and China," *Asian Perspective* 29, no. 1 (2005).
29. The contextual peculiarities of the Cuban missile crisis led Eliot Cohen to argue in 1986 that it held no valuable lessons. But cf. Blight, *The Shattered Crystal Ball*.
30. Graham T. Allison, Albert Carnesale, and Joseph S. Nye, Jr., eds., *Hawks, Doves, and Owls: An Agenda for Avoiding Nuclear War* (New York: Norton, 1985); Joseph S. Nye, Jr., "Nuclear Learning and U.S.-Soviet Security Regimes," *International Organization* 41, no. 3 (1987).
31. Carl von Clausewitz, *On War*, trans. Michael Howard and Peter Paret (Princeton, NJ: Princeton University Press, 1984), 119–121. Perhaps the most brilliantly graphic descriptions of what Clausewitz called "friction" may be found in Leo Tolstoy, *War and Peace*, trans. Constance Garnett (New York: Modern Library, 1994).

Section II

Comparing National Views on Strategic Context, National Security Priorities, and Doctrines

3

THE U.S.-CHINA STRATEGIC RELATIONSHIP

Michael May

What strategic roles have nuclear weapons historically served? What are the key determinants of deterrence? What is strategic stability and what factors enhance or undermine it? Will the existing international regimes and understandings remain stable despite the advent of additional nuclear powers? How might we expect the nuclear world order to evolve in the future?

These questions are not easy to answer. Nevertheless, some answers to them have been provided over the first sixty years of the nuclear age. In this chapter, I will examine these answers in the context of the U.S.-China strategic relationship. The questions are centered on nuclear weapons, but nuclear weapons do not fully define a strategic relationship, so I start by discussing briefly what a strategic relation implies.

BASES OF THE US-CHINA STRATEGIC RELATIONSHIP

The strategic relationship between two countries is the interplay of their powers and goals. It consists first of political and economic relations, which have the greatest ability to translate into power on a day-to-day basis. To the extent it relies on military capabilities, the relationship relies mostly on conventional forces and factors affecting their potential deployment. Lastly, it is defined by nuclear capabilities, which experience has shown to be an unusual and limited instrument of national power, applicable to very few situations, albeit situations in which disaster is a possible consequence.

Thus, the most important factors affecting U.S.-China strategic relationship are, from the U.S. side, its position at the top of the relative power hierarchy, and, from China's side, its turn away from the autarchic ideological system it experienced from the time of Mao Zedong to its current broadscale international engagement. The U.S. position enables it to pursue more effectively its long-standing strategic goals of preventing a hegemon from rising on the Eurasian continent and controlling international air- and sea-lanes. Beyond that, relative superiority has permitted the United States to widely expand its military presence, alliances, and other arrangements over the past dozen years. It is likely that this expansion was the result of different contingencies rather than planning, but the resulting deployments and commitments remain.

China's turnaround has made it into an economic power with worldwide impact, particularly with an impact on the American economy. It has brought into being a Chinese middle class that is forcing the government to evolve and has allowed China to engage in useful diplomatic as well as economic relationships around the world. Any assessment of the military and nuclear aspects of the strategic relationship must take these basics into account.

Among the military aspects of the strategic relationship between the United States and China, perhaps the defining one is the fact that the boundary between them lies mainly over the ocean, rather than, for instance, down the center of Europe or Asia. Such a boundary is less difficult to manage than the boundaries that run through the middle of contested continents, because of China's avoidance of a naval challenge to the United States, such as the challenges Germany and Japan mounted so disastrously and the Soviet Union mounted so expensively and with so little success.

Although less tense than the cold war boundary or pre-World War II boundaries, this boundary is not free of problems. I will return to those problems when discussing strategic stability. Here, I will discuss only the basics. The United States has the most modern, and in most engagements the most powerful, air, naval, and ground forces in Asia. These forces hold sway over air and water, controlling the "global commons" in a current formulation,[1] and also perhaps the littoral, but they would fare poorly in a prolonged inland war. Unlike Europe during the cold war, when the richer half of the continent was solidly on the U.S. side, U.S. power in Asia has relied on a handful of bases in Japan and South Korea. The Global Defense Posture Review attempts to alleviate this problem in several ways, including moving U.S. forces to dispersed and more number of locations and relying more on force projection from Guam or the United States. For the future, the 2006 Pentagon Quadrennial Defense Review envisages a force structure better suited to control terrorism while maintaining control of the global commons, rather than one suited to fight two land wars simultaneously.[2]

Turning now to the nuclear aspect of the U.S.-China strategic relationship, the principal factor is that China has declined to enter into a nuclear arms race with the U.S., limiting itself to a minimal strategic nuclear force that does not pose a threat of surprise attack. China has eighteen DF-5 ballistic missiles capable of reaching the United States and twelve DF-4 missiles capable of reaching targets in Russia and elsewhere in Asia, but not the North America. All these missiles are liquid-fueled and none is capable of launch in less than a few hours. The number of missiles have not substantially changed in decades. Programs to develop a solid-fueled intercontinental ballistic missile (ICBM) and a nuclear submarine capable of launching ballistic missiles have been in progress since the 1980s. They qualify as the slowest successful strategic programs in any nation since the nuclear age began. China also has on the order of a hundred nuclear-capable medium- and short-range ballistic missiles. The exact number is not known and it may be changing.

Forecasts have historically overestimated future Chinese nuclear forces by large factors. The lower priority given to nuclear programs (and military investments in general) is brought into relief when compared to the trillions of dollars invested by China in its civilian infrastructure during the same decades. We are not dealing here with a new arms race.[3]

In theory, the ongoing U.S. ballistic missile defense deployment could spur China to build up its nuclear forces. However, the pace of U.S. deployment, the continuing need to test during deployment, and the limited nature of the deployment tend to make the U.S. system a minor threat even to today's highly limited Chinese strategic forces. Nevertheless, as the U.S. antiballistic missile (ABM) system comes out of its growing pains and becomes operational, it could be a factor for deploying a larger number of Chinese missiles or for putting multiple independently targetable reentry vehicles on those missiles.

The foregoing considerations together define some basics of the U.S.-Chinese strategic relationship in broad outline and must inform a more detailed discussion on the role of nuclear weapons and the stability of that relationship. Should any of these underlying factors change significantly, everything else would also change. However, China so far has given no sign that indicates any major change occurring in those basic factors over the next decade or two.[4]

Role of Nuclear Weapons

The main role that nuclear weapons have played in U.S. policy after Hiroshima and Nagasaki, and in every other nuclear power's policy to date, has been that of a deterrent of last resort. Since Hiroshima and Nagasaki, there have been enough discussions, books, and papers on what ought to be the policy on nuclear weapons, enough to fill a library. In light of that continuing debate, but not always in accordance with its received wisdom, a set of facts on the ground has been developed.

The first of those facts is that nuclear weapons, though effective deterrents of last resort, have otherwise been quite limited instruments of power. States increase their relative power mainly by increasing their ability to influence the actions of others. Nuclear weapons have mainly helped induce states to avoid actions that would prove utterly destructive should they be attempted even in the absence of nuclear weapons. Thus a U.S.-Soviet war, or a Soviet-China war, or a U.S.-China war would have been, and would be today, destructive to every goal those three countries might have, regardless of whether they possessed nuclear weapons or not. Nuclear weapons reinforce that message. Hiroshima and Nagasaki were the exceptions.

Some parts of the U.S. Nuclear Posture Review (NPR) that were leaked in 2002 also seem like exceptions, although some current and former Administration members do not agree with that interpretation.[5] Because the change in declaratory posture has not been reflected in a change in strategic nuclear weapons, however, it would not significantly alter the U.S. deterrent posture regarding China.

Emphasis on deterrence does not mean that the United States or the former Soviet Union has renounced hopes of military victory, however pyrrhic, should deterrence fail. War is not desired, but defeat in any sense is desired even less. During the cold war, weapons were procured and deployed on both sides so that, should war occur, the other side's capacity to wage that war would be destroyed as far as possible. Both sides had actual, not simply in rhetoric, nuclear options that, though limited in effectiveness and unable to prevent widespread destruction, were not militarily meaningless. The existence of those options would have been a destabilizing factor in any crises serious enough to make either side realize that war was possible. This is not the case with China.

The second fact that developed over the past sixty years is that the possession of nuclear weapons induces caution and communication. The main cost of nuclear forces is not money, but the risk of catastrophe. To alleviate that risk, nuclear-armed powers to date have not been willing to push their adversary into a corner, though they have been willing to push their adversary to some degree. This balance required a nicety of judgment, which may not always be available in the future. The nuclear threat has at times forced communication between adversaries, and is indeed doing so now in the case of the United States and North Korea. The most effective means of U.S.-Soviet communication involved arms control, which signaled not an intent to disarm, but an intent to coexist.

The third element of nuclear policy in the nuclear age has been the search for security through universal international pacts and organizations. That search dates back at least to the czar's attempt to agree on peace in 1905, which was in part prompted by the invention of the machine gun. Machine guns have claimed more lives than nuclear weapons, though not enough to scare us into peace. Nuclear weapons may scare us into peace, as Winston Churchill predicted, but the balance of terror is fraught with dangers. Nuclear weapons policies have sought to alleviate that danger not only by deterrence, restraint, and communication but also through international pacts and organizations.

These pacts and organizations have received relatively broad and steady support. However, their effectiveness is in question now, for two reasons. First, while the only nuclear-weapons-capable countries in the early years of the nuclear age were either members of the Western or of the Soviet blocs, or (as in the case of China) large enough to deter a direct attack, today more insecure and alienated governments are also nuclear-weapons-capable. Second, in the past seven years the United States, for reasons good or bad, has lent only selective support to international pacts and organizations aimed at nuclear security. As a result, the international effort is now at a juncture from where it might either get much better or much worse. I shall return to this point at the end of this chapter.

The elements of nuclear weapons policy that I have noted do not comprise all that has evolved in the past sixty years, but they are possibly the most important facets of a history that is familiar to the audience. Today, the existence of nuclear weapons policies continues to imply deterrence against major attack and contributes to restraint between adversaries. U.S. leadership in the search for international norms and cooperation has faltered. The question is this: will nuclear weapons policies continue to lead to stable relationships among nuclear-armed powers? I consider next the stability of the U.S.-China strategic relationship.

STRATEGIC STABILITY

Stability in a relationship does not mean that the relationship is static (which it cannot be), but that, when faced with change and the accidents of history, it tends to return to peace rather than degenerate into war. Stability is measured by the ability to deal with change and disorder without catastrophe. For instance, the strategic stability of the U.S.-Russia relationship was, and still is, measured by the ability of both sides to deal with the crises in the Middle East and the collapse of the Soviet Union. The strategic stability of the U.S.-China relationship is measured by their ability to deal with problems in North Korea, Taiwan, and elsewhere.

Such stability has depended historically on several factors, of which I will note five: (1) the relative status of forces; (2) geography; (3) alliances and other relationships; (4) domestic perceptions of the relationship; and (5) economic relationships, or lack thereof. These are not listed in their order of importance: their relative importance depends on current circumstances. Let us see what those factors are in the current U.S.-China relation and then provide an assessment of U.S.-China strategic stability.

RELATIVE STATUS OF FORCES

As already noted, China, unlike the Soviet Union, has not attempted to match the United States either in conventional or nuclear capability. While China is modernizing its conventional forces, which are decades behind those of the United States, it has not attempted any expensive initiatives such as a blue-water navy, a long-range air force, or integrated projection forces to rival those of the United States. On the nuclear front, as noted above, China has deployed short and medium range forces that would have a bearing on any war in East Asia, but it has continued to limit its intercontinental force to a dozen or so antiquated and vulnerable missiles.

These forces do exist, however, and, if not destroyed in the first hours of a war, would threaten the existence of half a dozen or more cities in the United States. More relevantly, they could readily destroy U.S. military assets in East Asia, should those assets be used against China. As with nuclear weapons during the cold war, but to a much lesser extent, they reinforce the perception that a U.S.-China war would inflict an extraordinary cost on both countries in people, money, and future influence in the world, a cost that dwarfs any relative advantage that anyone could think might be derived from such a war.

The United States, while significantly reducing the number of its nuclear weapons, has supposedly named China as a possible nuclear target in the Nuclear Posture Review and has stated several times that military assets over the long term would be shifted from other theaters to East Asia because that is where a greater likelihood of conflict exists. Iraq has distracted the United States from that judgment, but not changed it.

Could U.S. vulnerability to the Chinese missiles that could reach the United States make for instability in a serious crisis? The crisis would have to be quite serious for the United States to contemplate an attack on these forces, with all its uncertainties and the consequences that would ensue. Nevertheless, unlike the situation with the Soviet Union, an attack to neutralize Chinese nuclear forces could be thought of as feasible. The Chinese may remedy that situation by improving the survivability of their forces or considering defenses. Those steps may in turn worsen the stability of the relationship on counts other than technical.

On the whole, and under most circumstances, however, the balance of forces makes for stability. The point at which the United States traditionally becomes seriously alarmed is when a potential hegemon rises on the Eurasian continent or when its naval and other means of projecting power abroad is seriously challenged. China has not chosen to pose that kind of challenge. No doubt, some will continue to sound the alarm over China's increasing ability to counter American (and other states') forces deployed in its vicinity. But in itself, aside from its effect on domestic perceptions, which is discussed below, modernization should not make for instability as long as the Taiwan situation can be managed.

Geography

I have noted that China has not and probably cannot successfully challenge the United States in the naval and air global commons, and that the United States has not and probably cannot successfully challenge China inland. Nevertheless, some geographically related problems do exist.

Neither the United States nor China is self-sufficient in essential resources. It is sometimes said that the traditional rivalries for resources that led to so much warfare have been lessened by globalization of trade, information, and communication. The effect of globalization on strategic stability is limited, in my view. There is only limited trust in the proposition that adversaries will not misuse global economy.

For instance, neither the United States nor China fully trusts that the global oil market will suffice their need for oil. On the contrary, there is a continuing discussion in both countries about the merits of a so-called strategic approach to the oil and gas question (which actually means buying properties abroad and making exclusive marketing arrangements) versus a market-based approach. Both the United States and China are oil and gas importers and, from an economic point of view, their interests are similar: to maintain an open, flexible world market for petroleum products and investments. This view has limited political resonance. Economic reality, unfortunately, has had little to do with strategic stability. As a result, we cannot rule out oil wars, although they probably won't be nuclear. So far, rationality has held, but rationality is fragile in the marketplace of political ideas.

Alliances and Other Relationships

In respect to alliances, the U.S.-China relationship is potentially less stable than was the cold war U.S.-Soviet relationship. During the cold war, U.S. alliances, despite occasional alarms, were founded on fundamental shared political and economic interests, as well as on security. European countries may have had a greater incentive to maintain peace in Europe than the United States did, but they had no incentive to deal with the Soviet Union in ways that would weaken the alliance. Japan and South Korea were even more faithful and financially supportive U.S. allies than the Europeans.

The Soviet alliances were based on the dominance of Soviet force and were resented by the people who were subjugated. They broke up as soon as the Soviet grip weakened. Only client states that had nowhere else to go, such as Cuba, North Korea, and Iraq at the time, remained faithful, but the Soviet Union abandoned them. The Soviet allies had little or no capability to affect the stability of the overall relationship, which was also true of Cuba after 1962. The Middle East remained dangerous, but American and Soviet leaders were of one mind as to the necessity of limiting that danger.

In the U.S.-China case today, the situation is different. All the major countries involved, North and South Korea, Japan, Russia, and to an increasing degree India, have changing capabilities and agendas, and those agendas do not predictably align with the agendas of either the United States or China in the most important matters affecting strategic stability. While the United States and China have shown their interest in managing the Taiwan situation, China and Taiwan have said that the status quo is unacceptable. Unfortunately, it is difficult to believe that any attempt to change the status quo would not make the situation worse for all participants.

The Six-Party Talks involving the U.S., China, Japan, Russia, and North and South Korea are continuing and may succeed. If they do not, the existence of a nuclear-armed North Korea could threaten the stability of U.S.-China strategic relations, particularly if the United States were to attack North Korea. Recent Chinese pressure on North Korea, however, makes that outcome unlikely.

India in the past has been peripheral to the U.S.-China relationship, but this may be less so in the future. Both the United States and China have been making overtures to India, whereas India has been able and willing to chart an independent strategic course. Which way will India's strategic path eventually go, and to what extent will India's choice affect the stability of the U.S.-China relationship, is an additional changing factor that is not easy to predict.

Pakistan in the past has been an important cause of disgreement between China and the United States. The twin dangers of nuclear exports from Pakistan and Islamist takeover have not ended. U.S. and Chinese policies on these matters are better aligned now than they were in the past, but it is unclear to what the extent remaining differences exist—or how they matter.

Finally, while the United States is likely to remain the dominant economic and military power in the next twenty years, it will not have the kind of ascendancy it once enjoyed. Barring surprise developments, the United States will probably continue to grow economically at perhaps half the rate at which the major developing Asian powers will grow. As a result, the overall strategic position of the United States vis-à-vis the Asian powers is bound to decline over the long term. Harbingers of growing Asian independence from the United States have been here for some time in the economic sphere. This process does not threaten the stability of the U.S.-China relationship, or any other U.S. relationship, in any direct way. The threat to stability will arise if either the United States or any major Asian power fails to adjust to this change.

Domestic Perceptions in the United States and China

Domestic perceptions in the United States about the U.S.-China relationship are on the whole a negative factor for strategic stability. Even moderate to liberal domestic U.S. opinion views China as a future rival, if not a present one, and is on the whole suspicious of the Chinese form of government and intentions. The right-wing opinion makers who are now politically dominant in Washington are even more strongly anti-Chinese. Only a minority, admittedly influential, of better-informed politicians, China scholars, business leaders, and economists think that strategic rivalry between the United States and China is not inevitable, and that the United States has more to gain from partnership rather than rivalry with China. But people who hold those views are primarily influential in business rather than political matters.

That being said, the situation is not uniformly dark. For one thing, neither U.S. producers nor U.S. consumers want Chinese imports or the resulting Chinese capital to disappear from the market. Another factor is that there is no serious popular sentiment against the Chinese people. Finally, there is some sort of an East-West divide within the United States, with the Pacific Coast residents both more acquainted and less worried about China and Asia generally. Still, there is a long way to go and much spadework to be done before domestic U.S. opinion could be considered a stabilizing factor in the U.S.-China strategic relationship; moreover, domestic perceptions, while they do not determine policy, do set limits on it and can facilitate the growth of either a stable or an unstable relationship.

Discussion of Chinese domestic perceptions of the U.S. relationship is best left to Chinese observers. From this American observer's standpoint, it would seem that a similar cleavage between the perceptions of those who emphasize security and those who emphasize economics exists in China. As in the United States, popular sentiment is strongly nationalistic although not hostile to Americans.

Economic Relationship

From an economic viewpoint, China and the United States have become significantly interdependent, an interdependence that includes investors and managers in both countries and throughout East Asia and suppliers of raw materials and components from all over the world. Some 80 percent of the value of Chinese exports to the United States is added from other countries, and most exporting firms in China have non-Chinese partners. Any U.S. economic decline will affect China and its many suppliers and investors around the world negatively, and vice versa. In marked contrast with the U.S.-Soviet situation during the cold war, economic interdependence has developed between China and the United States. This interdependence also affects much of the rest of the world, and, with few exceptions, as either of these nations fare, to some extent so will the other. In addition, Chinese capital investments have been a factor for low interest rates in the United States and a source of capital for Western institutions.

However important and beneficial this interdependence may be from an economic point of view, it is not likely to be a significant factor for strategic stability. Famously, economists before World War I sounded clear warnings that Europe had become economically interdependent to such an extent that war there would ruin Europe. The war was fought, nevertheless, and Europe was ruined, and the ensuing political consequences haunted Europe till the end of World War II. Other cases exist. Modern war has been an economic disaster.

Economic realities, including economic interdependence, play little role in whether a country goes to war or not. Economic myths, however, certainly do play a role, and they usually affect strategic stability quite negatively. This is another reason why domestic perceptions matter: they determine which myths are believed.

While economic interdependence probably does not help stabilize strategic relationships, a breakdown in global trade and the ensuing economic setbacks would destabilize it. The forces that limit global trade are strong in the United States. Should these forces prevail, the recession or depression that would likely follow serious limits on global trade would make it politically profitable to blame some external actor, and China is a large and well-known external economic actor.

Analysis

What conclusion regarding the stability of the U.S.-China strategic relationship does all this lead to? There is no nuclear arms race and little in the way of a conventional arms race, albeit continuing Chinese success in limiting the effectiveness of American deployments close to its shores will look like an arms race to some. There is a relatively uncontested geopolitical boundary, except for the flashpoint at Taiwan. Relationships with and among other states in Asia are changing and unpredictable, which is not a stabilizing factor. The politically dominant domestic perceptions, at least in the United States, while certainly not in favor of war, generally view U.S.-China relationship as a rivalry, which is again not a stabilizing factor. The joint U.S.-Chinese interest in maintaining peaceful economic interdependence and open markets is unlikely to have much ameliorating or stabilizing effect on the politics of the situation, although a breakdown in this beneficial situation could worsen the perception of the problem in both countries.

Can we add up these disparate factors? States play a strategic game to maximize their relative power. They place security at the top of their priority list, being afraid (with good reason) that if they do not, they won't survive. The resulting mutual insecurity has led to endemic wars. Wars make no sense economically among major powers, and have not made sense for some time, but that has not prevented wars. This should make us pessimistic.

Two factors have altered the conditions of the game, although the game continues. First, the three major strategic powers today, the United States, Russia and China, are so large that it would be difficult, if not impossible, for another state to threaten their physical survival, except with nuclear weapons in sufficient quantity. Direct attack on any one of the three would probably be considered as an overreach rather than an addition to power. Second, nuclear weapons make direct attack far more dangerous even for the militarily superior side. This was most observers' conclusion sixty years ago, and it still remains the foundation stone of nuclear deterrence.

My tentative conclusion is that with realistic leadership stability should hold between the United States and China so long as four conditions are met:

1. China continues not to challenge the United States on the high seas.

2. The United States accepts that China, and indeed other Asian powers, will grow relative to the United States in relative influence and power.
3. The Taiwan situation can be managed.
4. Leaders in both countries do not turn their public against the other.

The nuclear balance is notably absent. Nuclear weapons help deter wars, but the details of the balance are, in my opinion, not terribly important.

Stability does not mean, I emphasize again, that the search for advantage in relative military power and other forms of power will end or even abate. It only means that it is not likely to lead to war among the participants.

The political leadership in both countries, rather than objective military factors, geopolitical factors, or economic factors, will determine the strategic stability of the relationship. There is nothing inevitable about U.S.-China conflict, notwithstanding much political science theory suggesting the contrary. England and France, England and Germany, and France and Germany were military rivals once, but are no longer so. Neither geopolitical nor economic realities have changed among them, but domestic perceptions have. Whether domestic perceptions will change in the United States and China any time soon, and how they will change, is questionable. What the leaders in both countries can do, and will do, is also something I cannot predict, however the future of U.S.-China relations lies with those who hold influence.

INTERNATIONAL REGIMES

The destructive power of nuclear weapons led states to attempt regulating the nuclear aspect of international rivalries by means of international regimes and understandings. The international order is famously anarchic and insecure for its participants. The search for relative power that this system induces has been strewn with disastrous errors. Disastrous errors on the scale of nuclear devastation scare governments, for good reason, and so the search for workable arrangements to avoid such nuclear devastation has been more popular among them than previous searches for cooperative security.

These attempts took the form of supply restrictions and security assurances of varying strength and effectiveness. They have been partially successful in limiting the spread of nuclear weapons. Today, owing to the spread of technological and other progress, supply restrictions have become less effective in ways that we are all familiar with. As a result, some of the countries that have become nuclear-weapons-capable are not only insecure, but have historically been made insecure in part by U.S. policy. Thus, both the supply and demand pillars of nuclear restraint by international agreement have weakened. In such a scenario, will international agreements and understandings be effective in the future as tools of international stability?

The nuclear nonproliferation regime in its present form, while still badly needed to preserve what has been gained in the past, is no longer adequate to deal with present and future challenges. The remedies proposed include a number of more stringent supply constraints, including constraints on facilities that could make nuclear weapons materials, tighter and better-enforced export controls, and more demanding accounting and inspection requirements.[6] Negotiations are underway with Iran and North Korea that could lead to security guarantees to both countries, as well as other benefits, in return for their abandonment of nuclear weapons programs. Other more or less ambitious demand-side measures have been suggested. The question here is how the success or failure of international agreements would affect strategic stability, in particular with respect to U.S.-China relations.

My answer to the above question is that it will only affect it marginally. Although it is important to provide the means for collective action and to confer some degree of legitimacy when political objectives are agreed, internationally agreed nonproliferation measures could only marginally affect whether North Korea decides to become a nuclear-armed state and, if so, whether other states will also acquire nuclear weapons. As discussed above, Japan and South Korea could react in various ways, but it is hard to see how their choice would depend in any important way on international agreements and institutions. Those agreements and institutions have been very helpful in North Korea's case, but only as a means to carry out agreed policies, not as independent political forces. The international community does not have the clout to enforce pacts and understandings among states as powerful and wealthy as those in East Asia, unless those states agree. As a result, the health and welfare of the nuclear agreements and institutions will probably not have much effect on the stability of the strategic relation between the United States and China.

There is a possible exception to this. Nuclear weapons are equalizers to some degree. A few are enough to make force projection extremely dangerous and costly. U.S. military policy, which emphasizes force projection, will be particularly hampered by the further spread of nuclear weapons. How the U.S. military and, in particular, nuclear policy react to the spread of nuclear weapons is an open and important question. If nuclear weapons continue to be used as a deterrent of last resort, stability would be maintained. If they are used otherwise, the floodgates to wider use could open.

Absent any reckless action (which I do not foresee), the major powers concerned should be able to deal with the consequences of nuclear spread, as they have done to date, without affecting the strategic stability among them. Whether they will act in concert through strengthened nonproliferation agreements, or via bilateral or trilateral agreements, is hard to predict. The latter has been the more common situation and has led to geographic divisions of responsibility reminiscent of the older spheres of influence. It has also led to wars.

At a level short of strategic stability, international agreements and institutions do affect states, even powerful states. A case in point is India, which needs to import more uranium for its existing and planned power reactors The proposed U.S-India agreement would alleviate this problem but create another in that it would also violate existing non-proliferation norms.

A modest proposal to avoid instability (in the sense that I have defined) would consist of an agreed roadmap between the United States and China (in the case of East Asian states), and probably also between the United States and Russia (in the case of Iran). This roadmap should spell out the pitfalls that both states would want to avoid and that provides alternative ways to negotiate crises when taking future decisions. It should be an ongoing exercise in which both the United States and China should become vested. It should recognize the fact that the United States, China, and every other country will continue to struggle to maximize their relative power, but that nuclear war serves no side's end. It should also recognize the fact that, absent effective demand-side measures to address state insecurities effectively, nuclear weapons will continue to spread.

Notes

1. Barry Posen, "Command of the Commons: The Military Foundation of U.S. Hegemony," *International Security* 28, no. 1 (Summer 2003).
2. Thom Shanker and Eric Schmitt, "Pentagon Weighs Strategy Change to Deter Terror," *New York Times*, July 5, 2005. See also M. Taylor Fravel

and Richard J. Samuels, "The United States as an Asian Power: Realism or Conceit?" *Audit of the Conventional Wisdom* 05-2 (Massachusetts: MIT Center for International Studies, April 2005).
3. For an overall assessment, see Harold Brown, Chair; Joseph W. Prueher, Vice Chair; Adams Siegel, Project Director; "Chinese Military Power," Report of an Independent Task Force, Council on Foreign Relations, 2003. For numbers and further references, see Jeffrey Lewis, "China's Arsenal, by the Numbers," *Bulletin of Atomic Scientists* (May/June 2005), 55.
4. Harold Brown, "Managing Change: China and the U.S. in 2025, "address to the RAND-CRF Conference, June 28, 2005.
5. *Nuclear Posture Review* (excerpts), Submitted to Congress on December 31, 2001. For a critique, see Roger Speed and Michael May, "Dangerous Doctrine," *Bulletin of Atomic Scientists* (March/April 2005), 38–49. For a counterargument, see Keith B. Payne, "The Nuclear Posture Review: Setting the Record Straight," *The Washington Quarterly* 28, no. 3 (Summer 2005) 135–151.
6. "Remarks by the President on Weapons of Mass Destruction Proliferation," National Defense University, Washington, DC, February 12. 2004; Mohammed El Baradei, "A New Security Framework," *The Economist*, (October 16, 2003); and Michael May and Tom Isaacs, "Stronger Measures Needed To Prevent Proliferation," *Issues in Science and Technology* (Spring 2004), 61–69.

4

The Changing Strategic Context of Nuclear Weapons and Implications for the New Nuclear World Order

Major General Pan Zhenqiang (Retired)[1]

Since the atomic bombing of Hiroshima and Nagasaki in 1945, nuclear weapons have become one of the defining elements shaping the world strategic situation—for better or worse. The end of the cold war has again led to dramatic changes in the world's security landscape. The international community, however, continues to grapple with many vital security issues involving nuclear weapons. The success or failure in dealing with these issues will greatly impact the threat perceptions and security policies of major powers as well as the future strategic stability of the world.

This chapter offers my perspective on the roles of nuclear weapons during and after the cold war period. It concludes by sketching an ideal future strategic context in which the nuclear world order might evolve and help strengthen an enduring international strategic stability.

Strategic Context of Nuclear Weapons During the Cold War

Two primary factors with a direct bearing on nuclear issues characterized the strategic international environment during the cold war.

The first was the emergence of a bipolar structure in which the two superpowers—the United States and the Soviet Union—competed for world domination. These two powers rapidly formed two confronting camps, NATO and the Warsaw Pact, with each superpower dominating its respective alliance. The antagonism between the two sides covered virtually all fields, made up the basic trends of the world situation, and rendered relations between the East and West zero in sum. Within this fiercely confrontational relationship, the scramble for military superiority was of particular significance, as security was primarily perceived in military terms.

The second phenomenon was that the nuclear superiority became the centerpiece of U.S.-U.S.S.R. competition, owing to the unprecedented destructive power of nuclear weapons. In fact, for almost the whole period of the cold war, relations between the United States and the Soviet Union developed around the struggle for nuclear supremacy. During the initial period of the cold war when only the United States possessed an atomic arsenal, it actively tried to consolidate a stable world order based on its monopoly of these horrible weapons. In 1946, the United States put forward the Baruch Plan in an attempt to block—once and for all—access to nuclear weapons by the Soviet Union and other countries.[2] Washington formulated a military strategy of mass retaliation—using nuclear weapons as a trump card vis-à-vis its adversary.[3] All these developments brought the U.S. strategic doctrine for world domination, based on nuclear superiority, into vivid focus.

The nuclear monopoly, however, was short-lived as the Soviet Union developed its own nuclear capability. A fierce race in nuclear buildup between the two superpowers ensued, and by the early 1970s each side was equipped with a nuclear arsenal sufficient to annihilate the other multiple times.[4] Not only had the danger of a nuclear war increased dramatically, the world faced a new risk of proliferation of these weapons to other aspirant nations.

Under these circumstances, the United States and the Soviet Union gradually found themselves locked in an ambivalent relationship. They were vying for military superiority while carefully avoiding a head-on confrontation. Antagonism in their relations remained, yet common interests also emerged and were pursued. These included putting their arms race on a more controlled and predictable track, preventing their rivalry from escalating into a nuclear war, and avoiding proliferation of nuclear weapons materials and technologies to other countries.

A similarly complex pattern existed in the international political arena at large. The race between the two superpowers forced the world to live under the shadow of a possible nuclear war. The tension between nuclear and nonnuclear weapon states became acute and led to growing calls in the world to halt the nuclear arms race. At the same time, the international community saw an increasing common interest among all nations to cope with the risk of nuclear proliferation.

Mutual Assured Destruction

In the cold war context, there were four important hallmarks involving the inescapable role of nuclear weapons in reaching strategic stability.

First, the nuclear balance between the United States and the former Soviet Union became the highlight for strategic stability. The Anti-Ballistic Missile (ABM) Treaty of 1972, together with other agreements limiting strategic offensive weapons, codified this nuclear balance.[5] Under the ABM treaty, development of extensive strategic defensive weapons was not allowed. In addition, toward the end of the cold war, there were constraints on the total quantity, although not quality, of offensive weapons imposed through the SALT and START treaties. This peculiar arrangement of allowing the development of an offensive capability, but not a defensive one, was deliberately aimed at consolidating a state of Mutual Assured Destruction (MAD). The rationale was easy and simple to understand. Since both superpowers had formidable nuclear offensive capabilities without significant defensive ones, nuclear war would mean mutual annihilation. By preserving and exposing each side's vulnerability, neither would dare to launch a preemptive strike, and nuclear war would be prevented.

Deterrence

Second, it was in the interests of both superpowers to pursue a strategy of deterrence—to turn the core doctrine of MAD into an operational reality. The primary aim was to prevent a nuclear war. Deterrence seemed feasible because it was based on a balance of terror—despite each side pursuing a formidable nuclear offensive arsenal.[6]

Nuclear Weapon Nonproliferation

Third, the balance between the nuclear weapon states (NWS) and the nonnuclear weapon states (NNWS) in terms of different rights and obligations constituted another pillar of strategic stability in the cold war. The nuclear Nonproliferation Treaty (NPT) of 1967, and other related multilateral treaties, codified this balance. Endorsed by the majority of the international community, the NPT in particular played a unique role in defining the rights and responsibilities of nuclear and nonnuclear states. Those without nuclear weapons pledged not to seek nuclear weapon capabilities. In exchange, the nuclear weapon states committed to work toward nuclear disarmament and to provide assistance to the nonnuclear weapon states in the development of nuclear energy for peaceful purposes. From the outset, the NPT had broad support from the overwhelming majority of the international community, and thus contributed greatly to international nonproliferation efforts.

Arms Control

Fourth, a series of arms control and disarmament mechanisms, as well as bilateral and multilateral regional security arrangements, institutionalized regulations on all nations—including the two superpowers. They included U.S.-Soviet bilateral negotiations on further limitation of their nuclear weapons, the Mutual Balanced Force Reductions talks in Central Europe between NATO and the Warsaw Pact, the multilateral arms control and disarmament negotiation conference in Geneva, peacekeeping activities under the auspices of the United Nations, and many others. Despite some discriminatory features in the aggregate, these legal documents reflected a convergence of interests of the majority members of the world community, as well as the political willingness to accept certain constraints.

However, not all nations faithfully observed the limitations placed on their actions. A few refused to participate in the international nonproliferation regime based on the NPT framework. Other nonnuclear weapon states pursued clandestine nuclear programs—even as members of the NPT. The nuclear weapon states, the two superpowers in particular, have yet to honor their commitments to work in good faith toward nuclear disarmament. These failures aside, arms control agreements and international legal mechanisms still contributed significantly to strategic stability during the cold war era.

Strategic Stability in the Cold War

Overall, the implications of strategic stability in the cold war were mixed. On the positive side, it contributed to maintenance of peace, in general, and the prevention of nuclear war, in particular. Even a large-scale conventional war between the two major powers—or between NATO and the Warsaw Pact—were prevented for fear that such a war would escalate to a nuclear exchange. Like two scorpions in a bottle, the two superpowers were virtually at an impasse called strategic stability.

Strategic stability in the cold war also helped develop a useful code of conduct—particularly for the major powers—regarding the involvement or noninvolvement in regional conflicts and regional peacekeeping efforts. Despite numerous regional conflicts and local wars, global strategic stability was not seriously jeopardized.

Last, but not least, arms control and disarmament mechanisms were indispensable in maintaining strategic stability and mobilizing the international effort for further arms control and nonproliferation progress. As Mr. Tang Jiaxun, former Chinese Foreign Minister, put it

> [T]hanks to joint efforts over the years, the international community has established a relatively complete legal system for arms control and disarmament. As an important component of the global collective security framework with the UN at its center, this system has increased the predictability of the international relations and played an important role in safeguarding international peace, security and stability.[7]

In the nuclear field, these mechanisms regulated the rules of the game and ensured that the ongoing nuclear arms race between the two superpowers was kept on a controlled track.

Even after the cold war era, the existing legal system continued to promote the arms control and disarmament processes. The international effort on arms control during most of the 1990s produced additional important instruments like the Chemical Weapons Convention (CWC), the Comprehensive Test Ban Treaty (CTBT), and the agreement for indefinite extension of the NPT. All these achievements will continue to be important elements in the establishment of a new strategic stability in the twenty-first century.

On the negative side, strategic stability during the cold war carried some inherently irrational elements. First, it catered to the convenience of the global competition between the two superpowers—accepting the legitimacy of the existence of nuclear weapons. Rather than renouncing conflict, the focus was on maintenance of a stable conflict.[8] With deep-rooted suspicion and fear of being overtaken in military superiority, deterrence became the primary rationale for continuing the arms race. In the strategic framework that they established, the arms race—the nuclear arms race in particular—between the two countries never ceased, and preparation for fighting a nuclear war never relaxed. The result was an ever-continuing expansion of the two major powers' nuclear overkill capabilities beyond any reasonable calculations.[9] In fact, the world is still under the shadow of the spread of nuclear weapons and the danger of a nuclear war. Strategic stability based on a balance of terror is fragile, to say the least.

This irrationality also found expression in the discriminatory nature of rights and obligations for nuclear and nonnuclear weapons states under the NPT. The treaty actually perpetuated division between these two groupings of the world's nations. The obligations for the former were vague and general, while those of the latter were explicit and specific. Furthermore, while the overwhelming majority of the nonnuclear weapon states have largely observed their commitments not to acquire nuclear capabilities, the nuclear weapons states have yet to honor their obligations. This failure by nuclear weapons states raised a serious moral obstacle in the strengthening of a nonproliferation regime.

In a larger security context, cold war strategic security focused so narrowly on the military balance between the United States and the Soviet Union that many regional conflicts and disputes were either set aside or forced to follow the ebbs and flows of superpower relations. Far from being solved, these largely abandoned issues contained potential instabilities that invariably surfaced and affected future stability. Developments in the post-cold war era amply demonstrate this weakness of cold war strategic stability. With the old framework eroded, there were over thirty local wars or violent conflicts ongoing in various regions of the world every year during the decade of the 1990s. In turn, persistent instability has been one of the primary sources for turbulence and instability in the world today.[10]

CHANGING STRATEGIC CONTEXT OF NUCLEAR WEAPONS IN THE POST-COLD WAR ERA

The end of the cold war has fundamentally changed the world strategic environment. These changes have been demonstrated in the whole spectrum of human affairs, including the arena of international relations.

Collapse of the Bipolar System

Politically, the Soviet Union has disintegrated. The bipolar system has collapsed. As a general trend, the world is heading for multipolarity. As the scope of participation in world affairs has broadened to include more nations, so have mutual interactions and constraints. At the same time, there is a single superpower remaining in the world, one with increasing might and ambition. As it sees no peers to compete with in the future, Washington's international behavior seems less and less constrained. Meanwhile, rising regional powers have intensified regional instabilities.

Economic Globalization

Ongoing economic globalization has profoundly changed economic and trade relations of many nations in the world, enhancing both interdependence and mutual restraint. However, in general, there is still inequality in economic competition, enlarging the gap between the rich and poor and between the North and South, owing to the inequality in economic development.[11] Economic security is increasingly conspicuous in the security outlook of all nations.[12]

Technology

Rapid development of high technology is a double-edged sword for world security. It provides the developed countries—and the United States, in particular—new material means to develop and deploy new weapon systems. A revolution in military affairs may fundamentally change the traditional mode of warfare and the orientation of military modernization efforts of the major powers. But the proliferation of high technology, and even medium technology, also gives rise to the possibility of proliferation of weapons of mass destruction (WMD). In a deeper sense, high technology provides a new impetus to economic development and social progress—as well as dramatically upgrading the military capabilities of various countries. It also greatly changes the ways of life and the thinking of average people, and, thus, has a strong impact on the traditional norms of operation in a civilized society. Nontraditional security threats are emerging as new security challenges to the world with such speed and magnitude that no nation can single handedly deal with them.[13] As 9/11 illustrated, even though a state builds great strength, its society and individuals are still vulnerable.

All these changes emphasize the increasing complexity of security perceptions in the post-cold war era. State-to-state relations are no longer simplistically defined in terms of foes and friends. Members of the international community are facing unprecedented opportunities for development, peace, and security. At the same time, the world is confronted with new problems, threats, and challenges. What adds to the complexity of the situation is that there is no international consensus on how to best address these issues. Power politics and cold war mentalities continue to be the coins of the international realm, generating deep-rooted suspicion and mistrust among the major powers. Military alliances continue to exist and are even strengthened. Nations are still divided based on differences in perceived values and geopolitical and economic interests.

For China, this pluralistic, diversified, and interdependent world has two implications for the strategic context of nuclear weapons in the future. Global trends indicate that Beijing is convinced that "peace and development remain the dominating themes of the times" and that the international situation, in general—and the Asia-Pacific one, in particular—"tends to be stable as a whole."[14] Under these circumstances, the possibility of a nuclear war among major powers becomes increasingly remote. A change within the political relations among major powers makes it more feasible for them to cooperate in addressing security issues—including the spread of nuclear weapons.

Challenges in the Nuclear Strategic Context

Complexity in international relations also gives rise to factors of uncertainty, instability, and insecurity. At least three major challenges can be discerned as far as the future strategic context of nuclear weapons is concerned.

Increased Reliance on Nuclear Weapons

First, almost all of the nuclear weapon states—and the United States, in particular—have shown greater reliance on the role of nuclear weapons in their security strategies. This will certainly set the stage for the future context of nuclear relations among world nations. It is ironic that while nuclear weapons moved further into the background of the political relations between the major nuclear powers, these same nations find even a greater value in the role of nuclear weapons to protect their security interests. In this regard, it is fair to lay particular blame on the policy of the Bush Administration—characterized by unilateralism, disdain for international norms, and double standards. In the nuclear field in particular, the Administration has been dramatically redefining its strategy, seeking maximum freedom of action and great flexibility in developing new military capabilities at the expense of the security of other nations.

In early 2002, the Bush Administration revealed part of its nuclear posture in the Nuclear Posture Review, which demonstrated that the United States would continue to argue for the legitimacy of nuclear weapons. Furthermore, it would be prepared to use them in a much wider range of circumstances than before—with a particular emphasis on tactical uses. Such an emphasis in declaratory policy has not been seen since the days of flexible response forty or so years ago when tactical nuclear weapons were deployed in Europe and elsewhere. To that end, the Bush Administration is determined to upgrade its nuclear weapons infrastructure, develop new warheads, and prepare for the possible resumption of nuclear explosion testing. Washington is also determined to accelerate efforts to deploy ballistic missile defenses and develop both offensive and defensive capabilities in outer space.

The attitude of the Bush Administration toward nuclear weapons cannot but have an important impact on the policies of other nuclear weapon states. The security policies of these countries continue to give nuclear force an important role to play, and modernization of the nuclear force continues to be a priority. Russia has backed off from its no first use policy. Additionally, all acknowledged nuclear weapon states, except China, claim they are ready to be the first to use nuclear weapons if a situation warrants. As a result, no nuclear weapon state is seriously thinking about implementing its obligations as stipulated in the NPT. Nuclear arms control and disarmament negotiations have stalled. The Conference on Disarmament in Geneva has been virtually deadlocked on all the items at the table. The situation has triggered growing anger and criticism on the part of the nonnuclear weapon states. The recent failure of the 2005 NPT Review Conference highlights the tension between the two sides.

Regional Powers with Nuclear Weapons

The second challenge is the emergence of regional powers aspiring to develop nuclear weapons. The international community has yet to find a way to cope with this problem.

There have been some regions where interstate relations have improved—like Latin America—or where social progress has been achieved—like Eastern Europe and South Africa. Within these regions, there has been progress in strengthening the nonproliferation regime, particularly in the last decade. During the 1990s, one state after another—Brazil, Argentina, and South Africa—renounced the nuclear option. South Africa actually even destroyed its nuclear weapons. The arrangement to prevent the spread of a huge nuclear arsenal after the disintegration of the Soviet Union also appears to have been successful to date. All these are positive developments as far as nonproliferation is concerned.

But there have been more worrisome, and indeed alarming, aspects of this issue as well. With the collapse of the bipolar world system, tensions and conflicts have surfaced in South Asia, the Middle East, and Northeast Asia—the Korean Peninsula in particular. These regional powers are more likely to consider a nuclear option, either in the hope of expanding their influence or for simply insuring their survival.

In May 1998 India conducted a number of nuclear explosions, which forced Pakistan to respond in kind. Although it was no secret that these two countries had long ago surreptitiously acquired nuclear capabilities, the emergence of these two new de facto nuclear states was still shocking to the region as well as to the world.

Elsewhere, other crises simmered. The nuclear crisis in the Democratic Peoples Republic of Korea (DPRK) in 2002 threatened to bring about deep confrontation and potentially even a military conflict with the United States. Although the Six-Party Talks have offered some hope for a peaceful resolution of the issue, the two principle antagonists still remain far apart, and uncertainty remains the hallmark of the present situation. Meanwhile, the international community has serious doubts as to Iran's nuclear policy orientation. Tehran has acknowledged a highly enriched uranium (HEU) program, which had been unknown to the outside world for a long time. Despite Iran's insistence on the program's peaceful nature, its true purpose remains ambiguous at best.

Nuclear capabilities of both the DPRK and Iran have serious implications for world and regional peace and stability, especially if ignored. These cases have revealed some serious vulnerabilities in the monitoring and verification capabilities of the international nonproliferation regime. Even after being proven inadequate in monitoring secret progress in the development of nuclear weapons, the international community could not reach a consensus on immediate and effective ways to correct the situation through punitive measures. Finally, even when a breaching country is eventually pulled back into the NPT fold by providing some rewards, the message to other nonnuclear weapons states would clearly be a wrong one. If you cheat, you can always expect rewards in the end; if you do not, you get nothing. So, what is the incentive for a nonnuclear state to remain a faithful member of the NPT? This inability to deal with the increasing spread of nuclear weapons has dealt a heavy blow to the international nonproliferation regime.

In a broader sense, the emergence of new members in the nuclear club points to a more unsettling risk. Long-standing, dangerous regional conflicts, like those in the Middle East, South Asia, and the Korean Peninsula, now have a dangerous nuclear element. This situation not only complicates threat perceptions and war strategies but also lowers the threshold for the use of nuclear weapons. In a seemingly unending cycle, the incentives for nuclear proliferation for others are increased.

Nuclear Non-State Actors

The third challenge comes from newly emerging roles for non-state actors—both as sources and as potential users of nuclear materials, technologies, and know-how. All the existing international nonproliferation regimes have dealt solely with the behavior of sovereign states. The international community is facing a new and very real danger of a nuclear weapon—or a crude or dirty bomb—falling into the hands of non-state actors such as international terrorists or organized criminal groups. In addition, the scenario of an explosion from such a device in a large city, killing hundreds of thousands of innocent people, is not too far-fetched—but it is simply an unacceptable one for humanity. There has already been the discovery of some documents in al Qaeda caves in Afghanistan suggesting these terrorists were studying the manufacturing process of a dirty bomb. Although there was no evidence to prove to what extent they were successful in their effort, the discovery of their revealed interest was enough to alert the world that this danger cannot be ignored.

What accounts for these new twin dangers of the emergence of new nuclear weapon states and potential nuclear terrorism? Undoubtedly, the rapid spread of science and high technology has played an important role. Many commercial companies and individuals either have access to nuclear related knowledge or have the know-how themselves. Some have become independent suppliers, outside the oversight of organizations such as the Zangger Committee, the London Club, and the Nuclear Suppliers Group—all of whose members are state-parties to the NPT. The independents have circumvented national export controls and have supplied nuclear material to states with ambitions to develop nuclear programs for military purposes. It is common knowledge that a number of Western companies from the United States, Germany, Switzerland, France, and the United Kingdom were the main sources of gas centrifuges for countries like Iraq, Libya, and Iran.

Since then, with the rapid development of science and high technology, clandestine nuclear transfers are even more convenient, efficient, and harder to observe. The recent discovery of A. Q. Khan of Pakistan as the principle organizer of a secret nuclear-supply network shows how important non-state actors can be in assisting countries like Libya—or even the DPRK—in developing their nuclear programs.

More importantly—and what is still not clear—is whether Western companies or A. Q. Khan's network have had any contact with non-state actors eager to have their fingers in the nuclear pie. Severing this connection has become the primary goal of concerted global efforts against international terrorism.

A New Nuclear World Order

These three challenges constitute the most unstable ones in the strategic context of nuclear weapons. Without solutions, it will be difficult to develop a healthy and enduring nuclear world order. There are several points to be considered in any prospective solution.

1. There must be universal agreement as to the immoral and illegal nature of the use of nuclear weapons. This means that nuclear disarmament and nonproliferation must prevail to the point of prohibition and destruction of all nuclear weapons. Measures to reduce, rather than to expand, the role of nuclear weapons in national security strategies would facilitate the achievement of this goal.
2. To achieve a new nuclear world order, there must be comprehensive change in all areas of international activity—political, economic, and military. Among these, the international political element is critical. In other words, an enduring nuclear world order would have to be embedded in a more propitious international political environment in which nations do not feel the need to resort to the nuclear option, because there are alternative solutions.

3. The nuclear weapon states—particularly the United States and Russia, as the two major powers with the largest nuclear arsenals—should bear special responsibility for taking the lead in working toward nuclear disarmament and ensuring nonproliferation.
4. The international community should also take practical and efficient measures to strengthen traditional export controls as well as verification and monitoring mechanisms. Clearly, both are inadequate for coping with the new challenges generated because of regional conflicts, impact of economic globalization, and rapid development of science and high technology. But the solution to the problem requires a multilateral and cooperative approach. Coercive prevention based on the threat of force or unilateral actions often backfires and aggravates tensions.
5. As the two major nuclear weapon states, China and the United States have important responsibilities in fostering a new nuclear world order. To that end, both nations should seek the establishment of a more enduring and propitious bilateral strategic stability. Although possible, this task will not be easy as their nuclear capabilities are disparate and their perspectives divergent.

From Beijing's perspective, several factors are paramount. First, nuclear stability should be part of the overall Chinese-U.S. relationship. As long as this is the case, it is likely that the two countries will continue to put their nuclear weapons in the background. Second, owing to its defensive nuclear posture, China will continue to exercise self-restraint and avoid taking provocative measures to challenge U.S. core interests—provided the United States does not threaten the credibility of China's small, nuclear retaliatory force. Third, the two capitals have a common interest in addressing the threats of nuclear proliferation. Cooperation in this area will strengthen strategic stability in the nuclear field.

Notes

1. The article is based on a couple of my previous papers, namely, "Reflections on the Rationale of Rebuilding the Global Strategic Stability" (in Chinese), *International Studies*, no. 4, Chinese Institute for International Studies (2002); and "Nuclear Nonproliferation-Past, Present and Future," *Research and Progress on Arms Control*, China's Association for Arms Control and Disarmament 3, no. 1 (2005). Views expressed in the present article are entirely of the author's, and do not necessarily represent the position of any organizations or any other individuals.

2. Stanford Arms Control Group, *International Arms Control*, 2nd ed., (Palo Alto, CA: Stanford University Press, 1984), 97–98.
3. Wang Zhongchun and Wen Zhonghua, "The Un-dissipated Nuclear Clouds" (in Chinese), (Beijing: NDU Publishing House, 2000), 111–113.
4. According to the estimate of the International Institute of Strategic Studies in London, in the early 1970s the United States deployed 294 ICBMs, 155 SLBMs, and 600 strategic bombers; the Soviet Union deployed 75 ICBMs, 75 SLBMs, and 190 strategic bombers. Ibid., 75.
5. These treaties include "Antarctic Treaty" in 1959, "Limited Test Ban Treaty" in 1963, "Outer Space Treaty" and "Latin American Nuclear-Free Zone Treaty" in 1967, "Seabed Arms Control Treaty" in 1971, and other nuclear weapons-free zone treaties. See *A Concise Guide to World Armaments and Disarmament*, ed. China Institute for Strategic Studies (Beijing, PRC: Military Translation Press, October 1986), 72–77.
6. See Darryl Howlett, "New Concepts of Deterrence: International Perspectives on Missile Proliferation and Defenses," Occasional Paper No. 5, Center for Nonproliferation Studies, March 2001, 19–20.
7. Tang Jiaoxun, at the Opening Ceremony of International Conference on A Disarmament Agenda for the twenty-first Century, sponsored by the United Nations and the People's Republic of China, Beijing, April 2, 2002.
8. Camille Grand, "Ballistic Missile Threats, Missile Defenses, Deterrence, and Strategic Stability," from *International Perspectives on Missile Proliferation and Defenses*, Occasional Paper No. 5, Monterey Institute of International Studies and Mountbatten Center for International Studies, March 2001, 6.
9. According to one estimate, in January 2001 the United States had deployed 9,376 operational nuclear warheads and 5,000 nonoperational nuclear warheads ; Russia deployed 9196 operational nuclear warheads and 13,500 nonoperational nuclear warheads. See Hans M. Kristensen, "The Unruly Hedge: Cold War Thinking at the Crawford Summit," *Arms Control Today* (December 2001) 8–12.
10. For the detailed description of these armed conflicts, see SIPRI Yearbooks in the 1990s, especially the sections on Armaments, Disarmament, and International Security.
11. See Charles E. Morrison, "Globalization, Vulnerability and Adjustment", paper presented to The Pacific Forum, CSIS, August 19, 2000. Morrison pointed out that "(i)t is widely argued that globalization increases economic disparities between those better able to take advantage of globalizing forces and those unprepared for it. The relative income gaps between and within countries are widening. The income ratio of the richest fifth of the world's population and its poorest fifth have increased from 30 to 1 in 1960, to 60 to 1 in 1990, and 74 to 1 by 1997."
12. See Zhu Yangming, *Asia-Pacific Security Strategy* (Beijing: The Military Science Publishing House, 2000), 181–182.

13. See Paul Stares "'New' Or 'Non-Traditional' Challenges," April 2002, available at www.unu.edu/millennium/stares.pdf. Accessed on February 22, 2008. Stares said, "the range of conceivable security concerns broaden dramatically—some would argue limitlessly—to include a host of economic, social, political, environmental, and epidemiological problems. Whether they emanate from outside or inside the boundaries of the state is immaterial to their consideration as security threats. Likewise, whether they are the product of the deliberate or inadvertent acts is irrelevant. The harmful impact on the individual or the surrounding ecosystem is what matters. What makes problem 'new' or 'non-traditional' threats, therefore, is not that they are truly phenomena or products but rather that they are now treated as security concerns."
14. For more details of China's security perspective, see "China's National Defense in 2004," State Council Information Office, Beijing, December 27, 2004, available at http://www.china.org.cn/e-white/20041227/index.htm. Accessed on February 22, 2008.

5

CONFRONTING GATHERING THREATS: U.S. STRATEGIC POLICY

Michael Nacht

The cold war is fast becoming a distant memory. Even the term "post-cold war era" is now rarely used in the aftermath of the 9/11 attacks and the launching by President Bush of the global war on terror. But for the United States, as the only nation-state at present with truly global interests and global reach, it is necessary to be consistently vigilant of not only immediate concerns, but also of those developments over the horizon that could pose major difficulties in the future.

Central to American power, obviously, are its enormous economic wealth and technological dynamism that have facilitated the deployment of extraordinarily capable conventional and nuclear forces. A critical partner of this power is the structure of international relationships—especially in Europe, East Asia, and the Middle East—that have been adroitly used by Washington in the furtherance of this power.

But as we move through the first decade of the twenty-first century, a global situation is emerging in which the United States does not face a single adversary—such as Nazi Germany or the Soviet Union, which together dominated American strategic thought for sixty years. Both of these states had political ideologies deeply antithetical to American values. Both states played limited or negligible roles in American economic policy. And, in each case, the United States was able to marshal important supporters throughout the world in advance of American policy being implemented.

Introduction

The gathering threats facing the United States in the contemporary era are qualitatively different.

Islamic Jihad

The threat of Islamic jihad is based on a particular interpretation of Islam that has spread to scores of countries throughout Europe, Asia, the Middle East, Africa, and probably even within the Muslim communities of Canada and the United States. The threat is not state based, and, indeed, the stated goal of its titular leader Osama bin Laden is to destroy the very system of nation states created in Europe in the seventeenth century. A new Islamic Caliphate stretching from North Africa to Southeast Asia, and eventually the world, would replace it. America's economic, military, and political support for Arab and other Muslim states is itself a rationale used by the jihadists to recruit adherents with the intention of overthrowing the very regimes that welcome U.S. support. And militarily, as evidenced in Iraq and elsewhere, the jihadist use of suicide bombers in urban areas and against critical infrastructure facilities has largely nullified the classical elements of U.S. military power.

New Nuclear States

New nuclear states pose another threat. From roughly 1960 to 1990, U.S. nuclear nonproliferation policy, while far from fully successful, focused on dissuading many of its allies—Germany, Italy, South Korea, Taiwan—from acquiring nuclear weapons. Pledges to maintain, strengthen, or withdraw U.S. security guarantees were instrumental in discouraging these governments from pursuing their nuclear programs to weapons deployment. Even when Ukraine found itself with a nuclear arsenal after the collapse of the Soviet Union, it was the fashioning of security, economic, energy, and political arrangements that were crucial. Later in the 1990s, when both India and Pakistan detonated nuclear devices and declared themselves to be nuclear weapons states, the sense of threat to American interests was considered minimal. Both states have since developed much closer strategic ties with the United States, although for very different reasons.

The current major nuclear proliferation cases—North Korea and Iran—represent much deeper concerns. By keeping targets like Seoul and Tokyo at risk, North Korea may demonstrate the successful policy of a new nuclear state that is able to deter the United States from implementing an effective counterproliferation policy. This would establish an enormous negative precedent. It could also trigger the development of a chain of new nuclear states that, if it included Japan, could fundamentally alter the security system of East Asia for the first time in a half century. Iran's possession of nuclear weapons capability could trigger armed conflict with Israel, stimulate additional proliferation in the Middle East, and reduce even further the low probability of bringing peace and stability to the region.

China as a Great Power

A third threat is the emergence of the People's Republic of China as a great power. In modern times, the United States has never faced a situation where one of its closest trading partners and direct foreign investment partners was also a strategic rival. With the resolution of Taiwan's status, an enduring source of potential Sino-American conflict, the intersection of the two states' complex economic interdependence will have substantial and unpredictable impacts on their overall relationship—which will be driven in both countries by important domestic constituencies.

In this context, the analysis that follows addresses the following questions:

- How has U.S. security strategy affected nuclear relations among the major powers over the last decade?
- Is mutually assured destruction among great powers, and especially in Sino-American relations, a relevant concept today?
- What do the Bush Administration's new national defense and military strategies mean for U.S.-Chinese relations?
- How is the U.S. strategic approach toward China likely to evolve in the coming years?

U.S. Security Strategy and Nuclear International Relations over the Last Decade

In the past ten years, the U.S. security strategy has witnessed a dramatic transformation during the Clinton and Bush presidencies.

The Clinton Years

Bill Clinton entered the White House in 1993, running on a political platform of "it's the economy, stupid." He and his senior advisors embraced the notion that, with the end of the cold war, the era would be dominated by domestic and international economic concerns. The then U.S. Ambassador to the UN articulated an approach of assertive multilateralism, a notion that collapsed after the fiasco in Somalia in which eighteen U.S. combatants were killed after the United States could not obtain UN approval to protect them. The highest priorities for the Administration were to assist in the democratization of Russia and the other states of the former Soviet Union; to encourage economic, political, and military engagement with China, in part in an effort to promote pluralism and democratic interests in Chinese domestic politics; and to complete the denuclearization of Ukraine, Kazakhstan, and Belarus.

Clinton turned out to be an activist and selective military interventionist as president, but with no apparent overall strategy. Besides Somalia, U.S. forces were sent to Bosnia and Kosovo in the Balkans, as well as to Haiti. There was a tense showdown with North Korea over its nuclear program until the Agreed Framework was reached in 1994, and a crisis in Sino-American relations over Taiwan not long thereafter.

On the nuclear front, Clinton moved cautiously, but unsuccessfully, to win U.S. Senate ratification of a Comprehensive Test Ban Treaty. He chose to implement a stockpile stewardship program to keep the U.S. nuclear deterrent reliable and credible without further testing or new weapons development. He sought to renegotiate the Anti-Ballistic Missile (ABM) Treaty with the Russian Federation. Never completed, it would have permitted deployment of theater missile defenses so that U.S. forces and allies could be protected against regional nuclear threats—notably Japan in the face of North Korea's projected capability.

With the exception of very selective strikes in Afghanistan and Sudan, Clinton failed to respond militarily to a series of terrorist attacks—the first World Trade Center bombing in 1993, the Khobar Towers attack against U.S. forces in Saudi Arabia in 1996, the devastation of the U.S. embassies in Nairobi and Dar as Salaam in 1998, and the attack on the U.S.S. Cole in 2000. Perhaps this smorgasbord of national security activities reflected both a time in which there was no perceived existential, or even significant, long-term threat, and also the president's and his senior advisors' eclectic approach to foreign policy. At the end of the Clinton years, it was difficult to offer a succinct definition of what constituted U.S. security strategy.

The Bush Years

This selective, cautious, and somewhat vague approach to security policy by the Clinton Administration was radically transformed by the Bush Administration, especially after the 9/11 terrorist attacks. President Bush, Vice President Dick Cheney, Secretary of Defense Donald Rumsfeld, and members of the National Security Council staff were all of the view that U.S. security policy had to have clarity, consistency, and an articulated commitment to a no-nonsense approach to the protection of U.S. national interests. When the Administration entered office, there was little doubt that the intent was to return to a focus on the major powers—as had been stated in *Foreign Affairs* articles written by Condoleezza Rice and Robert Zoelick before the election.[1]

In particular, U.S. withdrawal from the ABM Treaty was of a high priority toward facilitating a more rapid deployment of theater and national missile defenses—necessary to combat the growing missile threat from China and rogue states such as North Korea and Iran. There was also a clear emphasis on China as a strategic competitor more than a strategic ally. In addition, there was a commitment not to engage in the sort of nation building in developing countries that Clinton had conducted. Such activity was seen as an unnecessary distraction and diversion of resources from more central issues. More broadly, it is probably safe to say that the Bush team had an ABC—"Anything But Clinton"—approach to foreign policy and to policy in general. A clear, across-the-board break from the past was the new team's intention.

The terrorist attacks of 9/11 altered, and at times accelerated, a number of these approaches. Over the course of the next three years, the Bush Administration issued a set of important documents outlining its overall strategic approach. The statements outlined new emphases and follow-up actions related to national security strategy, counter proliferation of weapons of mass destruction, and homeland security. First, preemptive use of force against terrorist threats and those who support them leapt to the forefront as the nation's leading national security priority. "Those who support them" was the key rationale for the efforts to topple the Taliban regime in Afghanistan and Saddam Hussein's regime in Iraq. Those actions have led to far more elaborate nation-building efforts than had been initially envisioned.

Second, the Administration reiterated its intent to withdraw from the ABM Treaty to move rapidly toward deployment of theater and national missile defense in light of a missile threat defined by the Rumsfeld Commission in 1998 as far more serious than the one characterized by the Intelligence Community Staff in its 1995 National Intelligence Estimate. The United States withdrew from the ABM Treaty and signed the Moscow Treaty in June 2002, a treaty that called for a reduction in deployed strategic nuclear forces by the United States and the Russian Federation, but which provided limited details and no verification procedures.

Additionally, although allies will be included when feasible, the United States has indicated a willingness to act alone if the situation warrants. Over time, this has become known as an emphasis on unilateralism, whether that description is fully accurate or not.

Aggressive counterproliferation policies were established to remove weapons of mass destruction (WMD) from the hands of those who might use them against the United States. The Proliferation Security Initiative[2] led to the formation of a group of more than two dozen nations cooperating to interdict items directly related to WMD capabilities, including interdiction on the high seas in international waters. This emphasis on counterproliferation was a clear shift away from an emphasis on nonproliferation that relied on diplomacy and international law.

Finally, the United States has opened up the possibility of developing new specifically designed nuclear weapons with low yields that could target deeply buried, hardened, underground targets with limited collateral damage.

Relations with the other Great Powers

How have these security initiatives affected nuclear relations among the major powers? Consider the views of each state in turn.

Russia

Russia has found itself with limited capacity to influence major international events since the collapse of the Soviet Union at the end of 1991. It had no ability to limit the expansion of U.S. military and political influence in the Middle East and Persian Gulf, to lead the UN-supported coalition against Iraq in 1991, or to affect the subsequent effort to oust Hussein in 2003. Being itself a target of irredentist Chechen forces that often targeted innocent civilians,

Moscow was sympathetic to a number of initiatives by Bush in the global war on terror. As a result, it permitted the deployment of U.S. forces in different Central Asian states to facilitate the U.S. invasion of Afghanistan in 2001.

But at the same time, President Vladimir Putin and the Russian leadership have not been interested in being the lapdog for U.S. policies, and viewed many of these policies as contrary to Russian national interests. Important elements of the military high command saw the U.S. withdrawal from the ABM Treaty and the United States' emphasis on missile defense as direct threats to the credibility of the Russian nuclear deterrent. Russia's response is increased budgetary support for follow-on offensive missile systems, including those with maneuverable reentry vehicles (MaRV).

Russia's response on nonproliferation and counterproliferation is inconsistent. One would think it is in the Russian national interest to stop, and even roll back, the spread of nuclear weapons, in part because of possible linkages to the Chechen problem. But Russia has been highly enthusiastic, evidently for economic reasons, to support many elements of a sophisticated Iranian nuclear energy program that clearly has links to weapons development. Russia also remains a recalcitrant partner in the Nunn-Lugar-Dominici Cooperative Threat Reduction Program—reluctant to share information and moving far more slowly in securing nuclear materials at U.S. expense than either the Clinton or Bush team expected.

Geostrategically, Moscow interprets a number of American moves in Ukraine and Central Asia—coupled with the continued expansion of NATO right up to the Russian Federation border—as directly threatening their vital interests and as an attempt by Washington to create a permanent ring of states dedicated to containing Russian expansionism.

China

For some time, China has seen the United States as both a vital part in the engine of its economic growth and as its main strategic competitor, the one power that stands in the way of Beijing's rise to great power status and its reclaiming of Taiwan. No wonder that recent news accounts report the Chinese elite as divided into two camps—the economic modernists and the security hawks.[3]

> The modernists see China joining the United States as the second great economic power of the 21st century, and the two nations sharing

the gains from increased trade ties and global growth. The hawks regard that view as naïve, and fret that American policy is to remain the world's only superpower and to curb China's rise. So China's response, the hawks say, is to try to erode United States hegemony and reduce America's power to hold China down.[4]

While China also has its own Islamic irredentist movement in its westernmost province to deal with, many strategists in Beijing see U.S. counterterrorism policy as consistent with Washington's desire to contain China. The United States has deployed forces in Central Asia, including Afghanistan; has closer ties with India; has urged Japan to take a greater role in its use of military force, including participating in contingencies to protect Taiwan; continues its sales of sophisticated weapons to Taiwan; and is moving to deploy missile defenses in Japan, South Korea, and Taiwan. No doubt, all of these are seen as anti-Chinese policies, and they have helped stimulate the growth and development of more advanced Chinese nuclear forces and the deployment of more intercontinental range missile systems capable of striking U.S. territory.

Major Allies

Britain, France, Germany, and Japan have all been largely supportive of U.S. counterterrorism policies, including military action in Afghanistan. They were split bitterly, however, over going to war in Iraq. Britain—in fact, Prime Minister Tony Blair—sided enthusiastically with the United States and committed about 8,000 combat forces. Japan also supported the U.S. initiative and sent noncombatants. France and Germany were openly opposed. Indeed, France used its diplomatic leverage to persuade a wide range of countries not to support the U.S. proposal to use military force in Iraq until WMD inspections progressed much further. France and Germany have also not been willing to help in Iraq after the conventional conflict turned into a highly volatile insurgency.

There has been little relationship, however, between these debates and nuclear weapons policies in these countries. Britain and France retain—leftover from the cold war—what was termed minimum deterrence capabilities, although against whom they are directed is not entirely clear. Modernization efforts continue, but in no way alter the fundamental character of these systems. Germany, on the other hand, seems firmly committed to its nonproliferation policy, with no signs at all of any alteration for years to come.

India, Pakistan, and Israel

India, Pakistan, and Israel, the other three nuclear weapons states, have had their nuclear programs affected in subtle ways. India, seeking to become a global power in all fields, is using its nuclear capability as an argument for entry to and permanent status on the UN Security Council. It has growing economic, political, and military ties with the United States, a vast change from the cold war era. Then it was assiduously neutral in declaratory policy, but often sided with the Soviet Union—its principal arms supplier and trading partner.

Pakistan, on the front lines in the war on terror, is an ally of the United States, yet harbors terrorists and many virulent anti-American Islamic groups. The United States has sought to provide assistance to better secure Pakistan's nuclear forces, but there is limited public information about what, if any, has actually been provided. The revelations of the A.Q. Khan nuclear proliferation network has cast a shadow on Pakistan-U.S. relations, but has not necessarily affected the pace of Pakistan's own nuclear development program. The United States intervened diplomatically at very high levels in the summer of 2003 when it appeared that an Indo-Pakistan war seemed likely. Since then, bilateral relations between these two states have improved markedly. Both India and Pakistan continue to maintain and modernize their nuclear capabilities, with India deploying the larger force, but Pakistan perhaps having the more militarily capable one.

Israel, the only non-declared nuclear state widely thought to have nuclear weapons, says virtually nothing about its programs. A major factor of Israeli concern is the growing Iranian capability, in terms of both longer-range delivery systems and advancements toward nuclear weapons deployment.

IS MUTUALLY ASSURED DESTRUCTION A RELEVANT CONCEPT TODAY?

It is not crystal clear how relevant mutually assured destruction (MAD) was during the cold war, but it seems less relevant now—particularly with regard to Sino-American relations.

Note that it was U.S. Defense Secretary Robert McNamara who in the mid-1960s coined the term "assured destruction" as a criterion for sizing the U.S. nuclear forces. If a substantial portion of Soviet military and urban industrial targets could be held at risk even after a Soviet first strike, McNamara reasoned that this assured destruction capability would serve as a credible deterrent—assuming a rational Soviet leadership. The Soviets never publicly endorsed the concept. And U.S. operational planners—less concerned with declaratory policy, what we say, than with employment policy, what we would do—always planned to fight a nuclear war in which the United States would prevail. Whether realistic or not, it may well be that the most senior U.S. and perhaps Soviet decision-makers were deterred from acting because of assured destruction, but the systems below them were probably ready to fight to win if called upon to do so.

The situation in Sino-American relations today is quite different. Obviously there is a huge disparity in nuclear firepower, both quantitatively and qualitatively, favoring the United States. But this is beside the point. China has no interest in matching U.S. nuclear forces. It does have an interest in deterring the United States from intervening with conventional forces in case of armed conflict over Taiwan—or in some other contingency in the future. To accomplish this goal, Chinese strategists have sought to expand the number and range of nuclear-tipped ballistic missiles that could reach the United States.

Senior Chinese military officers have raised the prospect of Chinese use of nuclear weapons in a conflict situation over Taiwan. In 1995, during the Sino-American crisis during the Clinton years, General Xiong Guangkai (now deputy chief of the general staff of the People's Liberation Army) told Chas Freeman, a former senior Pentagon official and U.S. Ambassador to Saudi Arabia, that China would consider using nuclear weapons in a Taiwan conflict. Freeman quoted General Xiong as stating that Americans should worry more about Los Angeles than Taipei.

A recent Chinese statement on this matter further illustrates this situation. On July 15, 2005, Major General Zhu Chenghu stated,

> If the Americans are determined to interfere [in a conflict to defend Taiwan] we will be determined to respond. We Chinese will prepare ourselves for the destruction of all cities east of Xian. Of course, the Americans will have to be prepared that hundreds of cities will be destroyed by the Chinese…War logic dictates that a weaker power needs to use maximum efforts to defeat a stronger rival…We have no capability to fight a conventional war against the United States…We can't win this kind of war.[5]

General Zhu's statement raises many interesting questions. Is it a departure from China's policy of no first use of nuclear weapons, since he was referring to Chinese first use after the United States intervened with conventional forces in the Taiwan conflict? Would the Chinese leadership really be willing to sacrifice all cities east of Xian if that meant wiping out its entire modern economic base? Do the Chinese have enough deliverable warheads to actually destroy hundreds of U.S. cities when U.S. estimates, perhaps incorrectly, place the current capability in the range of 45–57 missiles that can reach U.S. targets? Is General Zhu telling us that the DF-31 ICBM, the DF-31A road mobile ICBM, and the Jl-2 submarine-launched ballistic missiles are much further along than we think they are, or are there other new Chinese systems deployed or about to be deployed, of which we are unaware?

It is the credibility of the Chinese nuclear force to deter U.S. conventional intervention in a conflict over Taiwan that is central to Sino-American relations, not some abstract and somewhat misleading notion of mutually assured destruction.

New Strategic Strategies and U.S.-Chinese Relations

At a recent meeting of Asian defense ministers in Singapore sponsored by the International Institute for Strategic Studies, the then secretary of defense, Rumsfeld, gave a hard-hitting speech on China and wondered aloud why China was devoting so many resources to building up its military capability when no country threatened it. He implied that China was perhaps harboring aggressive intent and that Asian nations as well as the United States needed to take notice.

But a somewhat different interpretation is worthy of discussion. China, given its size, population, history, and newly found economic strength, as well as its enormous economic potential, has every right to plan for and dream of becoming a major world power. Major world powers have strong military capabilities. Enhancing such capabilities goes with the territory, and does not necessarily include harboring aggressive designs. This could be one benign explanation for the modernization of the Chinese military.

A second interpretation is that the Chinese leadership, and perhaps all future Chinese leaderships, will continue to seek to resolve the Taiwan question. Having a military option is central to their planning. Since it is largely the threat of U.S. military intervention to defend Taiwan that has precluded China from taking action for five decades, China is in a continuous search to find ways to nullify this threat. Use of a Chinese nuclear deterrent to dissuade U.S. conventional force intervention is a plausible response.

A third interpretation is that, in part due to Bush Administration policies, Chinese leaders in Beijing see many new threats on the horizon. A reinvigorated Japan might acquire its own nuclear forces or seek to acquire new power projection forces. A U.S.-North Korean conflict would threaten Chinese national interests. Down the road, a unified Korea would be armed with nuclear weapons. Taiwan could acquire its own nuclear weapons. A much stronger India would have more advanced nuclear weapons. And, a resurgent Russia might again seek to dominate border areas of the Far East.

Bush Administration policies almost certainly strengthen the hands of the strategic hawks in China who see a U.S. envelopment strategy and claim that much greater Chinese military as well as economic power is needed to counter American policies. Indeed, the seemingly messianic approach of the President in support of the spread of democracy poses a direct rhetorical threat to a Chinese leadership that is still highly authoritarian—even if it is no longer totalitarian.

On the other hand, there are a number of positive contributions of the Bush Administration policies to U.S.-Chinese relations. China, in its own interests, is playing a useful, if limited, role in the war against Islamic jihad. China has been consistently encouraged by Bush to play a constructive mediating role with North Korea and has participated in, as well as hosted, the six-party talks that also involved North and South Korea, the United States, Russia, and Japan. As the primary external source of food and fuel for North Korea, China is considered to have leverage over Pyongyang's decision making and has been encouraged to play a constructive role that could resolve the crisis over the North Korean nuclear program. And, after much pressure from Washington, China claims to be a valued partner in stopping the spread of WMD—especially nuclear weapons and missile technology. This would be an important step forward, since China's support was vital in the development of Pakistan's nuclear and missile technologies.

Conclusion: The Evolution of the U.S. Strategic Approach Toward China

Since the start of the George Bush Administration in 1991, the United States has maintained a two-pronged approach toward China. The first approach is to foster trade, direct foreign investment, and greater societal interactions. The hope is that a more economically prosperous

China will become more politically pluralistic. The second approach, simultaneous with the first, is to remain steadfast that the Taiwan issue has to be resolved peacefully and to remain vigilant about U.S. military support should Taiwan need to defend itself. The U.S. commitment to Taiwan is part of the credibility the United States needs to demonstrate in order to keep the East Asian security system led by Japan and South Korea stable.

The economic relationship is now of huge significance to both countries. But as columnist Tom Friedman points out, it is highly asymmetric. China not only provides the United States with basic household goods but also finances America's debt. The U.S. economic connection, on the other hand, has permitted China to grow at 9 percent or more per year for several years. It needs this level of economic growth to provide jobs for all the new entrants to the labor force annually.[6] Unemployment could lead to huge political unrest, and regime change cannot be ruled out. It seems difficult, although far from unimaginable, to visualize a major U.S. departure from this dual approach—unless matters spin out of control in North Korea or Taiwan. In a Sino-American confrontation, all bets are off regarding the bilateral economic relationship—no matter how much it will hurt the U.S. economy.

It is best to think of U.S.-Chinese relations as a struggle between centripetal forces pulling the two countries together and centrifugal forces pulling them apart. In the former category are economic interests and the domestic groups that benefit from them and, to a much less extent, similarity in views on countering Islamic terrorism and some common interests on the North Korean question. After all, for China, a divided Korea reduces the likelihood of a Japanese military resurgence that would pose a major challenge. In the latter category is the classical rivalry of an established great power with a rising power, as well as specific differences over democracy and human rights, intellectual property rights, and, of course, Taiwanese security.

For a long time the centripetal forces have dominated, and the people of both countries have prospered as a result. A reversal of this condition could pose a grave threat to both China and the United States.

Notes

1. See Robert Zoellick, "A Republican Foreign Policy," and Condoleezza Rice, "Promoting the National Interest," *Foreign Affairs* 79, no. 1 (Jan/Feb 2000), 63–78, 45–62.

2. "Remarks by the President to the People of Poland in Krakow, Poland, on May 31, 2003, (Proliferation Security Initiative)," (Washington, DC: The White House), May 31, 2003. www.whitehouse.gov/news/releases/2003/05/20030531–3.html. Accessed on February 22, 2008.
3. Lohr, Steve. "Who's Afraid of China Inc.?" *The New York Times*, Section 3, 1, July 24, 2005. http://www.nytimes.com/2005/07/24/business/yourmoney/24oil.html. Accessed on February 22, 2008.
4. Ibid.
5. Kahn, Joseph. "Chinese General Threatens Use of A-Bombs if U.S. Intrudes," *The New York Times*, July 15, 2005. http://query.nytimes.com/gst/fullpage.html?res=9902E7DB1E3DF936A25754C0A9639C8B63. Accessed on February 22, 2008. Gen Zhu is a dean at China's National Defense University.
6. Friedman, Thomas, "Joined at the Hip," *The New York Times*, July 20, 2005. http://www.nytimes.com/2005/07/20/opinion/20friedman.html?n=Top/Opinion/Editorials%20and%20Op-Ed/Op-Ed/Columnists/Thomas%20L%20Friedman. Accessed on February 22, 2008.

6

CHINA'S NUCLEAR WEAPON POLICY

Jia Qingguo

China has maintained a nuclear force primarily for two purposes: to free China from nuclear blackmail and to enhance its security at a minimum cost. Generally speaking, China's nuclear-weapon policy has nine basic components: minimum deterrence, no first use, nonproliferation, security assurance to nonnuclear weapon states (NNWS), security assurance to nuclear weapon states (NWS), nuclear disarmament, respect for the right of peaceful development of nuclear energy, opposition to ballistic missile defense systems, and peaceful resolution of nuclear crises.

MAIN COMPONENTS TO CHINESE NUCLEAR POLICY

Minimum Deterrence

For many years, China has pursued a policy of minimum deterrence. Although over time its technological sophistication and expanding resources have made it possible for drastic expansion of its nuclear arsenal, China has chosen not to do so. Instead, it has maintained the "barest of abilities to retaliate with nuclear force should they come under nuclear attack."[1] In the words of Chinese Ambassador Sha Zukang, "China's nuclear arsenal is the smallest and least advanced among the five nuclear powers."[2] As Lt. Gen. Li Jijun, vice president of the PLA's Academy of Military Science, put it in a speech to the U.S. Army War College on July 15, 1997, "A small arsenal is retained only for the purpose of self-defense." China's strategy is completely defensive, focused only on deterring the possibility of nuclear blackmail being used against China by other nuclear powers.³

No First Use

China announced its no first use policy when it tested its first nuclear bomb in 1964, and it has adhered to this policy ever since. According to its 1998 White Paper on National Defense, "From the first day it possessed nuclear weapons, China has solemnly declared its determination not to be the first to use such weapons at any time and in any circumstances, and later undertook unconditionally not to use or threaten to use nuclear weapons against nonnuclear weapon states or nuclear-weapon-free zones."⁴ China has not only strictly adhered to the no first use policy, but it is also a strong advocate for a no first use international treaty among nuclear weapon states. According to Chinese Ambassador Hu Xiaodi, "China initiated that nuclear-weapon states should conclude a treaty on no first use of nuclear weapons and undertake unconditionally not to use nuclear weapons against nonnuclear weapon states."⁵

Nonproliferation

For quite some time after China possessed nuclear weapons, Beijing was critical of the nonproliferation regime. China argued that the regime was an instrument of the nuclear weapon powers to maintain their monopoly over nuclear weapons. It was therefore unfair and unjust to the nonnuclear weapon states. Despite the critical view, however, China publicly stated that it would not engage in nuclear proliferation. Eventually, China formally subscribed to the nonproliferation regime in 1992. Subsequently, the Chinese government has taken many steps to ensure its compliance with nonproliferation rules.⁶ For example, in December 2001, the Chinese legislature adopted the Amendments to Criminal Law of the People's Republic of China, which designate as criminal offences such acts as illegally manufacturing, trafficking, and transporting radioactive substances, and stipulate commensurate criminal punishments for such offences. And in February 2002, the Chinese government promulgated the Provisions on the Administration of Safeguard and Supervision of Nuclear Import and Export and Foreign Nuclear Cooperation.

Security Assurance to Nonnuclear Weapon States

China provides nonnuclear weapon states with unconditional security assurances. It participates in several nuclear-weapon-free zone treaties in Latin America, the South Pacific, Southeast Asia, and Africa. In doing so, China assumes formal obligations to refrain from deploying, using, or threatening to use nuclear weapons in these regions. On April 11, 1995, in UN Security Council Resolution 984, China joined the other four declared nuclear weapon states (the United States, Russia, United Kingdom, and France) in providing legally binding positive security assurances to come to the aid of nonnuclear weapon states in the event of a nuclear attack against them.[7]

Assurance to other Nuclear Weapon States

In addition to offering assurances to nonnuclear weapon states, China has also provided security assurances to some declared nuclear-weapon states as their relations improved. For example, China has promised not to target its nuclear weapons against Russia in 1994 and the United States in 1998, and to keep its nuclear weapons at a very low level of alert.

Nuclear Disarmament

China believes in the goal of a nuclear-weapon-free world. It has been a long-term champion of nuclear disarmament. China's 1998 Defense White Paper advocates that "all states should negotiate and conclude an international convention on the complete prohibition and thorough destruction of nuclear weapons." In this regard, China believes that the countries that have the largest nuclear arsenals (meaning the United States and Russia) should take the lead in nuclear disarmament.[8] It has repeatedly urged these two countries to make deeper cuts in their nuclear forces.

Opposition to Bmd

China is opposed to the development of ballistic missile defense systems. It believes that development of such systems is destabilizing and encourages nuclear arms race. According to Ambassador Sha Zukang, China is opposed to the U.S. National Missile Defense program because it would weaken or neutralize China's very limited deterrence capability. "China will not allow its legitimate means of self-defense to be weakened or even taken away by anyone in anyway. This is one of the most important aspects of China's national security."[9]

Respect the Right of Peaceful Development of Energy

In principle, China respects the right of the nonnuclear weapon states to develop nuclear energy for peaceful purposes. The Chinese government believes that it is not only fair but also important for nonproliferation purposes to respect this right as long as the non-nuclear weapon states strictly observe the rules of the international nonproliferation regimes. This helps explain the positions China has held on the ongoing nuclear problems of North Korea and Iran.

Peaceful Resolution of Nuclear Crises

While China is firmly supportive of the nonproliferation regime, it does not favor use of force to deal with proliferation problems. It believes that such problems should be dealt with through negotiation and dialogue between and among the concerned parties. Force can only be used as a very last resort, and should be consistent with international law and with explicit authorization from the UN Security Council. Prior to the U.S. invasion of Iraq, China took the position that force should not be used until all peaceful measures were exhausted. Since the outbreak of the ongoing Korean nuclear crisis, China has, for the same reasons discussed above, repeatedly expressed its opposition to the use of force to deal with the crisis.

Alternative Views

Most people in the Chinese foreign policy circle share the views expressed in the nuclear weapons policy discussed in the previous passages. They agree that given the domestic and international circumstances China faces, the policy still represents the most sensible approach to dealing with the problem of nuclear weapons. Some people, however, do argue for changes to the policy so as to reflect the alleged new international and domestic realities.

To begin with, against a background of the development of the national missile defense and theater missile defenses on the part of the United States and some of its allies, some Chinese analysts point out that the real motive behind such efforts is to neutralize China's limited nuclear deterrence capabilities. In response, they argue, China should increase the number of nuclear weapons or improve its existing stocks to the extent that they can penetrate missile defense systems and maintain China's minimum deterrence capabilities. In his comment on the U.S. development of missile defenses on March 14, 2000, Sha Zukang, director general of the Arms Control Department at the time, said that China is opposed to U.S. development of missile defenses and would not tolerate weakening or deprivation of its limited means of self-defense in any fashion.[10]

In addition, in the light of the fact that none of the other four declared nuclear weapon states maintains the no first use policy, some Chinese argue that China's adherence to it only places China in a disadvantaged position. Therefore, it is time for China to change that policy so as to best defend China's security interests. The recent widely reported remarks by Maj. Gen. Zhu Chenghu on the possible use of nuclear weapons against the United States, should the latter attack Chinese targets in the event of a Taiwan Strait military confrontation, for example, are reflective of such a view.[11]

Finally, as the Taiwan separatists have pushed for independence more and more aggressively in recent years, some Chinese analysts take a more pessimistic view about the future of the cross-strait relations. Under the circumstances, they argue that China should sharply increase its nuclear arsenal so as to deter the United States from military intervention should military actions become necessary to remove the separatist problem in Taiwan. They point out that the United States did not intervene in Russia's military operations to deal with the Chechen problem primarily because Russia has a large nuclear arsenal.

Conclusion

Despite these and other views, the Chinese government has not changed its nuclear policy in any significant way. China still believes that its current time-honored approach best serves China's national interests. However, new international developments are making some Chinese to rethink about some components of this policy. Whether this will lead to any significant changes in its policy will depend on how China and the outside world interact and how such interactions affect Chinese perception of how effective China's current nuclear policy serves its national interests.

Notes

1. Bates Gill, "China's Nuclear Agenda," *New York Times*, September 7, 2001.
2. "Speech at the NMD Briefing by Ambassador Sha Zukang," Permanent Mission of the PRC to the UN Mission at Geneva, March 14, 2001.
3. "Traditional Military Thinking and the Defensive Strategy of China: An Address at the U.S. Army War College," Letort Paper No. 1, August 29, 1997, 7.

4. Information Office of the State Council of the People's Republic of China, "China's National Defense," July 1998, Beijing, http://russia.shaps.hawaii.edu/security/china-defense-july1998.html#5a. Accessed on February 12, 2008.
5. "Statement by Ambassador Hu Xiaodi, Head of the Chinese Delegation, on Security Assurances for Non-Nuclear-Weapon States at the 3rd Session of the PrepCom for the 2005 NPT Review Conference," April 30, 2004, at http://www.china-un.org/eng/xw/t94693.htm. Accessed on February 12, 2008.
6. Ministry of Foreign Affairs of the People's Republic of China, "Fact Sheet: China: Nuclear-Weapon Proliferation Prevention," April 27, 2004, http://www.globalsecurity.org/wmd/library/report/2004/prcnuclear-proli-prevention-factsheet_27apr2004.htm. Accessed on February 12, 2008.
7. "Statement by Ambassador Hu Xiaodi, Head of the Chinese Delegation, on Security Assurances for Non-Nuclear Weapon States at the 3rd Session of the PrepCom for the 2005 NPT Review Conference," April 30, 2004, at http://www.china-un.org/eng/xw/t94693.htm. Accessed on February 12, 2008.
8. Information Office of the State Council of the People's Republic of China, "China's National Defense," July 1998, Beijing, http://russia.shaps.hawaii.edu/security/china-defense-july1998.html#5a. Accessed on February 12, 2008.
9. "Speech at the NMD Briefing by Ambassador Sha Zukang," Permanent Mission of the PRC to the UN Mission at Geneva, March 14, 2001.
10. "Sha Zukang qiangdiao zhongguo fandui meiguo gao NMD" (Sha Zukang stressed that China is opposed to US development of NMD), http://www.chinamil.com.cn/item/nmd/content/news1987666-nmd.htm. Accessed on February 12, 2008. Professor Wu Xinbo also said that the U.S. development of the NMD would encourage China to increase its nuclear weapons and their penetration capability. December 15, 2001, http://www.zaobao.com/special/us/pages1/nmd151201b.html. Accessed on February 12, 2008.
11. "If the Americans draw their missiles and position-guided ammunition on to the target zone on China's territory, I think we will have to respond with nuclear weapons," said General Zhu Chenghu. *Financial Times*, July 15, 2005, http://www.ft.com/cms/s/2/28cfe55a-f4a7–11d9–9dd1–00000e2511c8.html. Accessed on February 12, 2008.

7

U.S. NUCLEAR POSTURE REVIEW AND BEYOND: IMPLICATIONS FOR SINO-AMERICAN RELATIONS

James J. Wirtz

The 2001 Nuclear Posture Review (NPR),[1] in conjunction with the 2001 decision to abandon the Antiballistic Missile (ABM) Treaty, marked the first significant effort to change U.S. strategic doctrine in a decade.[2] Both policies drew much criticism when they were first announced, but they have received relatively little attention in the aftermath of the 9/11 terrorist attacks on the world trade center and the pentagon, the coalition invasion of Iraq, and the ongoing global war on Terrorism.[3] In announcing their new strategic policies, however, members of the Bush Administration were largely silent on how the People's Republic of China (PRC) fit into U.S. nuclear doctrine and planning, leaving several questions unanswered about the NPR and U.S. missile defense. Were the NPR and the associated ideas of preventive war and preemption adopted with a future Chinese nuclear force in mind? Are the programs in the NPR and nascent U.S. missile defense intended to negate the relatively limited nuclear force China deploys today? Is the world about to see a nuclear arms race between China and the United States, prompted by a strong reaction to the 2001 Nuclear Posture Review?

Although many observers are prone to see danger in both Chinese and U.S. nuclear programs, the reality of the Chinese-American nuclear relationship is rather benign. Chinese officials continue to pursue a modest nuclear force modernization program that remains more of a political, rather than a military, issue in contemporary American thinking about nuclear weapons. There is of course a Chinese-American nuclear balance in the Pacific, but there is insufficient political discord to make that balance particularly salient. Despite the claims made by some observers about U.S. nuclear primacy,[4] the post-cold war draw down of U.S. nuclear forces will continue until it meets the limits set by the Moscow Treaty. By 2012, the United States will field roughly 20 percent of the strategic nuclear weapons it had deployed when Ronald Reagan left office, a development that seems to meet with approval on the part of officials in Beijing and Washington. China and the United States are both nuclear powers, but they have managed to prevent nuclear issues from dominating their relations. So far at least, Chinese and U.S. officials have muted the role played by nuclear weapons in the relations between their two countries, thereby reducing the possibility that a full-blown nuclear arms race might emerge in Asia.

This chapter describes recent American thinking about nuclear weapons and Asia by exploring why U.S. strategists are not particularly preoccupied by the threat posed by contemporary and future Chinese nuclear doctrine and capability. The first section describes the 2001 Nuclear Posture Review, exploring how the planning document clearly was not designed with a "Chinese contingency" in mind. It also will describe how the Bush Administration has made little progress in achieving its more ambitious objectives of transforming the U.S. nuclear arsenal. The second section explores the ongoing debate about the future of Sino-U.S. relations, highlighting how the nuclear balance seems to matter little in the way observers estimate the likely trajectory of events in the Pacific. The chapter also identifies the factors that have contributed to what amounts to a benign nuclear relationship between the United States and the People's Republic of China. The chapter concludes by identifying the potential risks both countries face when it comes to maintaining their nuclear relationship.

The 2001 Nuclear Posture Review

The Bush Administration's vision of the American nuclear future, articulated in the 2001 NPR, was part of a broader effort to restructure U.S. defense policy. The NPR thus reflected the key concepts of dissuasion, deterrence, defense, and denial articulated in the 2001

Quadrennial Defense Review (QDR). The NPR and the 2001 QDR established strategic priorities for U.S. defense and foreign policies.

The 2001 NPR incorporated a new framework for Russian-American strategic relations and a response to the ongoing proliferation of nuclear, chemical, biological weapons, and long-range ballistic missiles. It called for a reduction in the overall number of deployed nuclear forces, while at the same time it placed a renewed emphasis on U.S. nuclear systems as weapons to be used in battle. It identified the potential need for new types of nuclear weapons and delivery systems, while at the same time it suggested that precision-guided conventional weapons could accomplish many existing nuclear missions. It downplayed the threat posed to the United States by the largest nuclear arsenal in the world and instead highlighted the threat posed by weak states or non-state actors armed with rudimentary nuclear, biological, and chemical capabilities. It is a nuclear policy that makes a concerted effort to consign the defining feature of the cold war—the Soviet-American strategic relationship of Mutual Assured Destruction (MAD)—to the history books. The NPR apparently made no reference to China as a threat and it failed to use China as a justification for either current or proposed U.S. nuclear programs.

The NPR unveiled a new strategic triad, consisting of nuclear weapons and nonnuclear precision-strike capabilities, passive and active defenses, and a revitalized nuclear infrastructure. The new strategic triad is intended to integrate defenses (i.e., missile defense), nuclear weapons, and "non-nuclear strike forces"[5] into a seamless web of capabilities to dissuade potential competitors from mounting a military challenge to the United States,[6] to deter adversaries, and to fight and win wars if deterrence fails. The NPR noted that the strike elements "... can provide greater flexibility in the design and conduct of military campaigns to defeat opponents decisively. Nonnuclear strike capabilities may be particularly useful to limit collateral damage and conflict escalation. The NPR emphasizes technology as a substitute for nuclear forces that are withdrawn from service. Global real-time command and control and reconnaissance capabilities will take on greater importance in the new strategic triad. Nuclear weapons could be employed against targets able to withstand nonnuclear attack, (for example, deep underground bunkers or bioweapons facilities)."[7] Planners called for the new triad to rely on "adaptive planning" so that it could quickly meet emerging threats and contingencies. Advanced command, control, and intelligence capabilities were intended to integrate the legs of the triad, facilitating flexible operations. This emphasis on adaptive planning differs from the traditional approach taken to the development of the U.S. nuclear war plan, the Single-Integrated Operations Plan, or SIOP. The SIOP reflected a deliberate planning process that often took months or even years to complete and which generated a finite number of nuclear employment options for consideration by the president in his capacity as commander in chief.

The 2001 NPR thus comprised three different initiatives that reached for somewhat incompatible objectives. First, the NPR called for reductions in the overall size of the U.S. nuclear arsenal and the elimination of nuclear deterrence as the centerpiece of Russian-American relations. This first initiative actually justified further reductions in the U.S. nuclear arsenal by de-emphasizing the role and importance nuclear weapons played in U.S. defense policy. By de-linking the need to maintain U.S. nuclear forces as a counter to the relatively large Russian nuclear arsenal, the Bush Administration reduced the ability of defense planners to justify maintaining a large nuclear force based on parity with Russian nuclear forces. Second, the NPR called for the emergence of a new strategic triad that comprised active defenses, a responsive nuclear infrastructure, and the integration of the conventional precision global-strike complex and new "boutique" nuclear weapons designed to meet threats posed by emerging nuclear states. This second initiative was intended to increase the utility of nuclear weapons by integrating existing and potentially new specialized weapons into operational planning. Third, it called for the adoption of new planning principals and techniques designed to meet a dynamic threat environment, specifically, an array of known and even "unknown" threats that made traditional deliberate planning appear obsolete. This third initiative was a response to the uncertainty that continues to permeate planning in the Pentagon: most defense officials believe that the deliberate planning must be replaced by more flexible procedures and assumptions.

Many observers were quick to label the NPR as a dangerous term in the "arms race," especially the apparent U.S. intention to begin to develop and eventually deploy new types of nuclear weapons. Nevertheless, as a national strategy, the 2001 NPR was coherent, which probably increased its credibility especially in the minds of its critics. It identified how the strategic environment was changing, described how the U.S. nuclear arsenal needed to change to meet this emerging threat, and then offered a plan to develop new capabilities, doctrines, and operating procedures to create a new "strategic deterrent." But the Bush Administration's plan to create a new strategic deterrent took center stage for a relatively short period. Events in Iraq would soon come to overshadow the NPR. The 2006 Quadrennial Defense Review redirected U.S. defense efforts toward stability, security, transition, and reconstruction operations while reemphasizing the nonnuclear programs contained in the 2001 NPR.[8] The shift in policy between the 2001 and 2006 QDR rarely gains much attention from observers of the Sino-American strategic relationship: the Bush Administration is now emphasizing the importance of improving U.S. capabilities to conduct low-intensity conflict, stability, and humanitarian operations. Improving global precision-strike capabilities no longer seems to have a priority on the U.S. defense agenda.

Implementing the NPR

The NPR represented a road map for an ongoing strategic program: many of the capabilities outlined by the NPR did not exist in 2001 and do not exist even today. Since 2001, the Bush Administration has made some progress toward implementing the NPR, but on balance, it has been unable to reverse a deeply rooted trend set in motion at the end of the cold war. The U.S. nuclear arsenal and associated infrastructure has been shrinking for well over a decade, and this trend is likely to continue to the foreseeable future. Although the NPR called for a new strategic triad, the Administration's nuclear modernization program has met with little congressional or public support. In fact, the Administration has only enjoyed significant success in terms of the first NPR initiative: diminishing the role of nuclear weapons in U.S. defense policy in general, especially in U.S. relations with Russia.

The Bush Administration's effort to develop the new triad never really got off the ground. Initially, the Administration proposed an R&D program to investigate future applications for low-yield nuclear weapons. It requested $7.5 million from Congress to assess the feasibility and cost of a Robust Nuclear Earth Penetrator (RNEP) and $6 million to begin advanced concepts work to determine whether existing nuclear warheads could be adapted—without nuclear testing—to hold deeply buried targets at risk. The RNEP program was an engineering study of the feasibility, design definition, and cost of conversion of two (nuclear) candidate weapons to be configured as a robust nuclear earth-penetrating weapon.[9] The RNEP program generated much opposition, in part because most observers mistakenly depicted it as a procurement program, not as a feasibility study.

On June 16, 2004, however, the RNEP program was effectively terminated when the Energy and Water Development Subcommittee of the House Appropriations Committee approved the FY 2005 Energy and Water Appropriations Bill and failed to include funding for RNEP or the advanced concepts work.[10] The Bush Administration subsequently shifted its nuclear force modernization priorities.

In May 2005, senior administrators at Lawrence Livermore, Los Alamos, and Sandia National Laboratories issued a White Paper titled "Sustaining the Nuclear Enterprise—a New Approach."[11] Although the paper emphasized that the U.S. Stockpile Stewardship Program (SSP) is working, its authors noted that the weapons in the U.S. nuclear arsenal were never intended to remain in service for many decades. All of the weapons in the current arsenal will probably have to be retired within the lifetime of the youngest person reading this chapter. In response to the need to revisit U.S. policy toward sustaining the nuclear force, the Bush Administration requested funding, in the FY 2007 budget requests, for a Reliable Replacement Warhead (RRW), which would be optimized for safe and reliable storage over many decades of service life.[12] According to Ambassador Linton Brooks, "the RRW would relax Cold War design constraints that maximized yield to weight ratios and thereby allow us to design replacement components that are easier to manufacture, are safer and more secure, eliminate environmentally dangerous materials, and increase design margins, thus ensuring long-term confidence in reliability and a correspondingly reduced chance we will ever need to resort to nuclear testing."[13] The switch from RNEP to RRW, however, has not altered the fact that there is minimal political support in the United States for a militarily significant modernization of the U.S. nuclear arsenal. Although the U.S. Senate approved $66 million for studies related to the RRW in June 2007, the House Appropriations Committee cut funding completely for the program the same month.[14] The RRW program seems destined to meet with the same fate as RNEP.

In November 2005, John Harvey, policy planning director of the NNSA, summarized the current state of U.S. nuclear forces and policy. The trends that Harvey identified have deepened since he offered these observations:

1. Nuclear forces, after the cold war, have been rightly deemphasized under the NPR.

2. They no longer compel the same attention from senior military or civilian Department of Defense officials, or from Congress for that matter (despite the controversy over RNEP).
3. The military career path for the nuclear mission has serious shortfalls.
4. The bipartisan consensus we had during the cold war has evaporated.
5. We have not designed or developed a new warhead in twenty years—as a result some key capabilities the nation has asked us to maintain are in jeopardy.
6. We stopped testing nuclear weapons in 1992.[15]

Harvey's points are important because they reflect the ground truth about current trends related to the U.S. nuclear arsenal, despite the official policies laid out in the 2001 NPR. In the foreseeable future, the United States will continue to remain as a nuclear power, but nuclear weapons will recede in importance in U.S. defense planning. Given this situation, it is difficult to imagine that U.S. officials will see nuclear weapons as playing an important role in Sino-U.S. relations.

THE CHINA THREAT AND THE NPR

Although U.S. officials monitor Chinese nuclear force modernization programs, concerns about Chinese nuclear capabilities have exerted only a minor influence on U.S. strategic policy. The 2001 NPR is a case in point. The NPR emphasized adaptive planning procedures and capabilities-based, not scenario-based, planning. If China had been identified by U.S. officials as the primary nuclear threat faced by the United States, neither of these planning principles would be appropriate. If Chinese nuclear forces were considered to be an important threat for the United States, it would make sense to adopt deliberate, scenario-based planning principles to respond to that known threat. It is also not clear if, or how, the RNEP addressed a target set presented by Chinese nuclear or conventional forces that could not already be serviced by existing U.S. nuclear weapons. It thus appears unlikely that members of the Bush Administration had China in mind when they devised the NPR.

There is also little to suggest that contemporary Chinese nuclear forces provide much justification for U.S. weapons procurement decisions. The fact that China only deploys an extremely modest strategic nuclear capability prevents U.S. planners from using Chinese nuclear forces as a benchmark for "right-sizing" the U.S. nuclear arsenal. It would be necessary to cut deployed U.S. nuclear forces by at least 70 percent from Moscow Treaty levels before they approximated the size of the Chinese strategic nuclear force. U.S. defense officials and planners recognize China as a nuclear power, but it makes little political sense to highlight the relatively small Chinese nuclear arsenal when making requests to Congress for U.S. nuclear force modernization programs or even funding for maintenance of the existing arsenal. Linking the U.S. strategic deterrent to China would only muddy the political debate about U.S. nuclear force sustainability and modernization. For example, beyond the fact that Chinese officials appear interested in maintaining their nuclear arsenal in the foreseeable future, Chinese nuclear capability plays virtually no part in contemporary arguments about the RRW program.[16]

Just as Beijing has shown restraint in its nuclear procurement and deployment policy, the current state of political relations between China and the United States also shows a similar moderation. As Aaron Friedberg explained in a recent article, the current debate about the prospects for Sino-U.S. relations identifies few political issues of immediate concern.[17] Liberal optimists, for example, hope that as China becomes more deeply embedded in the global world economy and participates in international institutions, democracy will follow in the wake of economic integration and prosperity. A prosperous, democratic China, in their view, simply will not pose a threat to the United States. For liberal optimists, nuclear weapons have little role to play in current or future Chinese-American relations. By contrast, realist pessimists are concerned that military and diplomatic expansionism follows in the wake of economic prosperity, and that Chinese military capability and objectives will inevitably clash with American interests in the Pacific. In the words of John Mearsheimer, as China's economic power is translated into military capability, "China, like all previous potential hegemons, [will] be strongly inclined to become a real hegemon."[18] Realist pessimists do not focus on clear points of contention between China and the United States, but on how their relations will deteriorate as they are captured by an increasingly severe security dilemma. Realist optimists, however, believe that the jury is still out when it comes to the future of China. They believe that conflict does not inevitably follow economic growth and that shrewd diplomacy or even a modicum of restraint exhibited by all parties could do a great deal to mitigate conflict. They also note that it would take decades of significant economic growth to bring all of China out of poverty, creating doubts about the willingness of the regime to devote increasing resources for building Chinese power projection capabilities. Foreign adventurism might in fact be a low priority for the majority of Chinese who still hope to enjoy a better life for themselves and their children. Moreover, if Robert Ross is correct, Taiwan, the only real potential point of serious conflict between the Untied States and China, might be slowly fading as an issue.[19] In Ross's view, the Taiwanese independence movement is losing favor in Taipei, and is being replaced by leaders with a more pragmatic view of integration with the mainland. If Beijing becomes increasingly democratic, the trends identified by Ross on Taiwan will probably accelerate, reducing the likelihood that the island will serve as a flashpoint for conflict in the Pacific.

In sum, few American observers view China as a current significant threat to the United States. Those who worry about China as a future threat, moreover, cite only a few specific political points of contention. Instead, they focus on the "logic inherent in peer competition" as China continues to grow in terms of economic and military power. Clearly, history indicates that a rising China could rekindle great-power military competition, but actions to reduce Chinese economic growth would damage the global economy and might actually produce a self-fulfilling prophecy. Economic and military "containment" of China could be seen as a profoundly unfriendly act by Beijing, leading Chinese officials to strengthen their military forces.[20] Realist optimists, by contrast, suggest that constructive U.S. engagement of China combined with further Chinese integration into the world political economy might facilitate a peaceful "rise of China." Realist optimists also point to an additional factor that would likely moderate the behavior of both powers: nuclear weapons. They contend that nuclear weapons will continue to provide both Washington and Beijing with an incentive to turn to diplomacy and dialogue in working out the issues that will inevitably emerge in their future relations.[21]

POTENTIAL FLASH POINTS

If nuclear weapons today play a modest role in limiting what are generally benign relations between Washington and Beijing, what risks does the presence of nuclear weapons create for the leaders of both nations? Because the very existence of a nuclear arsenal creates a possibility that nuclear weapons might be used, many observers worry that the risk of nuclear use is rarely justified by the issues at stake in a political conflict.[22] And given that the U.S.-Sino rivalry is relatively muted, do the risks created by both sides' possession of nuclear weapons outweigh the benefits of their deterrent effect? For purposes of deterrence, are Chinese and American officials running a risk of nuclear war in the Pacific that is unjustified by the general lack of animosity in their relationship?

There are a variety of events that could conceivably upset the nuclear balance between China and the United States. It is possible to imagine four ways that the strategic situation in the Pacific might deteriorate significantly: following a nuclear accident; through a process of inadvertent escalation; as part of a limited strike to reestablish intra-war deterrence; or in response to some sort of catastrophic event. Some of these scenarios might be far fetched, while others might be quite likely given changing circumstances. But because it is difficult to judge the resiliency and stability of the Sino-U.S. nuclear balance, it is difficult to predict how leaders in Beijing and Washington might respond to various insults in the region.

Normal Accidents

One potential path to nuclear weapons use is what Charles Perrow has termed a "normal accident."[23] In other words, despite the fact that both the United States and the People's Republic of China have proven to be good stewards of their nuclear arsenals, it is impossible to rule out the possibility that an accident with a nuclear weapon might occur, in spite of the presence of elaborate mechanical, operational, security and procedural safeguards. In fact, as Perrow points out by describing industrial accidents involving nuclear power plants, petrochemical facilities, aircraft and air traffic control systems, marine accidents (collisions), mines, dams, lakes, spacecraft, and genetic engineering, the presence of elaborate safety mechanisms and procedures actually makes matters worse by introducing new twists and complications into operating systems that were not fully understood or anticipated by designers. It also is difficult for designers to anticipate how humans will ultimately interact with the mechanisms and procedures they design, creating the possibility that human-machine interaction might produce completely unanticipated and disastrous results.

In his application of Normal Accident Theory to the realm of nuclear weapons, Scott Sagan has described how all three elements of the theory can be found in routine peacetime operations and in the maintenance of a nuclear arsenal.[24] First, *system complexity* denotes the degree to which various components of an industrial process can interact in unanticipated and unintended ways. Common-mode connections, interconnected subsystems, feedback loops, branching paths of connections, multiple and interacting controls, and jumps from one linear process to another characterize complex systems. Second, *tight coupling* denotes the degree to which operators can improvise and intervene to stop catastrophic accidents once things begin to go wrong. In other words, systems are tightly coupled when delays in processing are not possible, only one method is available to achieve a goal, little slack is available in supplies, or when equipment or personnel or buffers and redundancies are designed into the system. Third, *production pressures* measure the degree to which operators have incentives to ignore safeguards, warning indicators, and safety procedures, or abandon good housekeeping practices to keep processes operating.

Normal Accident Theory suggests that despite the best efforts of officers and officials, the accidental detonation of a nuclear weapon remains a constant possibility. Indeed, if a process of nuclear marginalization[25] takes hold in China and the United States, reducing the role nuclear weapons play in their respective defense strategies, the possibility of accidents increases as increasingly less experienced operators interact with aging equipment. Indeed, Harvey's description of the current state of the U.S. nuclear arsenal highlights aging equipment and a less experienced work force. In peacetime, it is unlikely that an accidental detonation of a nuclear weapon would lead to a catalytic nuclear exchange. But in a crisis, when conventional and nuclear forces are on a heightened state of alert, a normal accident could spark a nuclear exchange. As observers noted decades ago during the cold war, opposing nuclear command and control systems themselves form a complex, tightly coupled system whose operators are exposed to acute time (production) pressures. Nuclear accidents during a crisis or wartime could easily produce unintended and highly destructive consequences.

INADVERTENT ESCALATION

Inadvertent escalation is used to describe the use of force that is not under the control of legitimate political authority. Analysts believe that it is most likely to occur during a crisis when opposing conventional military forces are operating in close proximity to each other. As forces jockey for position, shots can be exchanged due to accidents, misunderstandings or miscalculations, or for more deliberate reasons (the opponent intends to obtain some position that would provide them with an insurmountable advantage should war occur). Fighting under these circumstances would be "inadvertent" because it is driven by local events and interactions that do not necessarily have anything to do with the political or military intentions of higher authorities.[26]

Inadvertent escalation also might occur due to the differences in "situational rationality" that are likely to emerge between national and field commanders during a crisis. National leaders might be unprepared or unwilling to use force, but local commanders might come under enormous pressure to initiate hostilities to arrest deteriorating local conditions or to protect themselves and their forces from immediate harm. The fact that responsiveness to higher authority must always be considered contingent and conditional was long ago recognized by Thomas Schelling's work on "threats that leave something to chance."[27] In other words, as forces are placed on alert and begin to interact, there is an inevitable increase in the possibility that fighting may break out regardless of the intentions of the national leadership.

Scholars also imagined that inadvertent escalation provides a discernable path to nuclear war. In a high-intensity conventional conflict, it is possible that conventional combat will destroy a country's nuclear arsenal.[28] Attrition could be inadvertent—nuclear infrastructure or delivery capabilities colocated with the conventional force structure could be destroyed in the course of conventional combat. By contrast, conventional counterforce strikes against nuclear infrastructure and forces could also be part of a deliberate counterproliferation policy on the part of one of the combatants. This type of strike might either be a primary or ancillary objective of an overall campaign. During the first Gulf War, for instance, U.S. planners incorporated the goal of eliminating Saddam Hussein's nuclear and chemical weapons programs into their overall campaign to expel Iraqi forces from Kuwait. National leaders, however, might begin to feel the pressure to use their nuclear forces before they lose the ability to do so as conventional combat runs its course. Moreover, a country suffering inadvertent attrition of their nuclear forces could see these conventional counterforce attacks as a prelude to a nuclear strike. They might suspect that the opponent is attempting to disrupt their command

and control and surveillance capabilities before launching an all-out nuclear attack.

INTRA-WAR DETERRENCE

Although it is difficult to imagine a situation in which Chinese and American political leaders would deliberately order the use of nuclear weapons during a crisis or during the course of a conventional war, the very existence of nuclear arsenals creates the possibility that either side might chose to use nuclear weapons in a conflict. Moreover, considering the relatively limited discourse about strategic nuclear matters taking place among the scholars and officials from the two countries, it is unlikely that either side has a deep appreciation of their competing nuclear doctrines and strategies. The Sino-U.S. nuclear relationship is not well understood even by experts who know some aspects about both sides' nuclear capabilities and doctrines. For instance, there is nothing to suggest that U.S. officials have a deliberate plan to detonate a nuclear weapon to further their interests, but the NPR does call for a more complete integration of nuclear weapons into a combined conventional-nuclear "strategic deterrent." This type of planning document and policy statement, however, has raised fears among Chinese observers that the Untied States might be increasingly willing to use nuclear weapons against China during relatively minor conflicts. Similarly, policy statements made by Chinese military officers and studies generated by various institutes of unknown standing have raised fears in the United States that the Chinese might be willing to resort to nuclear weapons in less than existential conflicts. A crisis might thus shatter the stereotypes or unwarranted fears that are sometimes heard in both capitals. But it also might be a self-fulfilling interaction if both sides act on their worst fears and suspicions. In other words, there is a possibility that Chinese or U.S. officials might be surprised by the role played by the other side's nuclear forces in a crisis or conventional conflict.

Nuclear weapons might play a part in a Sino-U.S. conflict in several ways. They might be used by either side if an opponent somehow crossed a threshold by conducting conventional strikes against national territory or deliberately or inadvertently threatening the other side's vital national interests. Because both Chinese and U.S. officials have been relatively quiet about their deterrence objectives vis-à-vis each other, there is a possibility that either side could unknowingly act in highly provocative ways in a crisis or a conventional conflict.

Nuclear weapons might also be used as a warning, demonstrating that an ongoing crisis or conflict is about to spiral out of control. Theory, not history, would be used to inform the judgment about whether a nuclear warning shot would contain hostilities or exacerbate them.

Nuclear weapons also might be used in the event of some catastrophic conventional military failure. Wars have a nasty habit of failing to unfold according to plan, and a nation's leaders might come to believe that nuclear weapons might have to be brought to bear to stave off disaster. Strategies or stratagems might fail to produce expected results. A state might suffer significant technological surprise or find itself outclassed across entire groups of military technologies, leaving it virtually defenseless in the face of a sustained conventional assault. Military "systems-of-systems" also might fail to yield expected synergies, leaving military forces outgunned, undersupplied, and facing a numerically superior opponent.

Catastrophic Events

Today, there is insufficient political animosity between the United States and China to generate much concern about nuclear crisis instability in their relations. Because there is no grave political hostility to make any salient "technical" estimates of the balance between competing forces, officials and officers alike have not payed much attention to the military incentives they would face to be the first to use, or not use, nuclear weapons in a crisis. During a crisis in Asia, however, technical estimates of the nuclear balance between the United States and China could become highly salient, which would itself heighten tension in the region. A crisis in Asia is not the best time to think about the nuclear balance in Asia, but in reality a crisis could force the leaders in Beijing and Washington to begin to think about the nuclear balance that exists among several actors.

Clay Moltz has recently presented a list of events that could conceivably spark concerns about the Sino-U.S. nuclear balance.[29] On the Korean peninsula, a North Korean nuclear test or the unification of Korea under an ultranationalist regime would, at a minimum, generate a fundamental reassessment of nuclear policies. Similarly, a breakdown of the NPT could reinvigorate nuclear weapon programs in Asia, especially if Japanese officials decided to develop a nuclear arsenal in response to ominous proliferation trends. A sudden U.S. withdrawal from Asia or a sudden surge in Chinese nuclear force deployments or programs might also prompt an arms race in Asia as governments scrambled to cope with a rapid shift in the conventional and nuclear balance of forces in Asia. A Russian effort to reemerge as a superpower—based on a resurgent nuclear capability—would, at a minimum, halt the draw down in U.S. nuclear forces that has been ongoing since the end of the cold war. An Indo-Pakistan war that pitted an American client (India) against a Chinese client (Pakistan) also could spark a wider war.

Because the military and political relationships among Asia's great powers are closely interconnected, systemic effects will likely occur in the wake of a major change in one element of the system. Although the initial military or political insult to the Asian balance of power might be localized, the international consequences of a North Korean nuclear test, for example, might be amplified as national responses produce a cascade of self-reinforcing effects. States that have few real political interests threatened by an ongoing crisis or conflict might find themselves drawn into the conflict or into a regional arms race in response to the actions of other parties to the dispute.

Conclusion

Since the end of the cold war, nuclear relations between the People's Republic of China and the United States have been benign. The Chinese government has not launched a vigorous nuclear modernization program. Beijing has not responded in a significant way to the deployment of modest U.S. ballistic missile defenses, which appear directed toward countering the threat posed by North Korea's nuclear and missile programs. The United States continues its nuclear force draw down in compliance with the Moscow Treaty, has made no effort to develop weapons systems that combine nuclear technology with the technologies made available by the information revolution, and has proposed a nuclear modernization program that actually reflects the growing marginalization of nuclear forces in its strategic planning. Moreover, the Bush Administration's entire nuclear program has met with virtually no congressional support—the Congress appears interested in only reducing the size of the U.S. nuclear arsenal. Despite occasional statements and declaratory policies that the other side finds disconcerting or unintelligible, both Washington and Beijing take their responsibilities as nuclear custodians seriously. Nuclear weapons remain a factor in the relations between China and the United States, but they remain in the background.

If, as nuclear optimists expect, nuclear weapons exert a moderating interest in Sino-American relations, what might upset the strategic status quo in the Pacific? The greatest threat facing Washington and Beijing in the region probably would emerge from a crisis not of their making, which somehow draws their conventional forces into close proximity. The eruption of war on the Korean Peninsula that leads to the rapid disintegration of North or South Korean forces would create this type of situation. In addition to the risk of inadvertent escalation created by this scenario, Chinese or American officials might face a decision to intervene massively in the conflict to prevent the immediate demise of their respective client, or even in response to the introduction of nuclear, chemical, and biological weapons by the regime in Pyongyang. Once weapons of mass destruction are used on the Korean Peninsula, or once U.S. or Chinese conventional forces enter the fray, officials in Washington and Beijing might decide that the time had come to bring nuclear weapons to bear in the conflict. However, considering that both Chinese and U.S. officials have only an incomplete understanding of the other's nuclear doctrines and expectations of the role nuclear weapons might play in a third-party conflict, this type of interaction would be fraught with danger. Instead of relying on a crisis to clarify competing nuclear doctrines and expectations, Chinese and U.S. scholars and officials should begin a constructive dialogue about the role of nuclear weapons in their bilateral relations.

Notes

1. Excerpts from the classified version of the report were first reported in the *New York Times* and the *Los Angeles Times*. Most of the NPR text has been posted on the globalsecurity.org Web site at http://globalsecurity.org/wmd/library/policy/dod/npr.htm. This quote is taken from that text cited as the NPR's Executive Summary on p. 1, which was released by the Department of Defense. Other quotes come from the global security Web site, although the author has no way to confirm whether this is the actual report.
2. James J. Wirtz, and Jeffrey Larsen (eds.), *Nuclear Transformation: The New U.S. Nuclear Doctrine* (New York: Palgrave Macmillan, 2005).
3. An exception to this lack of attention to the NPR is Charles L. Glaser and Steve Fetter, "Counterforce Revisited: Assessing the Nuclear Posture Review's New Missions," *International Security* 30, no. 2 (Fall 2005), 84–126.
4. Keir Lieber and Daryl G. Press, "The End of MAD? The Nuclear Dimension of U.S. Primacy," *International Security* 30, no. 4 (Spring 2006), 7–44.

5. Department of Defense News Transcript, January 9, 2002, 6. www.defenselink.mil/qdr/report/Report20060203.pdf. Accessed on January 4, 2008.
6. The concept of dissuasion suggests that U.S. military forces will be so technologically and operationally superior that potential competitors will abandon efforts to challenge the United States. Efforts at dissuasion, however, might simply channel the military strategies and capabilities of potential competitors away from U.S. strengths to attack U.S. vulnerabilities, i.e., to adopt asymmetric strategies.
7. NPR as cited. 12–13. Web site at http://globalsecurity.org/wmd/library/policy/dod/npr.htm.
8. U.S. Department of Defense, *Quadrennial Defense Review Report*, February 6, 2006.
9. Jonathan Medalia, *Robust Nuclear Earth Penetrator Budget Request and Plan, FY2005–FY2009*, CRS Report for Congress, Order Code RL323347 January 10, 2005, 5.
10. U.S. Congress, House Committee on Appropriations, *Energy and Water Development Appropriations* Bill, 2005 House Report. 108–554, 1108th Cong., 2nd sess., June 2004 (Washington, GPO, 2004), 115.
11. Bruce T. Goodwin, Frederick A. Tarantino, and John B. Woodward, "Sustaining the Nuclear Enterprise – a New Approach," UCRL-AR-212442; LAUR-05–3830; and SAND2005-3384, May 20, 2005. Jonathan Medalia, "Nuclear Warheads: The Reliable Replacement Warhead Program and the Life Extension Program," CRS Report for Congress (RL33748) updated July 16, 2007.
12. James J. Wirtz, "Do U.S. Nuclear Weapons have a Future?" *Strategic Insights* 5, no. 3 (March 2006). http://www.ccc.nps.navy.mil/si/2006/Mar/wirtzMar06.asp. Accessed on February 8, 2008.
13. Statement of Ambassador Linton F. Brooks, under secretary for nuclear security and administrator, national nuclear security administration U.S. department of Energy, before the House Armed Services Committee's Subcommittee on Strategic Forces on March 1, 2006.
14. William Matthews, "U.S. Senate OKs $55M for Reliable Replacement Warhead," Defense News, June 28, 2007. http//www.defensenews.com/story.php?F=2866866&C=america. Accessed on February 8, 2008.
15. John R. Harvey, "Moving the Nuclear Weapons Program to DoD?" Address to the Federation of American Scientists 60th University Celebration, November 30, 2005.
16. Jonathan Medalia, "Nuclear Warheads: The Reliable Replacement Warhead Program and the Life Extension Program," CRS Report for Congress (RL33748), updated July 16, 2007.
17. Aaron Friedberg, "The Future of U.S.-China Relations: Is Conflict Inevitable?" *International Security* 30, no. 2 (Fall 2005), 7–45.
18. John Mearsheimer, *The Tragedy of Great Power Politics* (New York: W.W. Norton, 2001), 400.

19. Robert S. Ross, "Taiwan's Failing Independence Movement," *Foreign Affairs* 85, no. 2 (March/April 2006), 141–148.
20. On the divergence between the logic of the capitalist world economy and balancing and containment, see Mark R. Brawley, "The Political Economy of Balance of Power Theory," in *Balance of Power: Theory and Practice in the 21st Century*, ed. T.V. Paul, James J. Wirtz, and Michel Fortmann (Stanford: Stanford University Press, 2004), 76–99.
21. Avery Goldstein, "Great Expectations: Interpreting China's Arrival," *International Security* 22, no. 3 (Winter 1997/98), 36–73.
22. Jonathan Schell, *The Fate of the Earth* (New York: Knopf, 1982).
23. Charles Perrow, *Normal Accidents: Living with High-Risk Technologies* (Princeton: Princeton University Press, 1999).
24. Scott Sagan, *The Limits of Safety* (Princeton: Princeton University Press, 1993).
25. Stephen A. Cambone and Patrick J. Garity, "The Future of U.S. Nuclear Policy," *Survival* 36, no. 4 (Winter 1994/95), 73–95; Lawrence Freedman, "Great Powers, Vital Interests and Nuclear Weapons," *Survival* 36, no. 4 (Winter 1994/95), 35–52.
26. Joseph F. Bouchard, *Command in Crisis: Four Case Studies* (New York: Columbia University Press, 1991).
27. Thomas Schelling, *Arms and Influence* (New Haven: Yale University Press, 1966).
28. Barry Posen, *Inadvertent Escalation: Conventional War and Nuclear Risks* (Ithaca: Cornell University Press, 1991).
29. Clay Moltz, "Northeast Asia," paper presented at conference on "Nuclear Weapons Proliferation: 2016," Naval Postgraduate School. Monterey, California, July 28–29, 2006.

8

CHINESE NUCLEAR POLICY AND THE FUTURE OF MINIMUM DETERRENCE

Yao Yunzhu[1]

The terms "nuclear strategy" and "nuclear doctrine" are seldom used in Chinese military and strategic studies literature. Instead, "nuclear policy" frequently appears to cover both the strategic thinking and the basic principles of developing, managing, and employing nuclear weapons. Indeed, this very difference in terminology highlights a core position of China's nuclear calculus: their political—but not military—utility. This chapter analyzes the current Chinese nuclear policy, describes some of the major factors that may affect nuclear thinking in China after the cold war, and speculates over the future of China's nuclear deterrence in the twenty-first century.

CURRENT CHINESE NUCLEAR POLICY

It can be safely said that among all the nuclear states, the declaratory nuclear policy of China has so far been the most consistent. From the day when China first exploded an atomic bomb, its nuclear policy-related doctrine has remained unchanged. Five major themes can be derived from these policies.

No First Use Policy

The policy of "no first use" (NFU) has been frequently and consistently repeated in numerous Chinese government statements ever since China became a nuclear weapon state in 1964. By abjuring the first-use option, China has limited itself to retaliatory nuclear strikes. China has also called on all nuclear weapon states to commit themselves to a NFU policy at all times and under all circumstances.

Security Assurance to Nonnuclear Weapon States and Nuclear Free Zones

China has been very critical to the use of nuclear threats against nonnuclear weapon states and nonnuclear weapon zones. It has repeatedly called on all the nuclear weapon states to agree to a legally binding, multilateral agreement under which they would pledge not to use (or threaten to use) nuclear weapons against nonnuclear weapon states and nuclear-free zones. This policy component limits China's potential to employ weapons against only the few nuclear weapon states existing today. Apart from negative security assurances, which China gives unconditionally to all nonnuclear weapon states, China issued its first formal positive security assurance, along with the other four declared nuclear weapon states, in April 1995, promising to come to the aid of any nonnuclear weapon state that is subject to nuclear attack and to pursue appropriate punishment against any attacking state, under the auspices of the UN Security Council. This policy became part of the UN Security Council Resolution 984.

Limited Development of Second Strike, Retaliatory Capability

China has repeated its intention to maintain a very small nuclear arsenal on many occasions. In its 2002 Defense White Paper, China stated that it "has always exercised utmost restraint on the development of nuclear weapons, and its nuclear arsenal is kept at the lowest level necessary for self-defense only."[2] However, to make this small arsenal a credible deterrent, China has to make it survivable in the face of a first nuclear strike, even if that strike is overwhelming and devastating. In the Chinese literature, "few but effective" (*jinggan youxiao*) are the words most frequently used to describe the necessary arsenal.

Opposition to Nuclear Deployment Outside National Territories

China is opposed to the policy of extended nuclear deterrence, or the policy of providing "nuclear umbrellas" by nuclear weapon states to their allies. Consistent with China's long-standing policy of not sending or stationing any troops outside China, it is also officially opposed to the deployment of nuclear weapons outside national territories, and has stated that China will never deploy nuclear weapons on any foreign soil.

Complete Prohibition of Nuclear Weapons

China first called for the complete prohibition and thorough destruction of nuclear weapons in its proposal for a world summit in 1963, before its first nuclear explosion. On the same day that China conducted its first nuclear explosion, it again stated as follows:

> The Chinese government hereby solemnly proposes to the governments of the world that a summit conference of all the countries of the world be convened to discuss the questions of the complete prohibition and thorough destruction of nuclear weapons, and that as the first step, the summit conference conclude an agreement to the effect that the nuclear powers and those countries which may soon become nuclear powers undertake not to use nuclear weapons either against non-nuclear countries and nuclear-free zones or against each other.[3]

This has evolved into China's basic position on nuclear disarmament, and the People's Republic of China (PRC) has never given up efforts in promoting an international convention to ban nuclear weapons.

NUCLEAR POLICY: SIX THEMES

The major components of Chinese nuclear policy described above, if interpreted in Western deterrence terminology, could be characterized by the following six themes:

- Strategic deterrence, rather than operational and tactical utility,
- Retaliatory rather than denial deterrence,
- Central rather than extended deterrence,
- General rather than immediate deterrence,

- Defensive rather than offensive deterrence, and
- Minimum rather than limited or maximum deterrence.

Strategic Deterrence, Rather than Operational and Tactical Utility

Mao Zedong, in elaborating the reason to develop nuclear weapons, said, "we will not only have possession of more aircraft and artillery pieces, but also atom bombs. In today's world, we must have this thing if we don't want to be bullied by others."[4] The original purpose of nuclear development in China was to "break up the nuclear threat and smash the nuclear blackmail (*dapo he weixie, fensui he ezha*)." As a political instrument, nuclear weapons were to be utilized mainly at the level of grand strategy, not as a winning tool in military operations. The military value of nuclear weapons lies only in their deterrent effect against nuclear attack. The officially declared missions of the Second Artillery Force are twofold: (1) to deter the use of nuclear weapons against China, and (2) to launch an effective nuclear counterattack in the event of such an attack.[5] No distinction has been made in categorizing nuclear operations. That is, a nuclear strike against China, whether conducted at the strategic, operational, or tactical level, utilizing high or low yield warheads, and regardless of how massive or limited its lethality, is perceived as the highest form of warfare in the Chinese categorization, and one which must be responded to strategically. In Chinese strategic literature, we see discussions only on how to deter a nuclear war from happening, how to prevent a conventional conflict from escalating into a nuclear war, and how to retaliate after suffering a nuclear attack, but never how to win a nuclear war. Most Chinese strategists think nuclear wars are not to be won, but to be prevented.

Retaliatory Rather than Denial Deterrence[6]

When discussing deterrence, many Chinese cite Deng Xiaoping when explaining China's nuclear thinking. As he said in a meeting with some foreigners in 1983:

> While you have some deterrence force, we also have some; but we don't want much. It will do just to possess it. Things like strategic weapons and deterrence forces are there to scare others. They must not be used first. But our possession will have some effect. The limited possession

of nuclear weapons itself exerts some pressure. It remains our position that we will develop a few [nuclear weapons]. But the development will be limited. We have said repeatedly that our small amount [of nuclear weapons] is nothing. It is only to show that we also have what you have. If you want to destroy us, you yourself have to suffer some punishment at the same time.[7]

Deng's statement echoed Mao's nuclear thinking in several aspects. First, nuclear weapons are desirable only for their deterrent value, not for battlefield utility. Second, nuclear weapons, if ever used, will be used to cause the enemy as much pain as possible, so as to enhance its deterrent value in the first place. Therefore China has to adopt countervalue, as opposed to counterforce, targeting strategies to strengthen its deterrence posture.

Third, only a small number of nuclear weapons will be required to satisfy China's deterrent needs—to convince a potential nuclear adversary of a possible nuclear retaliation. Both Mao and Deng were very explicit that deterrent effectiveness does not increase in proportion with numbers of nuclear weapons. A survivable and invulnerable small arsenal can be equally effective in terms of deterrence. Deterrence effect depends on invulnerability to nuclear strikes, not on a large degree of nuclear attack capabilities. Accordingly, what China has sought is a nuclear arsenal that is small in size but reliable in survivability. And given its adherence to a NFU policy, China has to focus its nuclear development efforts on "second strike capabilities" that must be credible and survivable to have a deterrent effect.

Central Rather than Extended Deterrence[8]

By declaring its policy to counterattack with nuclear weapons only after being attacked with such weapons, China preserves nuclear capabilities to protect its own most vital interests, that is, the survival of the nation. Even in the cold war years, China has never provided nuclear umbrella to any other country in the world. For China, the concept of extended deterrence has simply not entered into the nuclear calculus yet.

General Rather than Immediate Deterrence

The deterrence exercised by the two nuclear superpowers in the cold war had been aimed at each other. They formed a bilateral deterrent relationship in which each side was very clear in its objectives. This form of deterrence was of a more immediate nature. China had never been comfortably fitted into the "bipolar" context. It had aligned with the USSR for some time, then had been outside both the poles for a period, and then tried to be closer to the United States. China also did not have the luxury of a nuclear umbrella for most of the cold war years. Therefore China's nuclear deterrence had been more of a general nature, with which China tried to form a multilateral deterrent relationship with all the nuclear powers by making clear what China wanted to protect.

Defensive Rather than Offensive Deterrence

One famous tenet laid down by Chairman Mao Zedong is the Sixteen Character Guideline for use of force: "We will never attack unless we are attacked; and if we are attacked, we will certainly counterattack" (*ren bu fan wo, wo bu fan ren; ren ruo fan wo, wo bi fan ren*). Behind this guideline is a sober-headed analysis of power balances. The People's Liberation Army (PLA) and its predecessors entered and won most wars as an inferior side, against great odds. So a defensive posture had always been preferred to an offensive one. However, Chinese forces have managed to transform from a weaker to a stronger force in the course (usually a protracted course) of previous conventional wars.

When applied to nuclear policy, this guideline is seen as a rejection of preemptive thinking. The renouncement of the first-use option, willingness to accept vulnerability, confinement to retaliatory nuclear use, principle of attacking only after being attacked (*hou fa zhi ren*), focus on second strike capabilities, and reservation of nuclear means as the last resort to protect only the most vital national interests all point to the defensive nature of China's nuclear policy. When deterrence strategies are applied in accordance with China's policies, they promote a purely defensive posture, even though nuclear weapons are inherently offensive.

Minimum Rather than Limited Or Maximum Deterrence

If one were to choose from Western deterrence classifications to describe Chinese nuclear policy, one would have to use the concept of "minimum deterrence," as compared to maximum or limited deterrence. Personally, I think the word "minimum" has too strong a quantitative connotation, which is misleading. I mean to emphasize a qualitative standard. The word "minimum" has for some time been officially used in Chinese government documents.⁹ Chinese strategists take the concept as a relative one, defined not only by pure numbers but more importantly by such key criteria as invulnerability of nuclear forces, assurance of retaliation, and credibility of counterattack. When a Chinese document says that China intends to possess nuclear weapons only at the minimum (or lowest) level for the needs of self-defense, it means that they must have the minimum, but assured, capabilities for a retaliatory second strike. Some studies have suggested a shift in Chinese nuclear posture toward limited deterrence, where China could employ nuclear weapons to deter both conventional and nuclear wars, and even to exercise escalation control in the event of a conventional confrontation.¹⁰ However, the basic logic of China's nuclear thinking dictates nuclear weapons as deterring, not winning, a nuclear conflict.

Factors Shaping China's Nuclear Thinking after the Cold War

Many factors may have exerted an impact on China's nuclear calculus since the end of the cold war. Listed below are three major ones.

The Changing Nuclear Environment

The end of the cold war and the collapse of the bipolar international system led to the decline of nuclear weapons as a predominant strategic consideration. A major nuclear exchange has become a remote possibility. Local limited wars, national and ethnic armed conflicts, territorial disputes, nuclear and military technology proliferation, international terrorism, and transnational organized crime have risen in significance as major threats to international and regional peace and stability.

One implication of this is that China's nuclear environment has become more complex. First, the Strategic Partnership formed between China and Russia reduced the prospect of a Russian nuclear first strike. Second, the possibility for military conflict between China and the United States over Taiwan has increased. Third, there have emerged on China's periphery two new nuclear weapon states—India and Pakistan—with the former explicitly considering China as a nuclear adversary. Fourth, the Democratic People's Republic of Korea (DPRK) is seeking nuclear weapons, contrary to the demands of Northeast Asian nations that the Korean Peninsula be nuclear free. Such actions may result in cascading effects, including the requirement for more robust missile defense systems in Northeast Asia, which may reduce the deterrent effect of China's small nuclear arsenal and provide incentives for nations like Japan and South Korea to go nuclear.

In light of these major changes, China evaluates its overall nuclear security as improving instead of worsening. It holds this view even though it has more nuclear weapon states on its borders than any nation in the world. There are several reasons for this evaluation. First, it would be too far-fetched to envision a military conflict between China and Russia, let alone one involving nuclear confrontation. Second, from the moment India went nuclear, India and China have been in a very credible mutual deterrent relationship. Pakistan, a long time friend of China, has also been locked in a mutual deterrent relationship with India. These two deterrent relationships have brought about a more earnest effort from both India and China for settling territorial disputes by political means and have reduced the danger of large-scale conventional conflicts between India and Pakistan. Third, China was relatively less concerned about the two new nuclear neighbors, for the general nature of China's nuclear deterrence can readily accommodate this changed nuclear environment. Fourth, China is actively engaged in the Six-Party Talks and is confident that a nuclear-free Korean Peninsula is a possibility, which is in China's best interests. In the foreseeable future, changes in nuclear environment pose no challenges significant enough for China to reconsider its nuclear policy.

Taiwan

Taiwan was not a predominant issue until the mid-1990s when the pro-independence forces gained momentum on the island. Cross-strait conflicts were a continuation of the 1945–1949 civil war, and nuclear weapons had no role to play in civil war scenarios. However, the Taiwan issue has been complicated by possible U.S. intervention in case of a military crisis. This constitutes the only conceivable scenario in which two nuclear weapon states might fight face to face. China has always complained, with good reason, that the United States is the largest external factor impeding China's reunification, peacefully or by force. With the *Taiwan Relations Act*, the United States has committed itself to the defense of Taiwan. The 2002 *Nuclear Posture*

Review (NPR) released (or leaked) by the U.S. Department of Defense even implied the use of nuclear weapons in "military confrontation over the status of Taiwan." Such confrontation is categorized as one of the "immediate contingencies" for which the United States has to set "requirements for nuclear strike capabilities."[11] So far, China has never (in any government statements or official documents) threatened nuclear use in a cross-strait conflict.

Taiwan is China's top security concern, and the only scenario for which China seriously considers the use of force.[12] Do nuclear weapons really have any role to play in such a scenario? This author's judgment is that it does not. If what we are talking about is a "local war under the conditions of informationalization," it would be useless for China to deter U.S. conventional intervention by using China's nuclear weapons. It is the United States, not China, which has the nuclear capabilities to control and even dominate conflict escalation. To win a nuclear war over the United States is quite different from deterring a nuclear strike by the United States. China is definitely the much weaker side as far as nuclear balance is concerned. Faced with a similar situation, Mao Zedong and Deng Xiaoping had set the strategy for China decades ago: to use nuclear weapons only as a deterrent against the use of all types of nuclear weapons, be they strategic or operational. Preventing an opponent's nuclear weapon use is the only way to neutralize his nuclear superiority. China's long-standing nuclear policy continues to serve its national interests in the current times.

U.S. Development and Deployment of a Ballistic Missile Defense System

China's strong opposition to U.S. ballistic missile defense (BMD) development and deployment has been adequately conveyed and extensively studied in the United States, for the issue has been a decadelong topic of hot debate. Unlike other issues, Chinese concerns over BMD had the most vocal and vehement expression by government officials, scholars, military officers, and even ordinary people posting their views on the Internet. On December 13, 2001, President Bush officially announced that the United States would withdraw from the Anti-Ballistic Missile (ABM) Treaty, a cornerstone arms control regime set up in the early 1970s. Six months later, the United States was free of any legal bindings against its development and deployment of BMD systems. The deployment decision by President Bush came as no surprise.

China has not been successful in stopping the United States from setting up a missile defense system that threatens to break the delicate balance of deterrence between the two countries. A national missile defense system, no matter how limited it might be, would no doubt reduce the effectiveness of China's deterrent against U.S. nuclear use. American scholars have difficulties in understanding why the Chinese should worry about a shield that the United States deploys to protect their own homeland. However, this very defensive shield, when used against the only flying dagger the opponent throws at it while taking the deadly blow, would be very offensive in nature. We all know the famous paradoxical logic in deterrence relations: nuclear force that is to be used as a last resort against enemy cities is defensive in nature and stabilizing in function, while a leakproof umbrella against nuclear attack is offensive in nature and destabilizing.

China is also reasonably sensitive to any BMD systems covering Taiwan. Obviously, such a shield would reduce the effectiveness of China's military operations against the island. This situation could also encourage Taiwan to take more provocative steps toward independence, because of the reduced deterrent effect of PLA's missile force. And again, even a limited missile shield over the U.S. homeland might reduce American concern over possible Chinese nuclear retaliation, permitting it to intervene more readily and threaten nuclear use, as it did in the 1958 Taiwan crisis. Finally, it would signify a semi-alliance relationship between the United States and Taiwan.

China has a further reason to worry about BMD development cooperation and future joint deployment by the United States and Japan. This would be an indication of a closer relationship and a more coordinated course of action in a future Taiwan conflict between the two cold war allies. An upper-tier BMD system jointly deployed by the two countries in the name of protecting allies and overseas troops could be readily turned into a BMD system to offset a mainland missile attack against Taiwan. It would also be a complicating development when Sino-Japanese relations are worsening and there is genuine concern over Japan's rearmament.

Therefore, BMD development and deployment is by far the most significant factor impacting China's nuclear calculus. China has to think about how to maintain a guaranteed, retaliatory, second strike capability in the face of a U.S. BMD system. It is also necessary to review the sufficiency and survivability of the arsenal. At the core of the Chinese concern is the credibility of the mutual deterrent relationship that China needs to prevent American nuclear threats or nuclear use in a cross-strait conflict.

Prospects for China's Nuclear Deterrent in the Twenty-First Century

The fact that China belonged to neither of the cold war blocs has some implications for anticipating the future of China's nuclear deterrence. Its general (rather than immediate) nature makes it easier for China's nuclear policy to adjust to the prevailing global situation in the twenty-first century. Never in the past had China focused on any particular nuclear adversary, nor does it do so today. Even the newly emerging nuclear threat from India can be readily dealt with under the existing policy.

The issue of Taiwan has forced the Chinese to face up to the possibility of military conflict with the United States over Taiwan. However, such conflict would have been assumed to be below the nuclear threshold, but for the issuance of the 2001 NPR by the U.S. Department of Defense and frequent media leaks that increasingly show China as the target country for U.S. nuclear planning.[13] Through the NPR, the Chinese know for sure that they are a nuclear target and Taiwan is the scenario in which nuclear weapons may be used. As a result, China must prepare itself for a nuclear confrontation with the United States in order to protect its most vital of all national interests. However, it would be totally wrong to assume China is going to deter U.S. conventional military intervention by threatening nuclear use, for China can hardly make such threats credible.

In the foreseeable future, the most significant factor that will influence China's nuclear calculus will be U.S. deployment of national and advanced theater missile defenses. China has to reevaluate the sufficiency of its nuclear arsenal to counter U.S. missile defense systems and retain a guaranteed ability to retaliate. However, such reevaluation will result only in the variation of the size of nuclear arsenals, not in any change to the policy's basic nature. What is of concern is the maintenance of China's retaliatory deterrence against a potential American nuclear attack.

Both Taiwan and BMD serve as important factors that will impact on China's nuclear calculus. The former highlights the necessity and urgency of ensuring a mutual deterrent relationship with the United States to prevent the use of nuclear weapons in a conflict scenario over Taiwan, which might not have been so important or urgent before.

Only in this way has Taiwan become relevant to China's nuclear policy. The latter issue of BMD emphasizes the concern over the credibility of Chinese deterrence against the United States. Concerns over Taiwan and BMD combine to form the focus of China's nuclear modernization—the maintenance of sufficient nuclear capabilities that can survive a first strike to inflict unacceptable damage on the enemy in a retaliatory strike. Put more accurately, China's nuclear modernization serves to validate its long-standing nuclear policy. China's nuclear policy in the twenty-first century will retain all the characteristics that are specified in the first section of this chapter, and nothing suggests any future deviation. Thus far, the three factors discussed in this section provide insufficient reasons for China to move beyond its minimum deterrence posture.

Another issue of interest is how China would translate its nuclear deterrence requirement into concrete numbers (number of warheads and delivery vehicles, etc.). A discussion on this subject is beyond my ability. However, the most important thing is to understand the underlying logic, not to guess the numbers. It implies that China has to keep a credible retaliatory nuclear force that can survive a massive first strike and launch a counter strike at the enemy. If the nuclear logic for China does not change fundamentally, the nature of the policy would not change. Slight increases or decreases in the numbers will only reflect the changes in calculating the sufficiency of China's second strike capability. All three generations of Chinese leaders have expressed their intent to keep the arsenal small, only "at the minimum level for self-defense." Any excess in quantity would be an unnecessary drain on the nation's limited budgetary resources. On the other hand, even if the size of the arsenal does not vary, a change in the underlying logic could trigger a major shift of China's nuclear policy, such as a shift from a minimum to a limited deterrence posture, where nuclear weapons could be designed and planned for winning wars instead of deterring them.

The last point concerns the nuclear relationship between China and the United States. It is in China's vital interest to have a certain degree of deterrent effect over other nuclear weapon states, be they Russia, the United States, or, potentially, India. At the same time, China is willing to accept vulnerability, as its NFU policy indicates. China had such a deterrent relationship in the cold war period with the Soviet Union since the 1970s, and later with the United States after the mid-1980s, although the significance of that deterrent relationship lessened as China and the United States enjoyed an improvement in their relationship (until 1989). Starting in the mid-1990s, however, both Taiwan and BMD have threatened to break this Sino-U.S. relationship, the former by gaining an enhanced, albeit informal, U.S. defense commitment (and perhaps also the U.S. provision of an extended deterrent commitment as implied by the NPR), and the latter by offsetting China's ability to retaliate. Both these factors are the result of American policy.

Conclusion

If China, the United States, and all the other nuclear weapon states want to share regional and global security, peace, and stability, they have to share a certain degree of insecurity first. In other words, nuclear powers must accept vulnerability by pledging to adhere to a no first use policy, so as to form a multilateral deterrent relationship among the "haves," and offering an enhanced security assurance to the "have nots." In today's world, security, like many other situations, is relative. If one party seeks absolute security and overwhelming superiority, it can only do so at the expense of others, which results in the overall loss of trust and security for all.

Notes

1. Senior Colonel Yao Yunzhu is currently the Director of the Asia-Pacific Office, Department of World Military Studies, Academy of Military Science, People's Liberation Army, China.
2. *China's National Defense in 2002,* Released by the Information Office of the State Council of the People's Republic of China, December 2002, Beijing.
3. "Statement of the Government of the People's Republic of China," October 16, 1964.
4. "A Brilliant Page in New China's History," *China's National Defense Daily,* May 31, 1999.
5. *China's National Defense in 2002,* Released by the Information Office of the State Council of the People's Republic of China, December 2002, Beijing.
6. Chinese strategists seldom make the distinction between retaliatory and denial, but their nuclear logic follows the same path as that of Glenn Snyder, who made the most thorough elaboration of the distinction between denial and retaliatory use of nuclear weapons, *Deterrence and Defense* (Princeton: Princeton University Press, 1961), 3ff.
7. Wu Tianfu, ed., *Schools of Nuclear Strategic Thinking in the World* (Beijing: Junshi Yiwen Press, 1999), 207.

8. Patrick Morgan contributed to this distinction in his *Deterrence: A conceptual Analysis* (Beverly Hills, CA: Sage Publications, 1977), 25–47.
9. In April 2003, the Chinese delegation issued a statement to the Second PrepCom for 2005 NPT Review Conference, saying, "China has always exercised [the] utmost restraint towards developing nuclear weapons, [and] kept its nuclear arsenal at the minimum level only for self-defense."
10. Alastair Iain Johnston, "China's New 'Old Thinking': The Concept of Limited Deterrence," *International Security* 20, no. 3 (Winter 1995/96); Paul Godwin, "China's Nuclear Forces: An Assessment," *Current History* 98, no. 629 (September 1999); Bates Gill, James Mulvenon, and Mark Stokes, "The Chinese Second Artillery Corps: Transition to Credible Deterrence," in *The People's Liberation Army as an Organization: Reference Volume* 1.0, ed., James C. Mulvenon and Andrew Yang (2001).
11. U.S. DOD, *Nuclear Posture Review Report (Excerpts)*, submitted to Congress December 31, 2001. Downloaded September 5, 2005 from www.globalsecurity.org/wmd/library/policy/dod/npr.htm.
12. *China's National Defense in 2004*, Information Office of the State Council of the People's Republic of China, December 2004. The White Paper listed four security concerns China has to address. The other three are as follows: technological gap resulting from new RMA, the risks and challenges caused by economic globalization, and the prolonged conflicting trends of unipolarity and multipolarity.
13. The issuance of Presidential Decision Directive 60 (PDD-60) in 1997 brought China back into the SIOP targeting process in 1998, sixteen years after China had been removed from the SIOP in 1982, to reflect Sino-American normalization of relations.

Section III

Regional Challenges and Threat Reduction Policies

9

EAST ASIA'S NUCLEAR FUTURE

Yang Yi

As shown in recent crises situations, international regimes preventing nuclear proliferation are facing continuous challenges and tests. Many international observers are anxious to know whether the present regimes can withstand the series of serious shocks and setbacks they have faced in recent years. Presently, there are two focal points in the international efforts against nuclear proliferation: the nuclear programs in the Democratic People's Republic of Korea (DPRK) and in the Islamic Republic of Iran. The DPRK's program is the more explosive of the two, given its disruptive impacts on the peace and stability in East Asia, as well as on the global nuclear arms control and disarmament regimes. Can the current crisis, imbedded in the deep-rooted hostilities between the DPRK and the United States, move beyond its current dangerous stalemate peacefully? What should the international community do to help prevent further deterioration of the present dangerous situation?

The likely nuclear future in East Asia is somewhat gray and very difficult to predict. Even prior to the October 2006 nuclear test, many observers believed that the DPRK would choose to cross the nuclear threshold and acquire nuclear weapons, as well as medium- and long-range missile capability. Many also believed that this would create devastating domino effects in East Asia. However, there was also another view that was relatively more optimistic. It argued that a peaceful solution to the nuclear crisis on the Korean Peninsula and the realization of a nuclear-weapon-free peninsula under the framework of the Six-Party Talks was not only desirable but also feasible.

In the spirit of working for the best and preventing the worst, this chapter aims at analyzing the future potential of nuclear proliferation in East Asia and its implications. It also attempts to explore the strategic choices of China and the United States to work together to meet their common challenges in the future.

Increasing Dangers of Chain Reactions of Nuclear Proliferation in East Asia

Presently a rigid confrontation and hostility exists between the United States and the DPRK, leading to continuing challenges in resolving outstanding issues through the Six-Party Talk framework. Some experts observe that time is on the DPRK's side, allowing it to move further toward weaponization if a solution based on mutual compromise cannot be reached. This would open a nuclear Pandora's box and create a domino effect of nuclear proliferation. The resulting situation would look very much like the one immediately after the nuclear tests by India and Pakistan in 1998. If such steps occur further, no matter how strongly the East Asian countries, the United States, and the international community at large react (including perhaps imposing sanctions upon the DPRK), it may be impossible to reverse the reality of the DPRK being a semi-member of the nuclear weapon club or to prevent the escalation of the chain of actions and reactions of nuclear proliferation in East Asia.

In such circumstances, major powers in East Asia, especially the United States and China, will be faced with ever-increasing challenges. These include dealing with a nuclear-armed DPRK, as well as the extremely difficult task of dissuading other countries from following suit. Some East Asian countries have the potential capability to develop nuclear weapons while others have available technologies and resources. Many international experts believe that Japan and the Republic of Korea (ROK) are the most likely countries in East Asia that will begin to develop nuclear arsenals.

Japan's Potential

The most worrisome country is perhaps Japan. As the victims of the only atomic strikes sixty years ago, Japan has been adhering to the "Three Principles of Non-Nuclearization." The Japanese peace constitution does not allow Japan to possess standing armed forces, let alone develop nuclear weapons. However, the peace constitution was violated fifty years ago when Japan established its Self-Defense Force. Since then, there have been talks from different corners of the Japanese community about developing nuclear weapons, but such extreme suggestions have never entered the mainstream opinion. However, this situation might change. As has been proved throughout history, the most seemingly impossible scenarios may emerge to surprise the vast majority of the populations. Thus, it may not be a far-fetched prediction that Japan could develop and deploy nuclear weapons in a very short period if the DPRK maintains a nuclear arsenal.

The political background and material conditions for the development of nuclear weapons in Japan are quite different from those of the DPRK. The latter has a very strong political demand and desire for the development of nuclear weapons in order to ensure survival, but Pyongyang lacks the necessary economy, technological resources, and nuclear materials. On the contrary, although Japan has not yet expressed its political demand and desire for developing nuclear weapons, it has both the economic and technological resources, as well as enough materials needed to produce nuclear weapons.

As far as outside observers can see, there are four political driving forces behind a possible Japanese decision to develop nuclear weapons. First, a nuclear-armed DPRK will make the majority of the Japanese people believe that Japan's immediate security is being threatened. The Japanese paranoia has a deep historical backdrop, as Tokyo has always had uneasy relations with its neighbors. The Japanese occupation of Korea before World War II instilled a deep-rooted hatred among the Korean people toward the Japanese. Furthermore, many leading Japanese politicians have been trying to gloss over Japanese atrocities during World War II. These factors have led to the prevailing anti-Japanese sentiments both in the DPRK and the ROK even sixty years after the end of Japanese occupation. In the minds of Japanese decision-makers, Japan will inevitably become one of the main targets of DPRK's nuclear weapons.

Second, Japan lacks both the sense of security and confidence in the U.S. nuclear umbrella. The Japanese people have always had doubts whether the United States would provide timely support for the defense of Japan. Rather, they would ask, is the U.S.-Japanese military alliance reliable? Is the U.S. government really willing to sacrifice the lives of American people to defend Japan? Even high-ranking officials of Japan pose these questions. Such sentiments will deepen when a hostile North Korea possesses nuclear weapons.

Third, Japan sees Chinese military forces as a potential threat and believes that its own conventional forces are far from being sufficient in assuring its national security—although it is widely accepted (even among Japanese defense circles) that Japan has first-class conventional forces that are among the best in the world, especially their naval forces. These forces are much stronger than China's. Yet, Japan still feels uncomfortable in the face of a China armed with a relatively small arsenal of nuclear weapons.

Fourth, Japan has a strong desire to become a major political power in the world and believes that it is necessary to also become a military power toward that end. To achieve this, Japan may choose to develop nuclear weapons as part of being "a normal nation." This may seem incredible to many experts, but it is true that such strange logic does exist in the minds of some Japanese politicians and defense officials.

Qualitatively and technologically, Japanese self-defense forces possess first-class weapons and equipment. It is worthwhile to note that since the 1980s, about 90 percent of Japan's weapons and equipment is produced in Japan, and only about 10 percent is imported from abroad. Japan has adopted a policy of combining industrial technologies and research for defense with those for civilian purposes. Many civilian enterprises, especially the giant ones, are also actively engaged in activities of defense-related research work and production. Presently, there are seventeen giant enterprises in Japan engaged in defense production and research that account for 95 percent of the purchases by the Japanese Defense Agency. They can perform different tasks in the research and production of various weaponry and electronic systems for military purpose. Many of the items manufactured in Japan, including satellites, rockets, missiles, fighters, tanks, warships, cannons, and munitions, are widely viewed as the most advanced in the world. Japan has even surpassed the United States in technology associated with semiconductors, robotics, photoelectricity, superconductivity, and plane instrumentation display. Tokyo's advances in technology related to communication, micro-electricity, computers, computer software, radar, and basic material are among the best in the world. Presently, Japan has developed integrated systems of research and production in the aerospace and missile industries. Japan now can manufacture almost all types of tactical missiles. Although the scale of their production is relatively small and the products are only meant for use of the Japanese self-defense forces (exports have traditionally not been allowed), their potential is great.

International observers are more anxious about the nuclear potential of Japan. It is estimated that Japan has accumulated 500 tons of weapons-grade plutonium, which is enough to make 1,000 "Hiroshima class" atomic bombs. In addition, it is reported that Japan could produce atomic bombs and hydrogen bombs within three to six months and 1,000 to 2,000 medium- and long-range missiles within a short period of time. In view of the technologies and nuclear materials available, Japan will not find it too difficult to cross the nuclear threshold. The only thing it needs is political will of the Japanese government.

South Korea

Owing to special historical, national, and geopolitical considerations, the ROK has perhaps the most earnest wish for a peaceful solution to the present nuclear crisis and the achievement of a nuclear-weapon-free Korean Peninsula. It will have to make a very difficult strategic decision if either the DPRK or Japan becomes a nuclear weapon state. The most likely choice for the ROK is perhaps to also develop nuclear weapons in the face of nuclear threats, both from the North and Japan. As seen by some international nuclear experts, the ROK has also the capability to become a nuclear weapon state on its own within a very short period of time, given its present technological and economic condition. What will happen next? It seems almost certain that nuclear proliferation will take place in East Asia and that the worst scenario, totally unacceptable to the international community, will become inevitable. The situation may well be spinning out of control.

How to Prevent the Vicious Circle of Nuclear Proliferation in East Asia?

The key to preventing nuclear escalation in East Asia is to keep the present crisis on the Korean Peninsula under control. A peaceful and comprehensive solution to the DPRK's nuclear weapons program must be found. Considering this, how can we stop the DPRK from joining the nuclear club by possessing a weaponized arsenal? Theoretically, four options could be considered.

The first choice could be the application of a comprehensive political, economic, diplomatic, and military pressure to force the DPRK to back down. There may be two possible outcomes. One is that the DPRK would give up its nuclear weapon program under increasing pressure from outside. Another possibility is that the DPRK becomes desperate and proceeds to carry out further nuclear tests at whatever cost. It will be an extremely difficult decision for the DPRK leaders to make. Historically, they have never succumbed to outside pressure of any kind. Importantly, the people of the DPRK have proven to be able to withstand extreme hardships. Therefore, enhancing pressure may turn out to be a stimulant to the acceleration of the DPRK's nuclear weapons program.

A second alternative would be to launch a preemptive strike on DPRK's nuclear facilities and root out any possibility of the DPRK developing nuclear weapons for a long time to come. The risk of such an option is obvious, and the outcome may be beyond anybody's expectation. A series of catastrophic and chaotic crises would most probably emerge in East Asia. There may be a large-scale regional war or armed conflict that may get out of control and lead to thousands of casualties and refugees in the region. The disastrous nature of such an option is easy to understand. Nevertheless, there seem to be voices raising this option, especially in the United States, where there are some who strongly advocate carrying out surgical strikes.

A third option calls for the United States, together with its allies, to accelerate research and development of missile defense systems in an attempt to construct an impenetrable shield. Such an option would be very expensive and unreliable. Moreover, this too may provoke chain reactions. The fragile global strategic stability will be further weakened. Will such actions be followed by a new arms race? What would the impact be on international efforts for arms control and disarmament?

The fourth option involves seeking a peaceful solution to the nuclear crisis within the framework of the Six-Party Talks, probing a more constructive way to build an enduring regional framework for the sustained strategic stability in East Asia in the future.

Many international observers are pessimistic about the future of the Six-Party Talks. In fact, no party has ever been satisfied with the achievements made in these talks. Nonetheless, it is the only official multilateral platform that directly deals with the nuclear crisis on the Korean Peninsula, and all six parties agree that the platform has been conducive to better communication between the hostile parties. There is no other channel that can replace it at present. Concerned parties, especially the United States and the DPRK, are haggling and bargaining with each other for their own maximum interests. It is a test of political will and wisdom. And the intense hostilities and confrontation often lead to a standstill in the dialogue process. However, a crisis is sometimes a turning point for opportunity. As a matter of fact, breaking through the deadlock is just a matter of political decisions by the United States and the DPRK, and room for the two sides to deepen dialogue still exists. The door for a nuclear-free Korean Peninsula has not yet been closed, and there is still a chance for a positive outcome as long as all participants of the Six-Party Talks and the international society continue to make joint efforts.

Possible Cooperation Between the United States and China in Preventing Nuclear Proliferation in East Asia

The United States and China are two major powers and both have the important responsibility of maintaining international and regional peace and stability. It is in the interest of the people of the two nations to make joint efforts in preventing nuclear proliferation in East Asia. On the other hand, there are other serious challenges in addition to the nuclear crisis on the Korean Peninsula that call for common efforts from these two nations. Thus, the Sino-U.S. cooperation should be oriented toward a wider range of issues. Four of them are discussed below. All of these issues are closely interconnected, and resolving all the four will all have a positive impact on the nonproliferation of nuclear weapons in East Asia.

Energy

With rapid economic development in the region, shortages of energy will pose a challenge of increasing proportions in the foreseeable future. Peaceful use of nuclear power may become a logical option for sustainable economic development for countries in the region. But no one should neglect the problem of the safety of nuclear power plants. The nuclear disaster in Ukraine in 1986 should not be forgotten, and the possibility for the reoccurrence of such disasters cannot be ruled out. In fact, the safety of nuclear power plants is not a problem solely for any individual country. It should be taken as a regional or even a global security issue. The United States has developed technologies needed to ensure such safety and has abundant experience in safeguarding nuclear power plants, whereas China is still in the very initial stages of developing such technologies. So the potential for the two countries to cooperate in this field is great. Although there have been agreements between the United States and China regarding cooperation in the field of nuclear power, actual implementation of these agreements seems to be very difficult for various reasons, primarily political reasons on the U.S. side. The Chinese government has been active in enhancing cooperation in this field.

Counter Terrorism

It is worthwhile to note that international terrorist groups may target nuclear power plants that are extremely vulnerable to surprise attacks. The terrorist attacks of 9/11 were an alarming signal for us all. International terrorist groups may exploit any point of vulnerability. The war against terror has made some progress. However, international terrorist groups are far from totally eliminated, and some of them are still actively seeking opportunities to launch terrorist attacks. The July 2005 terrorist bombing in London gave us a striking warning once again. The international community must maintain high vigilance. In this regard, close Sino-U.S. cooperation will help contain terrorist groups from engineering a nuclear disaster.

Nonproliferation

The prospect for bilateral security cooperation in East Asia between the United States and China is promising, especially in the area of nuclear nonproliferation. To that end, the two countries must see each other from a strategic perspective and respect the other's core national interests. They should establish strategic confidence between them first. Based on this, they can, in consultation with Russia, jointly provide negative security assurances for nonnuclear weapons states in East Asia, undertaking a "no first use" policy toward the use of nuclear weapons. They can also probe the possibility of signing the Nuclear Free Zone Treaty in Southeast Asia together and promote the establishment of a nuclear-free zone in Northeast Asia as well.

Arms Control

Strengthening the international regime of nuclear arms control and disarmament is also of great importance in containing nuclear proliferation. It is widely accepted that a nuclear-weapon-free world will be difficult to realize, and it will continue to remain only as a dream in the foreseeable future. However, there should be some kind of balance of interests between the nuclear *haves* and *have-no*ts. Members of the nuclear weapons club should be committed to nuclear arms control and disarmament. Perhaps the time has come for the United States and China to start a dialogue regarding how the two countries can work together to enhance the international regime of NPT and nuclear arms control.

10

SINO-INDIAN STRATEGIC RELATIONS

Shen Dingli[1]

By any measure, Sino-Indian relations are steadily improving.[2] This has been manifested by a number of factors.

In the political arena, both China and India have been accommodating each other in their respective "rise." India has been unwavering in committing itself to the "One China" position, and China seems to be supportive of India's bid for a permanent seat in a reformed United Nations Security Council (UNSC).[3] The two countries have overcome the difficulty that arose from India's nuclear weapons testing when China was implicitly pointed out by the Indian side to justify its tests. In the economic field, Sino-Indian bilateral trade is rapidly expanding, and carrying out mutual investments is no longer a new phenomenon. In the nuclear and security sphere, China joined the Nuclear Suppliers Group (NSG) in 2004, which has more or less relieved India's concern over a China-Pakistan nexus involving sensitive technology transfer. With regard to the U.S.-India cooperation deal on civilian use of nuclear energy, China and India agreed in 2006 that they too would follow suit.[4] The two countries have also carried out joint military exercises and India has even contributed its defense assets to aid China in combating SARS (Severe Acute Respiratory Syndrome).[5]

While Beijing and New Delhi have yet to resolve their border disputes, they have strengthened their military confidence building measures (CBMs) and have designated Special Representatives to engage in well-authorized talks on the border question. India has stated unequivocally that Tibet is a part of China while China has virtually admitted India's annexation of Sikkim. The two Asian giants have even officially declared their intention to forge a "strategic partnership."

Sino-Indian relations are also influenced by the policies of the United States. China used to work with the United States in denouncing India's nuclear weapons tests, but now China has to consider how the United States moves forward to accommodate India's nuclear status. Actually, the past few years have witnessed a growth in U.S.-India political and military rapprochement. While maintaining its interest in analyzing this development, China has shown no hesitance in adjusting its own India policy.

In the India-U.S.-China trilateral context, there has been a mixed picture thus far. On one hand, China noted that India has received the AWACS (Airborne Warning and Control System) that Israel originally built for China but was later disallowed by Washington to be delivered to China for political reasons. It is also noteworthy that India has shifted its official view toward the U.S. missile defense, which is quite a strategic move that repositions New Delhi in the world system.[6] On the other hand, India has condemned the U.S.-led NATO's bombing of the Chinese Embassy in Belgrade in 1999, and China has been impartial in covering the Kargil conflict in its press, at least by not tilting toward Pakistan, which gained it India's respect.

The impressive shift in Sino-India relations over the past two decades would not have occurred if it were not for the transformation of the world political landscape as well as China's and India's respective "rise" and also the pragmatic rather than rigid approaches of their respective leadership. This chapter will analyze various dimensions of the Sino-Indian relations that have become increasingly strategically defined, as well as the factors that have led to the formation of such a new relationship.

POLITICAL RELATIONS

China and India have worked out their first document regarding the principles of border dispute settlement. The political leaders in both countries have committed themselves to search for mutually acceptable solutions to the border disputes. If this issue is truly resolved, this part of Asia may find long-term peace and tranquility. Even prior to resolving the border dispute, China and India have agreed to build a strategic partnership, and are now cooperating in India's bid for a seat at the UNSC.

India's UNSC Bidding

China has enjoyed, for decades, its privileged position as the sole Asian representative in the permanent chamber of the UN Security Council. This has been augmented by China's unprecedented economic development since the late 1970s that has empowered it as a new competitor in the world economy. In parallel, during much of the late twentieth century, Japan successfully rehabilitated and reconstructed itself significantly and established itself as an economic superpower in the world. Today, it seems that Tokyo has concluded that it has qualified for a permanent membership of the UNSC and is lobbying forcefully for such a position.

So far India is neither a strong international economic power nor in the forefront of the world political stage. Nevertheless, India has longed for this and has been enjoying impressive economic growth. It has been maintaining a growth rate of 6–8 percent of its GDP (gross domestic product) for nearly a decade.[7] That brings India, in terms of PPP (purchasing power parity), as a new and respectable player in Asia's economy. Like Tokyo, New Delhi currently also deems it to be the appropriate time to bid for a UNSC permanent seat.

The challenge is thus for both the United States and China. As the current permanent members enjoying veto power, none of the P5 (permanent five members of the UNSC) would be truly interested in having their power further shared and their freedom of action complicated. Beijing and Washington may welcome a limited expansion of the Security Council at no cost to their veto privilege. However, the two capitals have divergent views on who should qualify for the new permanent slots. In 2005, Washington allowed an increase of only two seats, and included its close ally in the Far East, Japan, while rejecting India's bid. In contrast, Beijing may be more flexible in accepting an enlarged permanent chamber in the Security Council, but China seems conservative concerning Japan's bid.

Beijing's concern over Japan is rooted in the latter's refusal, especially by its latest leaders including the former Prime Minister Junichiro Koizumi, of East Asia's call for respecting history, in particular, of Japan's refusal to accept the facts of its wartime atrocities committed during World War II and subsequent need to assume its responsibility.

With fourteen A-class war criminals resting in Yasukuni Shrine, the yearly official visit by the Japanese Prime Minister and cabinet members leads most Chinese, as well as many other East Asians, to think that Japan is not politically suited to hold a permanent seat at the UNSC. Obviously, the U.S.-Japan security alliance that helps deter mainland China's freedom of action on the question of Taiwan also contributes to China's cool attitude toward Japan.

Beijing's theory about reforming the UNSC is that the new permanent members should have a fair regional representation and that developing countries should merit adequate consideration. Given these criteria, India seems better qualified, as it represents 1 billion people in Asia's developing world whose economy is improving and as it maintains a fairly independent foreign policy. Comparing the popularity of India and Japan in their neighborhoods in the context of bidding for the UNSC seat, India seems to be opposed only by Pakistan in all of South Asia, whereas Japan is disapproved by almost all its Northeast Asian neighbors: China, Democratic People's Republic of Korea (DPRK), and Republic of Korea (ROK).

Therefore, China seems to be more inclined to opt for India and is preparing for its *strategic* consequences—getting ready to share Asia's leadership and responsibility at the Security Council with New Delhi someday. Their political baggage of Pokran nuclear tests seems to be left behind. India has withstood international pressures for years—despite the "illegitimacy" of its development and possession of nuclear weapons, as viewed by the Nuclear Nonproliferation Treaty (NPT). India's nuclear status has been gradually accepted as a fait accompli, and China has to be realistic in this regard. For its own part, India has progressively officially distanced itself from viewing China as a "threat," though such arguments surface from time to time, especially when the border dispute still remains unresolved.

Settling the Border Dispute

The perennial headache of the Sino-Indian border dispute represents a seemingly insurmountable barrier to complete normalization of their relations. Indeed, there exists certain military confidence building measures between the two armed forces along the line of actual control (LAC).[8] However, without total settlement of the border dispute, it is hard to dispel distrust completely between the two countries.

Conforming to the strong commitment from each government toward shaping a new relationship in this new century, China and

India designated Dai Bingguo, the then vice foreign minister of China, and Misra,[9] national security advisor of India, for the first round of talks on the border question held from October 23, 2003. Their talks reached the climax of an *Agreement on the Political Parameters and Guiding Principles for the Settlement of the China-India Boundary Question* on April 11, 2005.

This agreement indicated in its preamble that "an early settlement of the boundary question will advance the basic interests of the two countries and should therefore be pursued as a *strategic* objective." It also noted that "[T]he differences on the boundary question should not be allowed to affect the overall development of bilateral relations."[10] It is worth mentioning that the agreement made it clear that "[T]he two sides will take into account, inter alia, historical evidence, national sentiments, practical difficulties and reasonable concerns and sensitivities of both sides, and the actual state of border areas."[11] With the ongoing progress in affirming the current LAC, it is reasonable to expect that the status quo of the LAC will be chosen to be the legal base of future negotiations for leading to an eventual border settlement.

On the territorial question, the then Indian prime minister, Atal Bihari Vajpayee, declared in June 2003 when he visited China that "Tibet Autonomous Region is a part of territory of the People's Republic of China (PRC)."[12] Though India may consider that it has been holding this position for over half a century, this statement per se has been viewed widely as India's first unambiguous assertion of this view. Consequently, Beijing made a quid pro quo action by withdrawing the status of Sikkim as a sovereign state from the Chinese Ministry of Foreign Affairs' official Web site, thus reverting from a long-held PRC principle that had denied India's sovereignty over the former Himalayan kingdom. Contrary to its Japan policy, Chinese idealistic foreign policy yields more to realism in the case of India. With Chinese Premier Wen Jiabao's visit to Delhi in 2005, the two sides furthered their exchange through the Joint Statement of April 11: India repeated its rhetoric on Tibet made two years earlier,[13] and the Chinese used the term "the Sikkim state of India."[14]

Moving Toward "Strategic Partnership"

China and India are the two most populous nations in the world. Given the size of their territory and population and the level and potential of economic development, the relationship between these two de facto nuclear weapons states cannot be trivial. Both nations' leaderships would accord their bilateral relations a global and strategic significance. In 2005, the two countries decided to refer to their relationship as a "strategic partnership."

A Sino-Indian cooperative partnership could have been nurtured decades earlier, as Zhou En-lai and Jawaharlal Nehru initiated, as early as in 1954, the "Five Principles of Peaceful Co-existence," which also laid their own foundation of relations. However, due to the problematic handling of the border dispute and the twist of the cold war, China and India missed their opportunity to build a partnership throughout much of the cold war period.

Two significant steps have been taken since late 1990s for the forging of a Sino-Indian cooperative partnership. The first step followed Jiang Zemin's visit to Delhi in November 1996. During this first visit by a Chinese head of state, the two countries agreed to establish "constructive cooperative partnership in the twenty-first century," signaling China's strategic shift to a balanced foreign policy toward South Asia in the post-cold war period. Vajpayee's visit to Beijing in June 2003, following the visit of the then defense minister, Fernandes, in April (despite SARS) consolidated this newly created partnership. Vajpayee's discussions in Beijing elevated Sino-Indian relations to a new height: his visit first set the tone of mutual recognition of Tibet and Sikkim and then set up the mechanism of Special Representatives to decide the principles of future border dispute negotiations.[15]

The second step is the outcome of Wen Jiabao's visit to India in April 2005. In the entire history of the PRC and the Republic of India, the two countries for the first time agreed to establish "a strategic cooperative partnership for peace and prosperity." This visit led to the signing and publishing of twelve bilateral documents, including the *Protocol of Implementing Military CBMs in the Border Areas along China-India LAC* and *Five-Year Plan of Sino-Indian Comprehensive Economic and Trade Cooperation*.

To be honest, China-India rapprochement has much to do with an evolving world order and multipolarity in the international system. This has reduced, though not necessarily removed, their mutual apprehensions. Both sides recognize the need to tap the opportunities their economic development and interaction have provided them in an interconnected world. Interestingly enough, this trend has been expanded to a Sino-Indian-Russo framework. In June 2005, the foreign ministers of these three countries met in Vladivostok and affirmed the need for democratization in international relations and a fair world order.[16] It remains to be seen how far this trilateral relationship can be advanced.

Economic Relations

China-India trade relations started from a very low point. In the aftermath of the then prime minister R. Gandhi's visit to Beijing, China-India trade was only worth 200 million U.S. dollars. The border trade was resumed from 1992, primarily with barter standing at a level of 5 million Chinese yuan per annum.

However, over just a decade, Sino-Indian trade relations have developed and expanded fast. In accordance with the statistics from China's General Administration of Customs, the total trade column between China and India reached 4.9 billion U.S. dollars in 2002, up 37 percent from 2001; 7.6 billion in 2003, up 54 percent from 2002; 13.6 billion in 2004, up 79 percent from 2003; 18.7 billion in 2005, up 37 percent from 2004; and 24.9 billion in 2006, up 33 percent from 2005.[17]

Reportedly, Vajpayee's visit to China in 2003 was in line with the Chinese official position that in three years the two countries shall double their trade from 5 billion (2003) to 10 billion U.S. dollars (2006). Apparently, this ambition has been met in less than two years. The April 2005 *Joint Statement* targeted 20 billion and 30 billion U.S. dollars for 2008 and 2010, respectively. In fact, the target of 20 billion was met by 2006. Given the actual average annual increase in the level of trade, 32 percent over the decade from 1995 to 2005, one could even linearly protract Sino-Indian trade volume to attain 43 billion U.S. dollars by 2008.

Realistically speaking, a yearly 43 billion dollar trade by 2008 is not impossible to attain given the current level of 24.9 billion (in 2006) and given the potential of trade between the two countries (they traded worth 8.2 billion U.S. dollars in the first quarter in 2007, up by 58.5 percent than the same period a year ago). It is almost certain that Sino-Indian trade will flourish significantly in the future, given their geographic vicinity and the vast scale of both their economies. Chinese and Indian governments have decided to launch a feasibility study for a bilateral free trade zone. This further bodes well for the future of their trade relationship.

Clearly, while China and India have managed to stabilize their nuclear relationship, they are blessed by their thriving economic relations through rapid expansion of trade. There is no doubt that Sino-Indian "strategic relations" will be strengthened and further stabilized through economic cooperation and trade. The two governments are encouraging the expansion of trade areas and reduction of trade barriers. They are also expected to strengthen cooperation in high-tech areas of mutual interest. Cooperation in infrastructure construction could possibly represent one more opportunity for near-term collaboration.

Security Relations

Putting the border issue aside, China and India have left the liability of India's nuclear weapons tests behind. They cannot talk officially about their nuclear relationship, but each has been watching the nuclear policy of the other side as it will shape their mutual responses to some extent. China and India still have much to do in reassuring each other of their intentions.

Nuclear Relationship

India and China are both promising economic powerhouses of the world, and their economic relations are easier to manage than their nuclear relationships. As an accepted nuclear weapons state, it is not easy for China to accept India as a de jure nuclear weapons state. As a member of the NPT, China is not in a position to accord India with an official recognition of its nuclear status because China has to conform to the norm of nuclear nonproliferation. India won't be encouraged with such a situation but both countries have agreed that nothing shall forestall their relations from moving forward. In fact, India doesn't care much if its nuclear weapons status is recognized or not.

Despite the fact that China cannot accept India's nuclear weapons status, it is clear that Beijing will not ignore that fact when making its strategic calculations. As both are nuclear weapons neighbors whose border disputes are yet to be resolved, China and India will find that they have to develop a multifaceted nuclear relationship that would include the following:

- *Understanding respective nuclear doctrines.* Allegedly, both countries have embraced No First Use (NFU) strategy. China is believed by most western strategists to be employing a minimum nuclear deterrence, while India seems to be pursuing a similar course. Understanding and ascertaining their respective nuclear doctrines concerning the strategic requirements, use and deployment, and the ramification of such development on regional and global disarmament and nonproliferation will remain their long-term strategic objectives.

- *Avoiding nuclear misunderstanding.* India may have acquired an adequate amount of fissile materials to build a nuclear arsenal of a few hundred weapons, while its civilian reactors are accumulating even more plutonium in spent fuels (though less militarily useable due to higher levels of isotopes of plutonium in the mix).[18] The potential to expand their nuclear arsenal exists, so it is important that China and India don't have misunderstandings or miscalculations in their strategic planning.
- *Employing a responsible nonproliferation system.* As nuclear weapons states, it is of utmost importance for the two countries to implement a nuclear nonproliferation policy and set up a national system of nonproliferation export control. China has had a relatively rich experience in this regard and it will be productive for them to engage in such cooperation. Meanwhile, it is imperative that the two countries develop enough physical protection for their nuclear assets, assuring the safety and security of their nuclear assets and minimizing the risk of nuclear theft and terrorism.

The Pakistan Factor

As an "all-weather strategic partner," Pakistan has rendered comprehensive support to China for decades. Likewise, China has delivered strategic support to Pakistan whenever it has had a need. Beijing-Islamabad relations were developed during the cold war period when security alignments were the key consideration in formulating foreign policy. The U.S.-Soviet confrontation was embodied in South Asia as Pakistan-India confrontation, and China's strategic relations with Pakistan have much to do with India's territorial conflicts with both China and Pakistan.

Allegedly, in much of the 1980s and early 1990s, China's nuclear-related exports, particularly to Pakistan, were of "major international nonproliferation concern" and clouded China-U.S. and China-India bilateral relations.[19] However, China made notable strides in the 1990s by joining formal arms control and nonproliferation regimes, and in the 2000s by joining informal nonproliferation export regimes. In the wake of the ring magnet issue, the Chinese government announced on May 10, 1996, that "it will not provide assistance to un-safeguarded facilities."[20] In May 2004, China joined the NSG in committing fully to full-scope safeguards (FSS), that is, not to provide any nuclear assistance to any country that refuses to accept FSS. By taking this measure, China has committed not to cooperate with India, Pakistan, Israel, and the DPRK as they remain outside of the NPT.[21]

India and Pakistan remain confrontational time and again, though their political relationship is improving. In the post-cold war era, maintaining a strategic partnership with Pakistan while limiting Sino-Indian relations undercuts China's important interests. Beijing might decide to redefine its strategic interests and build simultaneous partnerships with both Islamabad and New Delhi. Its strategic partnership with Pakistan could be redefined to include a wider range of subjects but with limits to the transfer of sensitive technologies. China's effort to adjust its nonproliferation stance and apply FSS upon itself helps to clear India's fundamental concern. This in turn creates trust and confidence between China and India that promote their strategic trust building.

Antiterror

The 9/11 attacks transformed the world political landscape, and antiterror issues have been increasingly a part of the new Sino-Indian security relationship.

Both China and India have taken notice of the terrorism threat in the bilateral, regional, and global context. The two have worked together in supporting the antiterror military action in Afghanistan. They both share their disagreement on the "unilateral" military action in Iraq under the pretext of counter-WMD (weapons of mass destruction) proliferation or antiterror. The two countries launched an antiterror dialogue in April 2002 (second round in June 2003, and another round in late 2005), and China has supported India's accession to the Shanghai Cooperation Organization (SCO) as an observer in mid-2005. It is understood that the Indian government has enhanced the security of Chinese diplomatic compounds as they may be under threat by the "Eastern Turkish Independence Movement" (ETIM), a UN-listed international terrorist group.

The Sino-Indian military-to-military contact is emerging with antiterror in mind. In November 2003 China and India carried out a joint search-and-rescue naval exercise in the East China Sea near Shanghai. In August 2004 Indian soldiers joined Chinese soldiers for a joint mountain-hike training. In December 2005 the Chinese navy conducted a joint exercise with India in the northern Indian Ocean for search-and-rescue operations. During December 19–27, 2007, the two armies had their first joint military exercise, called "Hand-in-Hand 2007." The purpose was for antiterror response and it was held in China's Kunming, Yunnan. It was the first exercise in the past 45 years in the two countries' relationship. Reportedly, a second round will be held in India in 2008. Such activities indicate a trend that the two countries are ridding traditional mindsets. The strengthening of China-India military relationship will place China in a better position in terms of establishing normal relations with other countries in South Asia.

THE DRIVING FORCES AND IMPLICATIONS

The aforementioned positive developments in Sino-Indian relations have been inspiring. They are derived from a number of factors, including the parallel rise of China and India that renders them more confident and mature in dealing with each other, and the post-9/11 developments that re-prioritizes threat perceptions and national interests. Obviously, U.S.-China and U.S.-India relations have affected Sino-Indian relations, inducing a change that is often positive regardless of the initial American intention.

It should be pointed out that the Sino-Indian relationship still needs time to mature. This relationship is not very fragile, as it enjoys wide support on the part of both countries, but it is not unshakable either, until the border dispute is resolved. As the border talks involve national feelings and are highly sensitive, one wouldn't expect this dispute to be settled anytime soon. Nevertheless, given the growing maturity of the two states, there is a good chance that they will be able to control any potential disruption in relations and that the current positive trend in their relations will continue.

Rise of China and India

The contemporary republics of China and India have only enjoyed a history of about half a century. On the part of China, it was only able to discover a flourishing path to success less than thirty years ago. For India, its democratic institutions have not delivered substantial economic goods for many years, and many resources have been diverted for non-civilian purposes. The two "newly" independent states so treasured their hard-won sovereignty that they collided militarily in 1962 over a border that has never been officially demarcated.

Nuclear weapons provide both China and India with security and pride. Presently they are still learning how to peacefully coexist, given their nuclear weapon assets. India's tacit accusation, in 1998, against China when India tested nuclear weapons was viewed as proof of its then "immature" foreign policy. However, India's possession of nuclear weapons has subsequently led it to handle relations with China and Pakistan more cautiously. India refrained in the early 2000s from aggravating confrontation vis-à-vis Pakistan after a terrorist attack outside its Parliament.

Following the nuclear weapons tests of India and Pakistan, both China and India have taken a forward-looking approach to deal with each other. The "China threat" rhetoric in India has been downplayed as Indian leaders and mainstream strategists are viewing China less as a threat and more as a partner. China has taken a more realistic view toward India, as it could not afford to leave relations cool for an excessively long time. One has to admit that both India and China are more confident and realistic now, which is driving their relationship forward positively.

World Strategic Landscape

The contemporary antiterror "warfare" will induce a strengthening of Sino-Indian relations. Such a global threat has allowed states to downplay their interstate competition and rivalry and presents ever unfolding opportunities for cooperation.

In the case of Sino-Indian relations, the previous section has suggested that the antiterror campaign furnishes the two countries with a common security objective in South Asia as well as Central Asia. When comparing Indian with Pakistani positions on the military actions in Afghanistan and Iraq, it is not impossible to infer that the Beijing-New Delhi policy coordination on antiterror probably has transcended the coordination and cooperation between Beijing and Islamabad.

China would not allow the improvement of Sino-Indian relations to sour its relations with Pakistan. However, China is facing more challenges due to terrorist attacks on Chinese nationals in Pakistan. In 2004 and 2007 Chinese engineers and workers were targeted in abductions, and on one occasion the kidnapping led to the death of a Chinese citizen. More recently, the Chinese government has requested cooperation from the Pakistani government in arresting and repatriating twenty-two key members of the East Turkestan Islamic Movement (ETIM) staying in the tribal areas of Pakistan.[22] In this context, it is likely that China will need to expand its antiterror cooperation with both India and Pakistan.

The American Effect

The role of the Unites States in Sino-India relations is unavoidable and its effect so far has been mixed. To elaborate, one needs to distinguish between intention, perception, and outcome.

First, the American intention, both professed and real: The published policy of the United States is readily available, while their "real" intention keeps others speculating. Then, how will China perceive American policy? Typically, China would perceive it from the negative angle, as the two countries continue to lack trust. Finally the outcome: China and India will continue to develop their bilateral relations under different external circumstances, and they will also analyze how the United States deals with each of them.

During the three terms of the Clinton and Bush Administrations, the United States continued to reform its relations with India: building bilateral defense relations, accommodating India's political standing (short of agreeing with India's bidding for UNSC permanent seat), extending civilian nuclear energy cooperation, and so on. Although China may be uninterested in seeing such developments, the PRC and India have continued to improve their relationship.

For the whole of the 1990s, China and the United States have only been briefly critical of India's and Pakistan's nuclear weapons tests. The United States lifted its sanctions on India quite quickly and started to accept India's minimum deterrence.[23] American realism kindled Chinese suspicion and, as a result, China presented its own realism: when the then Indian president K R Narayanan visited Beijing in 1999, the nuclear issue was not mentioned at all.

As mentioned above, the recent U.S.-India nuclear initiative makes China ponder. On July 18, 2005, President Bush agreed with the visiting Indian Prime Minister Manmohan Singh on the cooperation for peaceful use of nuclear energy. This marked a major departure from the U.S. precondition of compliance with full-scope safeguards for civilian nuclear cooperation with any foreign country.

As a new member of the NSG, China is obliged to comply with such full-scope safeguard requirements. Prior to joining the NSG, China had supplied low-enriched uranium to India, and light-water reactors to Pakistan, with both materials and facility exported under IAEA (International Atomic Energy Agency) safeguards but not full-scope safeguards, a prerequisite that neither India nor Pakistan would accept and qualify. With China joining the NSG in 2004, China has relinquished its rights to engage in nuclear cooperation for peaceful purposes with non-NPT states. Nevertheless, considering the current U.S. policy, China must speculate on the intentions of the United States and review its current full-scope safeguards requirement under NSG obligation. In fact, China has sought the same departure vis-à-vis India, or the expansion of FSS exception unilaterally to Pakistan as well. Apparently, American policy toward India affects Sino-Indian relations when Beijing envisions its relations with New Delhi.

Conclusion

The rise of China and India has become the defining phenomena of our contemporary world order. Despite deep difficulties concerning border dispute settlement and so on, China and India have embarked on a course of dialogue and cooperation.

China and India have been working on fostering their strategic partnership. Forging such a tie between Beijing and New Delhi, possibly still premature and likely to be consolidated over the next few decades, will serve to improve bilateral relations between the two countries and will also continue to affect American interests in the region.

Sino-Indian relations will benefit more than two billion people living in these two countries. The United States will foresee some uncertainties due to the rise of China and India and will play the statecraft of balance of power between China, India, and itself. However, given the tradition of Chinese and Indian independent foreign policy, they will find their own way to adjust policy developments to fit their own best interest. One can reasonably predict that no two nations among these three will form any bilateral alliance against the third nation. Sino-Indian strategic relations are unlikely to be directed against American interests, just as U.S.-India relations shall not be targeted against the People's Republic of China.

Notes

1. Shen Dingli is a professor of international relations at Fudan University. He is the Director of Center for American Studies and Executive Dean of Institute of International Studies at Fudan.
2. For some good review papers on Sino-Indian relations, see Richard Weixing Hu, "India's Nuclear Bomb and Future Sino-Indian Relations," *East Asia* 17, no.1 (Spring 1999), 40–68, and Sun Shihai, "Sino-Indian Relations toward the 21st Century," in *Asia Report 2000* (Changchun: Changchun Press, 2001, in Chinese).
3. *Joint Statement between the People's Republic of China and the Republic of India*, April 11, 2005. Article 16 stated, "[China] understands and supports India to play active role in the U.N. and international affairs."
4. *Joint Declaration between China and India*, New Delhi, November 21, 2006. Article 17 reads, "Considering that for both India and China, expansion of civilian nuclear energy program is an essential and important component of their national energy plans to ensure energy security, the two sides agree to promote cooperation in the field of nuclear energy, consistent with their respective international commitments." This entails revision of NSG, as its current shape doesn't allow, even for peaceful purpose, nuclear energy cooperation between NSG members and any nonmembers of NPT (Nonproliferation Treaty).
5. Indian Defense Minister George Fernandes visited China in spring 2003, despite the SARS that Beijing was suffering from. He announced that India will provide China with Indian military medicine.
6. Shen Dingli, "India's Intention Suspect" (Cover Story), *Outlook* (The Weekly Magazine), India, May 21, 2001, 52
7. By 2006, India attained US$1 trillion GDP a year.
8. Two previous documents signed by Chinese and Indian governments have played a pivotal role in stabilizing their relations. First, *Agreement on the Maintenance of Peace and Tranquility along the Line of Actual Control in the China-India Border Areas*, September 7, 1993. Second, *Agreement on Confidence Building Measures in the Military Field along the Line of Actual Control in the China-India Border*, November 29, 1996.
9. Special Representative Misra was later succeeded by former President Narayanan.
10. See Article I of the Agreement.
11. See Article V of the Agreement.
12. *Declaration on Principles for Relations and Comprehensive Cooperation between China and India*, June 23, 2003.
13. Article 12, *Joint Statement between the People's Republic of China and the Republic of India*, April 11, 2005.
14. Article 13, *Joint Statement between the People's Republic of China and the Republic of India*, April 11, 2005.

15. The two Special Representatives have held ten rounds of talks so far: October 2003, January 2004, July 2004, November 2004, April 2005, September 2005, March 2006, June 2006, January 2007, and April 2007.
16. See, *The Joint Communiqué of the Informal Meeting between the Foreign Ministers of People's Republic of China, the Russian Federation and the Republic of India*, June 3, 2005.
17. China's Ministry of Foreign Affairs, http://www.fmprc.gov.cn/chn/wjb/zzjg/yzs/gjlb/1328/default.htm, http://www.fmprc.gov.cn/eng/wjb/zzjg/yzs/gjlb/2711/. Accessed on February 4, 2008. China has registered trade surplus at US$0.2 B (2001), US$0.4 B (2002) and US$4.3 B (2006); and India has had trade surplus at US$0.9 B (2003), US$1.8 B (2004) and US$0.8 B (2005).
18. Nongovernmental estimates of India's fissile-material stockpiles are summarized in *Plutonium and Highly Enriched Uranium 1996: World Inventories, Capabilities and Policies*, by David Albright, Frans Berkhout, and William Walker (Oxford University Press, 1997). See also David Albright and Kimberly Kramer, "Fissile material stockpiles still growing", *Bulletin of the Atomic Scientists*, November/December 2004, 14–16.
19. For a Western viewpoint, see Chapter 7 "China," in Joseph Cirincione, Jon Wolfsthal, and Miriam Rajkumar, *Deadly Arsenals: Nuclear, Biological, and Chemical Threats*, 2nd ed., revised and expanded (Carnegie Endowment for International Peace, Washington, D.C., 2005,), 163–188.
20. According to press reports, the Clinton Administration determined in August 1995 that China had sold 5,000 ring magnets valued at US$70,000 to Abdul Qadeer Khan Research Laboratory in Kahuta between December 1994 and mid-1995. This unsafeguarded gas-centrifuge facility can produce weapons-grade, highly enriched uranium. *Reuters and UPI* reports, February 8, 1996.
21. The DPRK quit NPT on January 10, 2003. In the wake of U.S.-India agreement of peaceful use of nuclear energy of March 2006, China also agreed, in 2006, to cooperate with both India and Pakistan on peaceful use of nuclear energy. This can only be possible if and when China can rearrange its commitment of FSS toward NSG.
22. Lei Huai, "Chinese government requesting Pak cooperation", *Elite Reference* (in Chinese), June 26, 2007, http://qnck.cyol.com/content/2007–06/26/content_1805952.htm. Accessed on February 4, 2008.
23. Strobe Talbot, "Dealing with the Bombs in South Asia", *Foreign Affairs*, March/April 1999, Vol. 78, Issue 2, 110–122.

11

THE CHALLENGE OF A NUCLEAR NORTH KOREA

Scott Snyder[1]

The formative experiences of the Democratic People's Republic of Korea (DPRK) over sixty years ago are directly intertwined with the North Korean leadership's longstanding pursuit of a nuclear weapons capability. The DPRK Museum of Revolutionary History in central Pyongyang provides a silent tribute to the powerful lure of atomic weaponry as an essential tool for guaranteeing state survival. One large section of that museum catalogues and mythologizes two decades of Korean guerilla efforts to recover lost sovereignty and to escape from Japan's colonial rule, centering on the real and imagined exploits of an unparalleled guerilla fighter, Kim Il Sung. In the last room, one can find a call to national uprising issued on August 9, 1945, by Kim Il Sung. Within one week the nation responded, and Korea was liberated from Japanese imperialism, achieving Kim's ardent wish. Nowhere in this room is there any mention of the powerful assistance that the atomic bomb provided to Kim Il Sung in achieving the culmination of two decades of struggle. Likewise, the North Korean leadership knows how close the United States came to considering the use of nuclear weapons to break a protracted stalemate during the Korean War. North Korea's leadership also witnessed the advantages China gained from its successful nuclear achievements in the 1960s. It should be no surprise that Kim Il Sung made it a priority to pursue nuclear weapons capabilities following the North's recovery from the devastation of the Korean War.

One result of North Korea's ongoing efforts to pursue its nuclear program has been a protracted crisis over that program since the end of the cold war. Shorn of allies following the collapse of the Soviet Union and China's dedication to economic reforms, the North Korean leadership's survival dilemmas have only grown deeper since the early 1990s; at the same time, its nuclear program has become the center of international attention and the focal point of a protracted international crisis. This chapter will review the key elements of the North Korean program and how the experience of the first North Korean nuclear crisis has influenced the handling of the current crisis. It will assess the current status of the North Korean program and make a range of projections for its growth through 2010. It will also discuss implications for a Korean peace process, which has been explicitly linked to the North Korean nuclear crisis through the latest diplomatic efforts to resolve the crisis, represented by both the Joint Statement of the Six-Party Talks, issued on September 19, 2005, and the February 13, 2007, implementation agreement.[2]

THE FIRST NORTH KOREAN CRISIS: TACIT ACQUIESCENCE TO A NUCLEAR NORTH KOREA?

After the first Persian Gulf War and the discovery that Saddam Hussein's Iraq was further along in their nuclear weapons program than anticipated, the Clinton Administration touted counterproliferation as the new post-cold war threat to global security. The International Atomic Energy Agency (IAEA) made North Korea the test case for setting a new international standard through demands for "special inspections." Under Soviet pressure, North Korea reluctantly joined the IAEA in 1985, but it did so with the idea that IAEA inspections were pro forma inspections based on North Korea's voluntary declaration. Due to bureaucratic snafus, it was not until 1992 that the North Koreans finally accepted on-site IAEA verification of their program, just at the point when the IAEA was reviewing its inspection procedures following the embarrassing revelations in the aftermath of the Persian Gulf War that Saddam Hussein's nuclear development efforts were far more advanced than the IAEA inspections had indicated. The IAEA's efforts to utilize more thoroughgoing inspection techniques after their embarrassment in Iraq led them to focus on discrepancies between the DPRK's declared nuclear activities and the story told by a swipe of the glove box of an experimental 5 MWe graphite reactor at Yongbyon.

The North Koreans responded to the IAEA's demands for special inspections poorly, eventually choosing to exercise their right to withdraw from the treaty rather than be exposed as violators. At the same time, the way the investigation was handled exacerbated North Korean paranoia since U.S. intelligence given to the IAEA played a role in stiffening the IAEA's position. In fact, the North Korean case was being used to set a new precedent for the use of "special inspections" in the wake of the IAEA's failures in Iraq. Following North Korea's announcement that it would leave the NPT in March of 1993, the matter was referred to the United Nations Security Council, which requested all interested parties negotiate with the North Koreans to stay in the NPT. American and North Korean delegations met in June of 1993 in a last-ditch effort to keep the latter in the nonproliferation regime. Only months later, President Bill Clinton stood at the demilitarized zone (DMZ) and said that if the North Koreans were to acquire nuclear weapons, "it would be the end of their country."[3]

Alarming media stories over the ensuing months warned of the nuclear domino effect that would engulf Northeast Asia, as Japan, South Korea, and Taiwan were projected to go nuclear if North Korea did.[4] After an extended crisis and over eighteen months of sporadic negotiations between North Korea and the United States, the two sides finally came to an agreement. They laid out a process whereby the North Koreans would shut down and eventually dismantle their facilities capable of making weapons-grade plutonium in return for the supply of two light-water reactors by an international consortium and the promise of progress toward normalization with the United States. However, the issue of "special inspections" that had been at the heart of the crisis was kicked down the road and linked to the stage of completion "before the delivery of key nuclear components" of the light-water reactors under construction.[5]

The agreement itself would have achieved the objective of dismantling North Korea's nuclear weapons development program if it had been pursued to its completion by both sides. In this sense, the parties to the agreement could argue, and the international community could accept, that the North Korean nuclear program had been brought under control and that it was just a matter of time before North Korea was brought back into the NPT as a nonnuclear weapons state.

However, in the absence of mutual trust and performance by both sides, the terms of the agreement were not pursued to completion. Instead, the agreement was beset by delays, and it eventually broke down with the discovery of, and confrontation over, North Korea's covert uranium enrichment efforts in October of 2002. Shortly thereafter, the Agreed Framework unraveled as the United States led a campaign to end the Korean Peninsula Energy Development Organization's (KEDO) supply of heavy fuel oil to North Korea because of their noncompliance with the Agreed Framework (i.e., their pursuit of an alternative uranium-based path to nuclear weapons status in direct contradiction with the spirit of the Agreed Framework). In response, the North Koreans kicked out IAEA inspectors and regained control of 8,000 stored fuel rods that had been stored in anticipation of their removal from the country and North Korea's return to full compliance with its safeguards obligations under the NPT.[6]

By taking these actions in late 2002 and early 2003, the North Koreans forced the international community to come to terms with a dirty little secret. The international community—and especially North Korea's immediate neighbors—had chosen for the most part to ignore that North Korea had attained all the elements necessary to become a de facto nuclear weapons state from as early as the mid-1990s. The Agreed Framework allowed North Korea's nuclear status to remain ambiguous until a certain unspecified date—the point at which the North would have to come into compliance with its safeguards obligations in return for the supply of critical nuclear components for the two light water reactors constructed by KEDO. By doing so, the United States and the international community had tacitly affirmed that it could live with the ambiguity that North Korea may indeed have become a nuclear weapons state. The U.S. intelligence community had assessed that the DPRK may have enough fissile material from plutonium produced prior to 1992 to build one or two nuclear weapons.[7] At the same time, all of North Korea's neighbors could sleep easier knowing that North Korea's nuclear capacity had been capped and that there was a point in the future at which it might be brought back fully into the NPT as a nonnuclear state.

The dispute over the amount of plutonium may have made it easier to live with this ambiguity, since North Korea's available stock of plutonium was only sufficient for at most two bombs—reducing the likelihood of a North Korean nuclear test. The slow development of the North Korean nuclear crisis—in particular, the seven-year period of apparent success—also may have made it easier to live with the ambiguity. The protracted nature of the crisis has given North Korea's neighbors time to get used to the idea of a North Korea that had some nuclear capabilities, even in a limited form. This has become a particularly important factor as one considers the preferences of the various parties to the Six-Party Talks in terms of what they might be able to live with; that is, the apparent willingness of North Korea's neighbors to accept a "gray" North Korea.[8] North Korea's October 9, 2006, attempt to test a nuclear device has no doubt provided North Korea's neighbors with a renewed opportunity to consider their ability to respond to a nuclear North Korea.

The Current Status of North Korea's Nuclear Program 2007 and Projections For 2010

The current status and projected development of North Korea's nuclear weapons program can be roughly grouped into three stages or thresholds of development, each of which have progressively more serious implications for regional security in Northeast Asia. The first stage would be a scenario when North Korea might have a limited amount of nuclear material, possibly sufficient to make a bomb or two but not enough to test without severely limiting additional future development of the program. This was the stage that culminated in the first North Korean nuclear crisis, because the Agreed Framework prevented the North Koreans from reprocessing spent fuel rods that would have moved the North Korean program beyond the first phase.

The second phase would be a situation in which North Korea has enough material on hand to test, but has not yet built its nuclear arsenal to the point that it could safely risk losing material or take actions that might compromise its capacity as a nuclear weapons state. This is the stage that the international community is currently trying to manage through negotiation of the February 13, 2007, agreement that, if implemented, would freeze North Korea's continued acquisition of nuclear material and thus limit the likelihood that the North would proliferate nuclear materials to state or non-state actors. That agreement is backed by other efforts to institutionalize the nonproliferation of nuclear weapons or materials as an international norm pursuant to UN Security Council Resolution 1540.

The third phase would be the point at which the North Koreans might have accumulated enough material to make "n +1" nuclear bombs (where "n" represents the minimum necessary nuclear weapons the leadership determines will satisfy North Korea's own national security needs, be it deterrence or a sufficiently robust response capability to exact a price from any potential adversary); that is, it has enough nuclear material on hand to satisfy not only its own needs but also to export material to others. If the North Korean program is left to continue to produce fissile material unchecked by the international community, it is likely that North Korea would have crossed the third threshold in its nuclear development by 2010, at which point an economically desperate North Korea might conceivably choose to export fissile material for the cash necessary to assure its survival. The implementation of the February 13, 2006, agreement diminishes but does not completely foreclose the possibility that the North could export fissile materials.

The Agreed Framework froze North Korea's nuclear weapons development capability and placed fuel rods discharged from the five-megawatt reactor under international safeguards. Those fuel rods were placed in canisters and stored so as to stabilize the material. The rods remained under the watch of IAEA inspectors, but they were not physically removed from North Korea. The ambiguities surrounding North Korea's production of fissile material that it might have undertaken before 1994 remained unresolved, pending progress in the construction of the light-water reactors there. The chart below, derived from estimates by David Albright and Paul Brannan of the Institute for Science and International Security, provides estimates of the nuclear material acquired by North Korea through 2007. The discrepancies between the North Korean declaration and analysis taken from IAEA inspections conducted in 1992 yield estimates of the material that the North Koreans may have gained from its pre-1994 efforts, which is about six to ten kilograms of plutonium, or enough to make one or two nuclear weapons.[9]

The Agreed Framework provisions allowed North Korea to keep a sufficient and unspecified amount of nuclear material for a certain period of time. This allowed North Korea to preserve ambiguity that served as a deterrent by leaving potential adversaries unsure as to whether or not it might actually have developed a nuclear weapon. However, the Agreed Framework also ensured that the upper limit of North Korea's potential plutonium reserves was probably not enough for it to maintain a nuclear deterrent and also carry out a test. Recent reports by a high-level defector from North Korea reinforce this claim, although such statements cannot necessarily be regarded as accurate.[10]

The second stock of materials available for possible use in North Korea's nuclear weapons arsenal is derived from the 8,000 fuel rods that they removed from its nuclear reactors in 1994. These rods are estimated to be able to produce twenty-seven to twenty-nine kilograms of plutonium, or enough to produce an additional four

Table 11.1 Estimates of North Korea's Possible Nuclear Stockpile[11]

Year	Amount of Plutonium discharged from 5mw reactor (ISIS est., early 2007)	Plutonium separation	Weapon equivalents Estimate 5 kg of plutonium
1989	1–10 kg	0–10 kg in 1989–1992	0–2
2002–2003	27–29 kg	20–28 kg in 2003–2004	4–7
2005	13.5–17 kg	13–17 kg in 2005–2006	2–4
2006	10–13 kg	–	–
Total	46–64 kg	28–50 kg	5–12

Source: http://www.carnegieendowment.org/npp/publications/index.cfm?fa=view&id=16912. Courtesy of Jon Wolfsthal. Institute of Science and International Security. Accessed on July 19, 2005.

to seven nuclear weapons beyond the one or two weapons that the North Koreans are already assessed to possess.[12] The rods had been under the watch of IAEA inspectors until the inspectors were kicked out by the North Koreans in December of 2002, and the DPRK claimed to have reprocessed these rods in 2003.

North Korea's reported decision to reprocess the spent fuel rods is significant because it provides the North Korean leadership with access to sufficient fissile material so that it could afford to conduct a nuclear test and still retain a credible nuclear deterrent capability. During the first North Korean nuclear crisis, the Clinton Administration drew its "red line" at the unloading of the five-megawatt reactor precisely because it was recognized that the plutonium contained in those fuel rods, after reprocessing, could be used to provide North Korea with sufficient material to conduct a nuclear test. This would, of course, remove any ambiguity about its status as a nuclear weapons state. However, even with access to the spent fuel that was safely stored with the assistance of the U.S. Department of Energy and monitored by the IAEA for over seven years, North Korea's access to plutonium would remain limited. In retrospect, it is clear that one big failure of the implementation of the Agreed Framework was that additional efforts were not made to remove the spent fuel rods from North Korean territory at an earlier stage in the process.

During the spring of 2005, the North Koreans announced that they had once again unloaded their five-megawatt reactor, removing the rods that had been loaded when they restarted the reactor in early 2003. The Institute for Science and International Security estimates these 8,000 irradiated rods, if they were reprocessed, could produce another thirteen to seventeen kilograms of plutonium. This plutonium could be used to produce another two to four nuclear weapons. The five-megawatt reactor can be continuously reloaded and operated to produce fuel for a nuclear weapons program at the rate of about six kilograms of plutonium per year, or enough material to add an average of a single nuclear weapon each year through the end of the decade.[13]

In addition to the plutonium produced by the five-megawatt experimental reactor at Yongbyon, there are two additional sources of fissile material that the North Koreans might be able to utilize to expand their access to fissile material for use in nuclear weapons. The first is the potential fissile material that North Korea might gain from its covert efforts to enrich uranium. There is no publicly available information that confirms precisely the status of the development of that program, but some estimate that North Korea's attempts to acquire centrifuges and other equipment that can be used to enrich uranium to weapons-grade quality through the A.Q. Khan network could potentially provide the North Koreans with sufficient uranium to provide them with an additional bomb per year once the program comes online.[14]

A second source of fissile material in North Korea could come from the construction of larger reactors that would produce exponentially more plutonium than the capacity of the five-megawatt experimental reactor at Yongbyon. Although there are serious questions at this stage about whether the original foundation of the partially built reactors could be used to support new construction or whether it would be necessary to rebuild the foundation, the prospect of any production of plutonium by larger reactors in North Korea is daunting. The U.S. Central Intelligence Agency (CIA) estimated in 2002 that upon completion those reactors could be used to produce up to 275 kilograms of plutonium annually, enough to build dozens of nuclear weapons each year.

With the completion of a fifty-megawatt or a 200-megawatt reactor, North Korean nuclear weapons production would rise exponentially once the reactor becomes operational. Even under the most conservative scenario, it is possible to imagine that if the North has available material to make fourteen to twenty nuclear weapons, there would be a sufficient stockpile both to test and to export nuclear materials in the event of regime-threatening economic hardship in North Korea. This might be a sufficient amount of plutonium that North Korea would need to secure in order to ensure its own deterrent and also be able to sell fissile material (although no state actor has ever chosen to export fissile material thus far) if it faced economic desperation, considering North Korea's missile export sales record.

One caveat to the assessment above is that despite considerable shared intelligence on the status of North Korea's nuclear weapons program, there are apparent differences between the intelligence assessments of South Korea and China on the one hand and those of the United States on the other. South Korean intelligence assessments appear to have judged that North Korea may have attained one or two nuclear weapons, but that capacity to deliver such weapons remains in a primitive state, even following the series of missile tests that were carried out by North Korea on July 5, 2006. This assessment leads South Korea's political leadership to draw the conclusion that there is still time for negotiation and room for the possibility that North Korea may be willing to bargain away its nuclear program—even following a nuclear test. In contrast, assessments in Washington increasingly are that the DPRK has already "crossed the Rubicon" and will never give away the nuclear capabilities that it has developed thus far. The differences in the South Korean and American respective intelligence assessments of the state of the North Korean nuclear program reveal an important underlying factor that has hampered effective policy coordination between the two countries in prioritizing the urgency and determining appropriate policy tools for addressing North Korea's ongoing nuclear weapons development efforts.[15]

REGIONAL RESPONSES TO THE SECOND NORTH KOREAN NUCLEAR CRISIS: HEDGING AGAINST A NUCLEAR NORTH KOREA

The first North Korean nuclear crisis served as a wake-up call for all of North Korea's neighbors in the region, but the second North Korean nuclear crisis and North Korea's nuclear test have served as a true test of whether or not parties in the region were willing to move from rhetorical opposition to North Korea's nuclear test to practical action in line with the consensus represented by the September 19, 2005, Joint Statement of the Fourth Round of Six-Party Talks.[16] The second crisis has propelled the region into a more dangerous phase, especially following North Korea's test of a nuclear device on October 9, 2006. Global terrorism has heightened concerns over nuclear weapons proliferation and extended a special focus to the possible intersection of these two concerns in the form of possible acquisition of nuclear materials by non-state actors. There have been changes in the preferred methods by which the United States pursues its nonproliferation objectives, but the fundamental concern with nuclear proliferation as the world's most dangerous security risk remains unchanged.[17]

As ambiguity has gradually been removed from North Korea's capabilities and as demonstrated North Korean capacities become more concrete, all the states in the region have been forced to take various sorts of actions in response. One response that some countries have taken, no doubt partially catalyzed by uncertainties deriving from the North Korean nuclear weapons development effort, has been to hedge by enhancing their own response capacities and by laying the groundwork for their own potential nuclear development efforts. The rapid international condemnation of North Korea's October 9, 2006, nuclear test and the rapid passage of UN Security Council Resolution 1718 condemning the test were clear illustrations of the extent to which North Korea's neighbors regard nuclear proliferation on the Korean Peninsula as undesirable. Even before North Korea's test there has been evidence of hedging among regional parties in response to the DPRK's continued nuclear development efforts.[18]

For instance, it was belatedly revealed that the first North Korean nuclear crisis prompted an internal review conducted by the Japan Defense Agency on whether to develop nuclear weapons, an idea that was rejected at the time as it was not in Japan's national interest to do so.[19] South Korean experiments with laser enrichment of uranium isotopes, although conducted sporadically on an experimental scale between 1982 and 2000, went unreported to the IAEA until that agency conducted inspections in 2004 that took advantage of more intrusive powers gained through South Korea's adherence to the Additional Protocol.[20] (The Additional Protocol is an additional inspections process that was created to enhance the IAEA's monitoring and verification capacity. It was developed partially in response to the "special inspections" fiasco with North Korea in 1992–1993.) It is well known that both Japan and South Korea have the technological capacity, the know-how, and the necessary materials to go nuclear in a matter of weeks or months. Thus, as states that have the technical capacities to develop nuclear weapons and extensive experience with production of nuclear energy for peaceful purposes, Japan and

South Korea have matched North Korea's nuclear development to a certain extent. As long as both states are allies of the United States and therefore under the U.S. "nuclear umbrella," there appears to be little likelihood under current circumstances that either Japan or South Korea would go nuclear.

A second influence of the North Korean nuclear challenge, in combination with ongoing North Korean long-range missile development efforts, has been to focus concerns on North Korea's WMD delivery capacity—the possibility that North Korea could deliver a weapon of mass destruction on the tip of a missile. The North Korean missile tests on July 5, 2006, catalyzed attention to North Korea's capacity to strike neighboring states. A stronger than expected response by the international community included the Japanese-led passage of UN Security Council Resolution 1695 condemning North Korea's missile tests and laying the groundwork for enhanced efforts to prevent North Korea from further nuclear or missile development efforts.[21] A domestic debate stimulated by the North Korean missile tests over whether Japan might need preemptive strike capabilities to defend itself from a prospective North Korean missile launch not only revealed a newfound sense of vulnerability derived from the reminder that North Korea had developed the capability to strike Japan militarily, but also provoked longstanding South Korean sensitivities stemming from the colonial legacy of Japanese aggression concerning the idea that Japan might again use military force on the Korean Peninsula. In light of the Roh Administration's low-key response to North Korea's missile tests, South Korea's sensitive response to Japan's reaction to North Korea's test seemed disproportionate and misplaced, but it is probably a good measure of the extraordinary sensitivity in South Korea to any Japanese efforts to build an offensive strike capability. The rapidity of the international response to the North Korean missile tests and China's decision to join in support of a strong resolution condemning the tests suggested the emergence of a consensus that the North Korea's missile tests, in tandem with its nuclear development efforts, were deemed a clear threat to regional stability.

Third, as part of the evolution of global norms and heightened concerns regarding the threat of nuclear nonproliferation, the UN Security Council has imposed new requirements on member states to report on nuclear proliferation related activities through requirements under UN Security Resolution 1540, while the Proliferation Security Initiative attempts to build a coalition of the willing to take a more activist bottom-up norm-building role through promotion of enforcement of counterproliferation activities such as export controls and possible interdiction of suspected WMD shipments. These measures have global reach, and in some instances have already had an impact on the DPRK's ability to procure certain items that could be used as part of its WMD development efforts. However, there is no existing effort that can fully prevent the DPRK from relying on homegrown technology to manufacture materials that could be used to expand North Korea's nuclear arsenal.

A fourth impact of the North Korean nuclear crisis was to catalyze the establishment of an on-again, off-again regional dialogue process among the six parties. Although the Six-Party process has received much criticism and has appeared to "die" on more than one occasion, the North Korean nuclear crisis catalyzed the formation of a regional security dialogue and the development of a regional consensus on core objectives embodied in the September 19, 2005, Joint Statement of Principles. This has committed all the regional parties to the objectives of the denuclearization of the Korean Peninsula; normalization of relations among all the regional parties, including the United States and Japan, with North Korea; economic development of North Korea; and the establishment of permanent peace on the Korean Peninsula. Although these broad principles may seem vague and rhetorical, they represent a consensus set of objectives among all the parties and are to be achieved through the principle of "action for action," implying simultaneous movement to meet the security concerns of the respective parties through a step-by-step process. These core principles represent a multiparty consensus around which all the parties can work to pursue practical, shared objectives.

NORTH KOREAN NUCLEAR TEST: CATALYST FOR MOVING FROM RHETORICAL CONSENSUS TO COLLECTIVE ACTION?

Many analysts expected that a North Korean nuclear test would constitute a paradigm shift in terms of regional responses to the North Korean nuclear challenge. Even prior to a North Korean nuclear test, Pyongyang's neighbors attempted to signal their desire to North Korea not to take this step. Intelligence concerns about a possible North Korean nuclear test first surfaced publicly in a *New York Times* story on May 6, 2005, which indicated the seriousness with which the intelligence community was watching North Korea in anticipation of an imminent test of its nuclear weapons capability.[22] That story highlighted the possibility of a test, along with American intelligence briefings to South Korea, Japan, and China.

The *New York Times* story stimulated unusually harsh and overlapping public responses of both South Korean and Chinese officials, representatives of the parties that are generally perceived as most willing to deny the seriousness of the North Korean nuclear program. A South Korean senior official was quoted as saying that in the event of a nuclear test, China would not tolerate a nuclear North Korea and would allow the issue to go before the UN Security Council, while the Chinese press noted South Korean Foreign Minister Ban Ki-moon's harsh comment that "If the DPRK makes hasty actions, such as conducting a nuclear test, it will isolate itself even further and bring itself onto a path with unpredictable future."[23] The Bush Administration requested that the PRC warn North Korea not to conduct a nuclear test, and senior Chinese communist party official Wang Jiarui is reported to have told Japanese lawmakers that the likelihood of a North Korean nuclear test is fifty-fifty, suggesting that the Chinese senior leadership took the American reports seriously and have conveyed their own concerns and "red lines" to North Korea, together with American views.[24]

The North Korean missile and nuclear tests in July and October of 2006 represented a direct challenge by North Korea to the rhetorical consensus embodied in the Joint Statement that had been negotiated in September of 2005. The tests catalyzed joint action among all the parties, utilizing coercion both multilaterally (UN Security Council Resolutions 1695 and 1718) and bilaterally (China and ROK withholding benefits promised to DPRK) in response to the DPRK challenge. The DPRK's nuclear test had been tactically successful in that it drew all parties back to the negotiating table, but a strategic failure to the extent that the other parties saw the DPRK test as having flouted shared interests in peace and prosperity that had been articulated in the Joint Statement. Only in the aftermath of the tests did the Joint Statement take on added significance as the basis for pursuing North Korea's denuclearization through the mobilization of a variety of forms of collective action in both bilateral and multilateral forms in the service of the common objective of maintaining regional stability—presumably through the eventual denuclearization of the Korean Peninsula.

The North Korean nuclear test proved to be a clarifying event and an immediate catalyst for tactical adjustments to policy in Washington, Beijing, and to a lesser degree, in Seoul. First, North Korea's nuclear test proved that two decades of U.S. efforts to deny North Korea a nuclear weapons program had failed. The clarity of the failure required adjustments in U.S. policy, if for no other reason than that a policy geared toward preventing North Korea from testing nuclear weapons was no longer applicable in a context in which a weapons test had already occurred. President Bush clearly warned of the dangers of proliferation and the certainty of retaliation if such proliferation were to put U.S. national security interests at risk. But the test also posed a tremendous challenge for the Bush Administration, since no state that has tested has ever voluntarily given up its nuclear weapons. Given the enormity and unprecedented nature of the challenge, the task of challenging the six parties to undergird their rhetoric with collective action remained as the only viable action available to the Administration in the immediate aftermath of North Korea's nuclear test. A more passive action risked acquiescence to North Korea's challenge and pursuit of the "Pakistan model" of gaining de facto acceptance as a nuclear weapons state, while a more active approach risked escalation that the Administration could ill-afford to pursue unilaterally in view of other commitments in the region. Enhanced promotion of cooperation/collective actions with other parties in the region was the only option available to the Bush Administration.

A second shift caused by North Korea's nuclear test concerns Chinese policy interests. China's willingness to utilize UN instruments to condemn North Korea in the aftermath of the North's missile and nuclear tests was unprecedented, but these actions did not signal that China was willing to promote or instigate political instability in North Korea. Nonetheless, the North had taken actions that directly impinged on Chinese security interests, primarily in the form of catalyzing further insecurity in Japan (and therefore a more rapid augmentation of Japanese military capabilities in response to the escalation of the threat from North Korea). China needed to find ways to restore its influence with North Korea while avoiding promotion of instability in the North. Rather than using economic sanctions or cutting off North Korea's energy or food lifelines, the Chinese took their own bilateral financial measures to freeze financial transactions with North Korea and withheld bilateral economic cooperation with the North. At the same time, the Chinese sought to restore top-level dialogue with Kim Jong Il, which had been cut following the missile test. Special envoy Tang Jiaxuan visited Washington, Moscow, and Pyongyang immediately following North Korea's nuclear test, and China was able to bring North Korea and the United States back to the negotiating table within three weeks of the test. The U.S. interest in cooperation with China required a willingness to show that Washington was doing all it could to work with the North in return for China's unprecedented willingness to join multilateral and bilateral measures designed to bring North Korea back into line.

North Korea's nuclear test appears to have had a lesser impact on South Korean policy than either that of the United States or China in the immediate aftermath of the test, but South Korea has taken clear actions to subordinate inter-Korean cooperation to the objectives of the Six-Party Talks, including withholding of rice (but not fertilizer) assistance to North Korea unless the North adheres to its commitments as a party to the Six-Party Talks. For instance, the resumption of inter-Korean ministerial talks occurred immediately after the conclusion of the February 13 implementing agreement, and South Korea has continued to raise North Korea's need to fulfill its obligations in order to improve the atmosphere for inter-Korean progress. A major test will be whether or not South Korea will continue to place the commonly held objectives of the Six-Party Talks as its highest priority, even over the desire to enhance inter-Korean relations.

The test also drove a division among U.S. policymakers, between the objectives of nonproliferation (state-based restraints on spread of technology) and counterproliferation (more aggressive international efforts to prevent transfer of materials such as interdiction, etc.) factions within the U.S. government. Such divisions came into relief most clearly in the context of questions about the implications of aggressive efforts to promote regime change in North Korea that might actually facilitate proliferation by causing the loss of assured command and control of weapons in the hands of a state actor.

These simultaneous adjustments in approach to North Korea were catalyzed by the North Korean nuclear test and created the atmosphere for the resumption of the Six-Party Talks in December of 2006 in addition to several rounds of U.S.-DPRK bilateral talks in Beijing and Berlin (in January of 2007).[25] Following a bilateral understanding reached in Berlin, the six parties reconvened in Beijing in February of 2007 and were finally able to arrive at an understanding of practical steps to be taken under the "action-for-action" principle embodied in the Joint Statement. The February 13 agreement committed North Korea to shut down its nuclear facilities at Yongbyon and place them under IAEA inspection within sixty days in return for 50,000 tons of heavy fuel oil or equivalent and to disable those facilities upon delivery of an additional 950,000 tons of heavy fuel oil or equivalent. Under a prior understanding between the United States and the DPRK in Berlin, the United States had also pledged to "resolve" the issue of North Korea's funds that had been frozen in the Banco Delta Asia (BDA), a sticking point that delayed actual implementation for several months. The February 13 agreement also called for the DPRK to make a declaration of its remaining nuclear facilities and established five working groups on denuclearization, energy resources, normalization between the DPRK and the United States and the DPRK and Japan, respectively, and a working group on regional security in Northeast Asia. Upon completion of those steps, the six foreign ministers would meet to discuss next steps in implementation of the joint statement.

The February 13 agreement came about in the context of North Korea's isolation and a lack of North Korean alternatives as a result of regional compellence toward North Korea as well as the offering of benefits through the agreement. For the first time, in the wake of North Korea's nuclear test, all the parties were willing to recognize their common strategic interest in maintaining a nonnuclear Korean Peninsula and to subordinate lesser (bilateral) interests to a common shared objective. The extent to which the shared objective of denuclearization of the Korean Peninsula can be achieved in the long run will depend on whether or not all parties hold firm to policies that place the collective interest in denuclearization, normalization, economic development, and peace above perceived bilateral strategic interests vis-à-vis other parties in the region.

However, it remains to be seen whether that unity of purpose among the five parties can be sustained in action in light of their differing strategic priorities. For such unity of purpose to be sustained, it will require that China and South Korea continue to subordinate their bilateral ties with North Korea to the common objective of North Korea's denuclearization, while it will require that the United States and Japan subordinate their respective antipathies to North Korea to the common will to improve bilateral relations with Pyongyang, including through offering of political and economic incentives that are referenced in the Joint Statement. The effectiveness of a "collective security" mechanism in Northeast Asia, as embodied through actions taken through the Six-Party Talks, will depend on whether or not all the parties are willing to hold to a shared strategic purpose and a willingness to subordinate their own strategic objectives to practical steps necessary to achieve the commonly identified objectives of the Joint Statement of principles. All the parties in the region prefer to address

North Korea's nuclear program through negotiations on the basis of the prior rhetorical agreements produced by a consensus among the six parties. However, the degree of adherence of all the parties to the collective actions necessary to achieve compellence of North Korea is likely to be the critical factor that determines the success or failure of the Six-Party Talks as a vehicle for addressing North Korea's nuclear gambit.

Conclusion

As the North Korean nuclear crisis has worn on, and especially with the development of a second crisis following October of 2002, a certain level of fatigue has set in among all the actors in the region regarding the North Korean nuclear program and its implications for regional security. Just as the North Korean humanitarian crisis unfolded over many months, revealing a systemic failure among North Koreans to be able to feed their own people, so also the North Korean nuclear challenge, well into its second decade, now appears to have been a creeping crisis, with all the regional partners gradually coming to accept discrete steps by North Korea that, in the end, add up to a North Korea that is nuclear capable and indeed has declared itself a nuclear weapons state. Following North Korea's test of a nuclear device, the passage of UN sanctions, and the negotiation of a regional agreement among the six parties, now it is up to all the parties to take practical actions outlined in the February 13 agreement that require some degree of perceived sacrifice of self-interests for the sake of the common good. If this effort fails, perhaps a bigger crisis will stimulate cooperation in the service of a common purpose.

If the North Koreans are able to pursue their slow-motion approach and gradually expand their nuclear stockpile while gaining acquiescence from their neighbors, the DPRK may indeed be able to expand the threat that it poses to the region instead of uniting the region in opposition to North Korea as a primary source of threat. To the extent that the United States is seen as either prematurely sounding the alarm or overreaching the willingness of the players in the region to confront the threat, the United States may become an obstacle to a regional recognition that concerted action must be taken to address this problem.

However, North Korea's nuclear pursuits may raise the ante by promoting an odd mixture of hedging and denial strategies in the region as it relates to nuclear proliferation. This mixture of strategies derives from uncertainties both about the future of the global nonproliferation regime and about the future of U.S. leadership in Asia. In essence, there remains a great deal of confusion and doubt in Asia about whether the core problem to be resolved is North Korea as a challenge to the global proliferation regime, North Korea as an obstacle to the spread of democracy and human freedom, North Korea as a pretext for maintaining regional U.S.-led hegemony, or the unresolved historical legacy of cold war confrontation that remains to be addressed by achieving a final end to the Korean War and to enmity between the United States and North Korea.

Notwithstanding the hedging, denial, and avoidance of shared responsibility that are the primary dangers that accompany the risks inherent in a nuclear North Korea, the most hopeful possibility is that the challenge of a nuclear North Korea may finally prove to be big enough that it acts as a catalyst for achieving regional cooperation in the service of denuclearization, normalization, economic development, and peace in Northeast Asia. The establishment of a six-party mechanism—and the convergence of a sense of shared responsibility among all the parties in the region in response to growing tensions—enhances U.S.-China cooperation (while it preserves U.S.-Japan and U.S.-ROK alliance coordination) and unites all parties in practical pursuit of a nuclear-free Korean Peninsula. Following North Korea's October 9, 2006, nuclear test, the primary question is whether all the parties are willing to take the necessary actions to back up the rhetorical consensus embodied by the September 19, 2005, Joint Statement. To the extent that any party puts its own interest above that collective consensus, such actions are likely to leave an open pathway for North Korea to utilize its nuclear program to reinforce its core objective of regime survival while sowing the seeds of renewed instability in Northeast Asia.

Notes

1. This is a draft prepared for the U.S.-China Strategic Dialogue Conference organized by the Center for Contemporary Conflict, U.S. Naval Postgraduate School and the Pacific Forum of the Center for Strategic and International studies for the Advanced Systems and Concepts office of the U.S. Defense Threat Reduction Agency. The views expressed here are those of the author and not the institutions with which he is affiliated. Comments or questions may be directed to Scott Snyder at SnyderSA@aol.com OR ssnyder@asiafound-dc.org., or by phone to 202-588-9420.
2. The text of the Joint Statement of the Fourth Round of the Six-Party Talks may be found at http://www.state.gov/r/pa/prs/ps/2005/53490.htm.

Accessed on May 22, 2007. The text of the February 13, 2007 agreement on initial actions to implement the joint statement, adopted at the Third Session of the Fifth Round of the Six-Party talks on February 13, 2007, was published as Nautilus Special Report 07–013A, and may be found at http://www.nautilus.org/fora/security/07013Statement.html. Accessed on May 22, 2007.

3. "The Hermit Kingdom Strikes Back," *The Economist*, July 17, 1993, 19. For an excellent background to the run-up of the first North Korean nuclear crisis, see Michael J. Mazarr, *North Korea and the Bomb: A Case Study in Nonproliferation* (New York: Palgrave Macmillan, 2003).

4. See Doyle McManus, "Column One: The New Dangerous Dominoes; Nuclear Wanna-Bees And Wary Bystanders are Caught in a Nuclear Balancing Act Over Who Has—And Who Soon May Get—Nuclear Weapons. The Rising Number of Players Raises the Risk of Disaster," *Los Angeles Times*, May 8, 1994, 1.

5. Section IV.3 of the Agreed Framework states that "When a significant portion of the LWR project is completed, but before delivery of key nuclear components, the DPRK will come into full compliance with its safeguards agreement with the IAEA (INFCIRC/403), including taking all steps that may be deemed necessary by the IAEA, following consultations with the Agency with regard to verifying the accuracy and completeness of the DPRK's initial report on all nuclear material in the DPRK." See http://www2.law.columbia.edu/course_00S_L9436_001/North%20Korea%20materials/agreedframework.htm. Accessed on July 26, 2005.

6. Barbara Demick, "North Korea Shows Its Bluster is No Bluff," *Los Angeles Times*, December 29, 2002, 1.

7. "CIA Estimate of North Korean Nuclear Capability," Prepared for Congress, 2002. See http://www.nautilus.org/DPRKBriefingBook/nuclearweapons/CIAEnrichmentNov-02.pdf. Accessed on July 25, 2005.

8. Brad Glosserman, "Living with a Nuclear North Korea," PacNet #29A, July 25, 2005.

9. The table is reproduced from David Albright and Paul Brannan, "The North Korean Plutonium Stock Mid-2006," dated June 26, 2006. Accessed on September 19, 2006, at Institute of Science and International Security Web site, http://www.isis-online.org/publications/dprk/dprkplutonium.pdf. For comparative reference, see also "CIA Estimate of North Korean Nuclear Capability." An updated version of this assessment was conducted in early 2007. See David Albright and Paul Brannan, "The North Korean Plutonium Stock, February 2007," http://www.isis-online.org/publications/dprk/DPRKplutoniumFEB.pdf. Accessed on May 22, 2007.

10. Anna Fifield, "Defector Says North Korea 'Has One-tonne Nuclear Bomb,'" *Financial Times*, July 20, 2005, 10. The defector is reported to have claimed that the North Koreans used four kilograms of plutonium to manufacture that bomb, and are now working on miniaturization techniques.

11. See Jon Wolfsthal, "Estimates of North Korea's Possible Nuclear Stockpile," available at http://www.carnegieendowment.org/npp/publications/index.cfm?fa=view&id=16912. Courtesy of Jon Wolfsthal. Accessed on July 19, 2005.
12. Jon Wolfsthal, "Estimates of North Korea's Possible Nuclear Stockpile."
13. CIA Estimate of North Korean Nuclear Capability.
14. Hearing of the Senate Armed Services Committee, "Current and future Worldwide Threats to the National Security of the United States," February 27, 2007.
15. These insights are drawn from comments made during a meeting with a senior South Korean government official, San Francisco, September 15, 2006.
16. Joint Statement of the Fourth Round of the Six-Party Talks.
17. Doyle McManus, "Column One: The New Dangerous Dominoes," and Sonni Efron, "Nuclear Arming Could Snowball; North Korea's Moves to Restart Its Own Program May Prompt Neighbors to Build Their Own Arsenals, Security Analysts Say," *Los Angeles Times*, January 6, 2003, 1.
18. United Nations Security Council S/RES/1718 (1718), October 14, 2006, http://daccessdds.un.org/doc/UNDOC/GEN/N06/572/07/PDF/N0657207.pdf? OpenElement. Accessed on May 22, 2007.
19. "'95 Study: Japan and Nukes Don't Mix," Asahi News Service, February 20, 2003.
20. Report by the Director General, "Implementation of the NPT Safeguards Agreement in the Republic of Korea," November 26, 2004. http://www.iaea.org/Publications/Documents/Board/2004/gov2004-84.pdf. Accessed on July 26, 2005.
21. United Nations Security Council S/RES/1695 (2006), July 15, 2006, http://daccessdds.un.org/doc/UNDOC/GEN/N06/431/64/PDF/N0643164.pdf? OpenElement. Accessed on May 22, 2007.
22. William J. Broad, Douglas Jehl, David E. Sanger and Thom Shanker, "North Korea Nuclear Goals: Case of Mixed Signals," *New York Times*, July 25, 2005, 1; David E. Sanger and William J. Broad, "U.S. Cites Signs of Korean Steps to Nuclear Test," *New York Times*, May 6, 2005, 1.
23. Jin Linbo, "The Stalemate of the Six-Nation Talks Has Yet To Be Broken," *Beijing Liaowang* [translation by FBIS from Chinese] May 2, 2005; No 18, 52–53, (FBIS Doc No. CPP20050517000060) and Yonhap News Agency, "China Will Not Tolerate N.K. Possessing Nuclear Weapons: Official," May 24, 2005.
24. Kyodo News Agency, "PRC Official Wang Jiarui Says Chances of DPRK Nuclear Test 'Fifty-Fifty,'" June 1, 2005.
25. Kyodo News Agency, "PRC Official Wang Jiarui Says Chances of DPRK Nuclear Test 'Fifty-Fifty.'"

12

CHINESE ARMS CONTROL AND NONPROLIFERATION POLICY

Gu Guoliang[1]

Chinese arms control and nonproliferation policy has been evolving since the end of the cold war. With a constantly developing situation both internationally and at home, greater importance has been placed on the role of arms control and nonproliferation in China's security strategy and foreign policy. China has in the past adjusted its arms control and nonproliferation policy to better serve its foreign and defense policy objectives, and to adapt itself in the changed international environment.

EVOLVING CHINESE ARMS CONTROL AND NONPROLIFERATION POLICY OVER THE LAST DECADE

During the cold war, China was not a major player in world affairs, and the issue of arms control and nonproliferation was not a major component of China's foreign and defense policies. For most of the cold war, China pursued an independent foreign policy, opposing the hegemony of both the superpowers—the Soviet Union and the United States. China was a bystander watching and criticizing the arms race and the arms control negotiations between the United States and the Soviet Union, and China held a suspicious view about the international arms control and nonproliferation regimes. Thus, during the cold war period, China remained outside of the key international arms control and nonproliferation treaties.

THE NEW INTERNATIONAL ENVIRONMENT CHINA FACES

After the end of the cold war, the world structure is no longer dominated by the confrontation of the East and West camps. The cold war has been replaced by regional conflicts. The world is faced with multiple uncertain threats. Especially after the terrorist attacks of 9/11, terrorism and the proliferation of weapons of mass destruction (WMD) have become a major concern of the international community. In its National Security Strategy published on September 20, 2002, the Bush Administration reckoned that, "With the collapse of the Soviet Union and the end of the Cold War, our security environment has undergone profound transformation.... The United States is threatened by terrorists and tyrants who may acquire weapons of mass destruction." Antiterrorism and nonproliferation have therefore become the "most urgent tasks" for the national security of the United States.[2]

After the end of the cold war and with the disintegration of the Soviet Union, the United States began to consider China its number one potential adversary. The Clinton Administration pursued a policy of engagement, trying hard to bring China into international networks including the arms control and nonproliferation regimes. Since then, arms control and nonproliferation have become the major issues between the United States and China (along with human rights and trade friction, aside from the situation in Taiwan). There were a number of discussions between the Clinton Administration and the Chinese government over the various problems of arms control and nonproliferation.

When the Bush Administration came to office, it pursued both a policy of engagement and containment toward China. The terrorist attacks of 9/11 have made antiterrorism and nonproliferation of WMD the most urgent task for U.S. national security strategy. Antiterrorism and nonproliferation of weapons of mass destruction have also become a common cause for the international community.

Facing the new international security environment, China has reviewed and adjusted its policy on arms control and nonproliferation. It now attaches greater importance to its arms control and nonproliferation policy to adapt to the changed international environment and renewed Sino-U.S relations.

The Domestic Factors that Shape China's Arms Control and Nonproliferation Policy

Since China started its economic reform and open-door policy in late 1970s, it has come to understand the importance of integrating itself into the international system and has realized the political and economic benefits of joining these networks. China has learned its lessons from the U.S.-Soviet arms race during the cold war period—that participating in such proliferation or an arms race is not in the country's best interest, and that it would not bring security or economic prosperity. Since China has stated it has no ambitions to be a superpower, its economic growth and expansion need not be paralleled in military power. Therefore, China needs to have arms control as well as balanced development of its economic and military prowess. China's modernization of national defense is based on this perspective.

In the past, China has also come to understand that proliferation of weapons of mass destruction and their means of delivery is detrimental to world peace and security, and therefore is also detrimental to China's own security. Nonproliferation is in the common interest of all countries, including China. In fact, terrorism is also posing an enormous threat to the security and order of China. China is very much concerned that terrorists could cause devastating consequences to the life of the Chinese people if weapons of mass destruction were used. Over a long period of time, especially since the 1990s, the "East Turkistan" forces inside and outside Chinese territory have planned and organized a series of violent incidents in the Xinjiang Uygur Autonomous Region of China, which included explosions, assassinations, arsons, poisonings, and assaults, with the objective of founding a so-called state of "East Turkistan." These terrorist incidents have seriously jeopardized the lives and property of people of all ethnic groups as well as the social stability in China, and have even threatened the security and stability of other affected countries and regions as well.[3] On September 11, 2002, the Security Council of the United Nations adopted the resolution to impose sanctions on the "East Turkistan" forces, and the United States formally put the name of "East Turkistan" forces into its list of names of terrorist groups. China and the United States have established long-term antiterrorist mechanisms of cooperation and have made major achievements in this field. These efforts have contributed to the maintenance of China's social stability and the improvement of relations between China and the United States.

In the past decade, owing to sustained rapid economic growth, China's political influence and its role in the world have considerably grown. The international community pays closer attention to China's behavior and expects China to play a greater role in world affairs, including activities related to arms control and nonproliferation. China has become more conscious of its role of a responsible major world power.

North Korea's Nuclear Program

It is based on the concepts discussed above, as well as its national interest, that China has pursued its policy toward the Democratic People's Republic of Korea's (DPRK) nuclear program on the following three principles: first, China stands for a nonnuclear Korean Peninsula; second, China stands for the maintenance of peace and stability of the Korean Peninsula; and third, China stands for a peaceful solution to the crisis caused by the DPRK's nuclear program through dialogue. China is concerned about DPRK's nuclear and missile programs because they do not wish to see another nuclear state emerging in its neighborhood. China needs a stable environment to concentrate on its own economic development. Nuclear and missile proliferation in East Asia does not serve the state's security interests. China is also concerned that DPRK's nuclear program may provide an excuse for other countries in the region to develop their own nuclear programs. Therefore, China has played an important part in bringing about the Six-Party Talks and has made great efforts in persuading North Korea to give up its nuclear program. They have worked together with the other members of the Six-Party Talks, as well as the international community, to counter both nuclear and missile proliferation in Northeast Asia and have supported the general goal of the Proliferation Security Initiative.

The Learning Process China has Gone Through

China's arms control and nonproliferation policy has undergone a learning process in recent years. Not having been familiar with all the rules associated with international arms control and nonproliferation regimes, China was cautious at first. But China has been quick to learn. Their accession to almost all the major international arms control and nonproliferation treaties, bilateral arrangements with the United States, and the introduction of domestic regulations governing the export of nuclear, biological, chemical, and dual-use materials and technologies in a relatively short period of time demonstrates the political will of China to integrate itself into the international arms control and nonproliferation regime and to shoulder the responsibilities of a major power. Two major examples follow.

The changing of China's attitude toward the Missile Technology Control Regime (MTCR) is an example in point. Since the early 1990s, the United States has conducted a series of talks on missile issues with China with a view toward persuading them to join the MTCR. China was critical of the discriminatory nature of MTCR since it was an arrangement of only a few countries, so they were reluctant to join in. After the United States gave China detailed explanations of the goals and the rules of the MTCR, China agreed in February 1992 that it would act within the guidelines of the MTCR for its export of missiles and related technologies. In 1994, China committed itself not to export ground-to-ground missiles featuring the primary parameters of the MTCR—that is, missiles capable of reaching a range of at least 300 km with a payload of at least 500 kg. In 2000, China further declared that it had no intention to assist any country in any way in the development of ballistic missiles that can be used to deliver nuclear weapons. In August 2002, The Chinese government promulgated the regulations of the PRC on the Export Control of Missiles and Missile-Related Items and Technologies and the control list.[4] When China had a better understanding of MTCR, it decided to apply for membership in early 2004. However, the United States changed its mind and refused to accept China's entry, as some U.S. officials believed that "there is still a problem concerning China's implementation of its regulation on missile export control."[5] The position of the United States contrasts that of the European Union (EU). On December 9, 2004, China and the European Union issued a joint declaration on nonproliferation and arms control, which explicitly stated, "The EU supports China's entry into MTCR."[6] The United States' changed position has puzzled China as to what America's true intentions are. The other example is China's changing attitude toward verification. When China joined negotiations on the Chemical Weapons Convention (CWC), it was very concerned that some countries might abuse the verification process to interfere with China's internal affairs. Yet, today, China has accepted hundreds of intrusive inspections and has been praised by the Chemical Weapons Convention Office (CWCO) for its full compliance with the treaty obligations.

China has been criticized by the United States for not fully implementing its export control regulations. The Chinese government, however, is determined to fully implement all such regulations and has made great efforts to educate and train its industry about international nonproliferation treaties and domestic export control regulations. The Chinese Foreign Ministry, Ministry of Commerce, and Customs have worked in close cooperation and taken serious measures toward stopping and punishing illegal exports. Chinese efforts have been successful and appreciated by the international community. Of course, there is room for improvement. The problem partly comes from China's decentralization and economic liberalization, which have brought some new problems to the enforcement of China's arms control and nonproliferation policies. There are thousands of small and medium sized enterprises that have spread throughout various parts of China. Some of them do not know or understand the regulations, and others try to seek profits by ignoring them. The Chinese government gets informed only after the U.S. sanctions are imposed on some Chinese entities, without being told the details of the violation.

China has Taken an Active Part in International Arms Control and Nonproliferation Efforts

Since the early 1990s, China has taken an increasingly active part in international arms control and nonproliferation efforts. China has signed most international treaties related to arms control and nonproliferation and joined most of the relevant international organizations. China has acceded to the Nonproliferation Treaty (NPT), signed and ratified the Chemical Weapons Convention (CWC), signed the Comprehensive Test Ban Treaty (CTBT), and joined the Zangger Committee and the Nuclear Supply Group (NSG). China is also considering joining the Australia Group, the Wassenaar Arrangement, and the Missile Technology Control Regime.

In recent years, China has implemented and enforced a number of laws and regulations, which form a complete system for the export control of nuclear, biological, chemical, missile, and other sensitive items and technologies, as well as all military products.[7] It has adopted international export control measures, including export registration system, end-user and end-use certification system, licensing system, list control method, and "catch-all" principle, and has stipulated corresponding penalties for breaches of these laws and regulations.

China's nonproliferation export control measures are in conformity with international practice.

China maintains that the international arms control and nonproliferation regimes should be safeguarded and strengthened, and that efforts should be made to promote these regimes' universality and authority. China believes the issue of WMD proliferation should be solved through political and diplomatic means on the basis of existing international laws. It also advocates that the social and economic root causes of WMD proliferation should be addressed.

The Role of Arms Control Policy in China's Security Strategy

Like most countries, China's arms control and nonproliferation policy serves its foreign and defense policies. China's arms control and nonproliferation policy also plays an important part in its national security strategy.

China's Arms Control and Nonproliferation Policy Serves its Foreign Policy Goals

China's arms control and nonproliferation policy projects the image of a responsible major power. China's proactive support of the international arms control and nonproliferation regime under the framework of the United Nations is in accordance with its foreign policy of supporting a multilateral, rather than unilateral, international structure. It also serves the general objective of maintaining a sound and stable relationship with the United States.

China's arms control and nonproliferation policy also reflects its broader security concept. China has recently been advocating a new cooperative security concept. In 1996, China put forward the initiative that countries in the Asia-Pacific region jointly cultivate a new concept of security, which focuses on enhancing trust through dialogue and promoting security through cooperation. In China's view, the core of this security concept should include mutual trust, mutual benefit, equality, and coordination. Mutual trust means that all countries should transcend differences in ideology and social systems, discard the mentality of cold war and power politics, and refrain from mutual suspicion and hostility. They should maintain frequent dialogue and mutual briefings on each other's security and defense policies and major operations. Mutual benefit means that all countries should meet the objective needs of social development in the era of globalization, respect each other's security interests, and create conditions for others' security while ensuring their own security interests, with a view to achieving common security. Equality means that all countries, big or small, are members of the same international community and should respect each other, treat each other as equals, refrain from interfering in other countries' internal affairs, and promote the democratization of international relations. Coordination means that all countries should seek peaceful settlement of their disputes through negotiations and carry out wide ranging and thorough cooperation on security issues of mutual concern to remove any potential dangers and prevent the outbreak of wars and conflicts.

Based on this new security concept, China has improved its relations with many nations, including its neighbors. China has also pursued a proactive arms control and nonproliferation policy and has uplifted its international status by improving relations with the United States through expanded cooperation in arms control and nonproliferation.

China's Arms Control and Nonproliferation Policy Serves its Defense Policy Goals

China pursues a passive national defense policy. China's arms control and nonproliferation stance is one of the major parts of its defense policy and security strategy.

In its fourth defense white paper, "China's National Defense in 2004," the national defense policy is made very clear. "The development goal for China to strive for in the first two decades of this century is to build a moderately prosperous society in an all-round way... China adheres to an independent foreign policy of peace and a national defense policy of the defensive nature."[8]

The main tasks for China's national defense are as follows: to step up the modernization of its armed forces, to safeguard national security and unity, and to ensure the smooth process of building a prosperous society. China's basic goals and tasks in maintaining national security are the following: to stop separation and promote reunification; to guard against and resist aggression; and to defend national sovereignty, territorial integrity, and maritime rights and interests. With rapid economic development at home, changing external environment, and the trend of military development in the world, it is essential for China to modernize its national defense and to improve its operational self-defense capabilities under the conditions of informationalization.

China's arms control policy, which consists of its nuclear policy and its policy on conventional forces, are the crucial components of China's security strategy. China's nuclear policy consists of two major components: maintaining a credible nuclear deterrent force, and the "no first use" doctrine. The Chinese government has repeatedly stated that the very small nuclear arsenal China possesses is for defensive purposes only, that China will not use nuclear weapons first under any circumstance, and that China will not use (or threaten to use) nuclear weapons against nonnuclear states. China has pledged not to enter a nuclear arms race with other nuclear states. Nevertheless, it wants to maintain an "effective nuclear counterattacking force in order to deter possible nuclear attacks by other countries."[9] China's signing of the CTBT and its positive attitude regarding the negotiation of a Fissile Materials Cutoff Treaty (FMCT) have shown its willingness to limit its nuclear weapons modernization programs. In the meantime, China has made it clear that it will strive to maintain the credibility of its deterrent nuclear force and will not allow its deterrent capability to be negated by the U.S. ballistic missile defense (BMD) program. In other words, the pace of China's nuclear development will be affected by the pace of development of the U.S. BMD program.

As for conventional forces, China has carried out major reductions of its armed forces in the past years. Since the mid-1980s, China has twice downsized its military by a total of 1.5 million, reducing 1 million troops during 1985–1987 and another half million during 1997–1999. In September 2003, the Chinese government decided to further reduce 200,000 troops by the end of 2005 to maintain the size of its armed forces at 2.3 million. While China has stressed the strengthening of its navy and air force with the intent of defending its territorial integrity and its natural resources, it has no intention of projecting military power beyond the region.

In recent years, China's defense expenditures have raised the concern of other countries. Yet, in the past two years, the percentages of China's annual defense expenditure in relation to its GDP and to the state financial expenditure in the same period have remained basically stable. China's defense expenditure was 170.778 billion yuan in 2002 (1.62 percent of gross domestic product, or GDP) and 190.787 billion yuan in 2003 (1.63 percent of GDP). Its defense budget for 2004 was 211.701 billion yuan. For most of the years since the 1990s, the growth rate of China's defense expenditure has been lower than that of the state financial expenditure. The absolute amount of China's defense expenditure has long been lower than those of some major Western countries. In 2003, China's defense expenditure amounted to only 5.69 percent of that of the United States, 56.78 percent of that of Japan, 37.07 percent of that of the United Kingdom, and 75.94 percent of that of France.

The Future Development of China's Arms Control and Nonproliferation Policy

The Chinese government has already decided on its long-term strategy of national development for the next few decades. China will continue to concentrate on its economic development while simultaneously building up a defensive force. China's arms control and nonproliferation policy is established and predictable.

China will Continue to Pursue a Proactive Arms Control Policy

China will not enter into an arms race and will continue to stand for complete prohibition and destruction of nuclear weapons. It will continue to pursue a policy of "no first use" of nuclear weapons and ban the use (or the threat of use) of nuclear weapons against nonnuclear-weapon states. It will continue to support efforts to build up regional nuclear-weapon-free zones. China will continue to support the adoption of the FMCT, as well as an international legal instrument on preventing the weaponization of outer space through negotiations. China will also continue to reduce the size of its armed forces.

China will Continue to Pursue a Proactive Nonproliferation Policy

China will continue to pursue a policy of not supporting, not encouraging, and not assisting other countries to develop WMD. While China supports the principle of peaceful use of nuclear energy, it will work together with the International Atomic Energy Agency (IAEA) to ensure this is done under full safeguards and oversight. China will continue to play its critical role and work together with the international community to solve the DPRK's nuclear issue under the framework of the Six-Party Talks. China will redouble its efforts to enforce its regulations of export control.

China will Continue to Support Multilateral, Bilateral, and Unilateral Arms Control and Nonproliferation Approaches

At present, there are multilateral, bilateral, and unilateral arms control and nonproliferation approaches. These approaches are mutually supportive. China supports global regimes in international arms control, as well as nonproliferation treaties under the framework of the United Nations. China also supports regional arms control and nonproliferation regimes, such as nuclear-free zones, the Six-Party Talks, ASEAN dialogues, Shanghai Cooperation Organizations, and other regional security regimes. China also supports trilateral or bilateral regimes or second-track dialogues, such as China-Japan-U.S. and China-U.S. strategic talks. China also supports unilateral force reduction and disarmament.

CONCLUSION

China's arms control and nonproliferation policy has undergone significant changes. The friction over arms control and nonproliferation between China and the United States has transformed into extensive cooperation between the two countries. China and the United States in the past years have established mechanisms of dialogue and crisis management at various levels. Both sides have had good cooperation in handling the DPRK's nuclear program and Iran's highly enriched uranium program. Nevertheless, major differences still exist between the two countries. Both sides need to carry out further dialogue to better understand each other's strategic intentions in order to build trust and confidence.

Recently, China's modernization of its national defense has again caused some concern mainly to the United States and Japan. The release of the "Annual Report on the Military Power of the People's Republic of China" by the U.S. Department of Defense has been delayed because of the exaggeration of China's military build up and its clamor of the "China threat." For the first time, Japan's 2004 White Paper on Defense and the new National Defense Program Outline explicitly names China as the major potential threat to Japan's security, it states, "China has been modernizing its nuclear and missile forces as well as its naval and air forces. Careful deliberation should go into determining whether the objective of this modernization exceeds the scope necessary for the defense of China, and future developments in this area merit special attention."[10]

With the changing international situation, China needs to modernize its lagging national defense solely for defensive purposes. The United States possesses one of the largest nuclear arsenals in the world, engages in revolution in military affairs, lists China as one of its targets of nuclear attacks, provides a nuclear umbrella to allies in Northeast Asia, and strengthens its BMD capabilities. China has to rely on itself to have a credible minimum nuclear deterrent force and an effective conventional force to defend its sovereignty and territorial integrity. China has neither the intention nor the capability to join the arms race. China will continue to be a contributor to world peace and stability and will continue to participate in international arms control and nonproliferation efforts.

Notes

1. Gu Guoliang is Deputy Director and Research Fellow of the Institute of American Studies and Director of the Center of for Arms Control and Nonproliferation Studies, Chinese Academy of Social Sciences.
2. The White House: *The National Security Strategy of the United States of America*, September 2002, 15.
3. "'East Turkistan' Terrorist Forces Cannot Get Away with Impunity," released by Information Office of the State Council of the PRC, January 21, 2002.
4. China's Nonproliferation Policy and Measures, Information office of the State Council of the PRC, December 2003, Beijing, 16–17.
5. Paul Kerr and Wade Boses, "China Seeks to Join Nuclear, Missile Groups," *Arms control Today* 34, no. 2 (March 2004).
6. Joint Declaration of the People's Republic of China and the European Union on Nonproliferation and Arms Control, December 9, 2004.
7. *China's nonproliferation policy and measures,* Information Office of the State Council of the PRC, December 2003, 9.
8. *China's National Defense in 2004*, the State Council Information Office, December 27, 2004, 11.
9. *China's National Defense in 2000*, the State Council Information Office, October, 2000, 13.
10. Outline points overseas for SDF to defend Japan, The Asahi Shimbun, December 11, 2004.

13

ARMS CONTROL AND SINO-U.S. STRATEGIC STABILITY

Brad Roberts

The centrality of arms control in U.S. nuclear strategy was clear in the cold war. Arms control was a tool for coping with instability in the nuclear relationship between the United States and the Soviet Union. After the cold war, arms control has been seen as both a tool for consolidating the new peace (by the Clinton Administration) and as a dangerous restraint on U.S. freedom of action (by the George W. Bush Administration). In the U.S.-China relationship, nuclear arms control has never played a significant role. Should it play such a role? Might it play such a role in the future? To explore answers to these questions, this chapter proceeds as follows. It begins with a short review of the limited current role of arms control in the bilateral relationship. It then examines first Chinese and then U.S. thinking about the potential future of nuclear arms control. The chapter then speculates about how conditions might change leading to a different view in the future of the role of arms control in enhancing strategic stability.[1]

BACKGROUND

During the period of significant arms control innovation in U.S.-Soviet nuclear relations in the 1960s and 1970s, China was deeply isolated from international affairs. Militarily, it was focused on creating a nuclear deterrent that would be effective against both the Soviet

Union and the United States, among others. Only in the 1980s did China begin to participate in multilateral arms control, joining the Law of the Sea in 1982, the Antarctic Treaty and the Outer Space Treaty in 1983, and the International Atomic Energy Agency and Biological and Toxin Weapons Convention in 1984. In 1986 it renounced atmospheric testing of nuclear weapons (although it did not sign the 1963 test ban treaty). Then, in the 1990s, Beijing acceded to the Nuclear Nonproliferation Treaty (NPT), the Chemical Weapons Convention, and the Comprehensive Test Ban Treaty (CTBT).[2]

As both China and the United States are party to the aforementioned treaties, the potential for military competition is somewhat moderated by the multilateral nuclear arms control framework. China has sought to expand the multilateral treaty system and to enhance its constraints on U.S. military developments, especially in outer space. At the same time, the Bush Administration has generally sought to halt the expansion of the treaty regime and to focus on more effective implementation of existing agreements.[3]

The multilateral regime, however, has done little to shape the specific nuclear weapons postures of China and the United States. The effects are of two kinds. First, the Article VI disarmament obligation of the NPT puts a general onus on all nuclear weapon states to end arms races and move toward full eventual implementation. Second, the CTBT inhibits the ability of both China and the United States to deploy new types of military nuclear capabilities with high confidence in their technical efficacy. The question then is whether additional nuclear arms control undertakings outside the multilateral regime are of any value to China and the United States.

CHINA'S ANSWER: NOT YET

China has regularly stated its willingness to join the process of nuclear reductions at some unspecified future time and has conditioned its willingness to do so on deep cuts in the arsenals of the "nuclear superpowers."[4] But the goalposts seem to keep moving. In 1982, China said that it would join nuclear arms control talks only after the United States and Soviet Union halted the testing, manufacturing, and deploying of nuclear weapons and also reduced their arsenals by 50 percent. In 1988, as the Strategic Arms Reduction Treaty (START 1) was being implemented, China modified its position and promised to join the disarmament process not at the 50 percent mark, but only after further "drastic reductions" in the superpower arsenals. In 1995, China stated that it would not accept additional formal nuclear arms control restraints unless the United States and Russia reduced their arsenals far beyond START II numbers, abandoned tactical nuclear weapons, abandoned ballistic missile defenses, and agreed to a joint no first use pledge (NFU). In 1999, President Jiang Zemin restated China's basic position: the United States and Russia should "substantially cut down their respective nuclear arsenals, thereby paving the way for other nuclear weapons states to participate in the multilateral nuclear disarmament process."[5]

Over the last decade the United States and Russia have continued, and indeed accelerated, the process of reducing their nuclear arsenals. But China's position remains unchanged. It continues to press the United States to embrace no first use (just as it continues to press Russia to return to its prior no first use pledge), and it continues to have deep reservations about the pursuit of missile defenses by the United States. The basic logic behind China's "not yet" answer—derived, as it is, from the great disparity in the size of the arsenals of the United States, Russia, and China—is generally accepted among Western nuclear scholars. China's nuclear arsenal has always been very modest quantitatively, especially in comparison to the huge buildup and the competitive and qualitative improvement of U.S. and Soviet arsenals. But the logic of China's evolving answer to "when?" is less generally accepted; indeed, it is seen as a hint to the possibility that China sees no serious possibility of joining the nuclear arms control process beyond its promise for eventual disarmament.

THE GEORGE W. BUSH ADMINISTRATION'S ANSWER: NOT EVER

The Bush Administration's thinking about the future of arms control with China is embedded within its thinking about the future of arms control more generally. The Administration arrived in January of 2001 with a well-formed view that the Anti-Ballistic Missile (ABM) Treaty was a dangerous constraint on the development of the U.S. strategic posture. Other existing treaties such as START I and the Intermediate-range Nuclear Forces Treaty were not seen in the same light, though START I, in particular, came to be seen by the Administration as imposing obligations on the United States (and Russia) that make little sense in the post-cold war setting (such as counting rules). The Administration accepted a new arms control obligation, the Strategic Offensive Reductions Treaty (SORT, or Moscow Treaty), only because it was willing to acquiesce to the strong desire of Russian President Vladimir Putin for some firm U.S. commitment to continue the process of reducing nuclear inventories. The Moscow Treaty obliges the United States and Russia to reduce their deployed nuclear forces by two-thirds—to between 1700 and 2200 warheads—at the end of 2012.

It is useful to elaborate in a bit more detail the strategic vision that led to this set of arms control choices. During its first year in office, the Bush Administration elaborated a "new strategic framework" (its words) encompassing the following main ideas:[6]

- In the language of the Administration's National Security Strategy, there was "an unprecedented opportunity" of historic proportions to put relations among the major powers onto a "new footing," by shifting away from the balance of power as the primary mode of interaction and onto "constructive agendas of cooperation" advancing common interests, common responsibilities, and "increasingly common values."
- Seizing this opportunity required moving the political relationship between Washington and Moscow away from its traditional focus on the military balance of power and problems of nuclear stability. These were the "wrong currency" of bilateral political discourse. It was increasingly important to move nuclear weapons out of the foreground and "into the background" of the evolving political relationship so that the two could stop thinking of each other as enemies.
- The vulnerability of the United States to nuclear-armed ballistic missiles in the hands of "rogue states" was seen as a far more potent threat to stability than the U.S.-Russian nuclear relationship and thus withdrawal from the ABM Treaty was deemed necessary and indeed essential to the new framework. But it was understood that the aggressive pursuit of missile defense would be done in a way that would not put the viability of the Russian deterrent at risk.
- Implementation of START I was seen as desirable and would continue.
- The United States would not become a party to the CTBT but it would sustain a test moratorium unless new reasons emerge to terminate it.

This framework was fully elaborated in the Bush Administration's first year and reflects its critique of the preceding Administration, which it saw as pursuing a wrong-headed focus on the maintenance of Mutual Assured Destruction in combination with an excess of restraint on missile defense and nuclear testing. The Administration emphasized the virtues of flexibility for America in meeting the challenges of an uncertain international environment—a flexibility that would be significantly impaired by arms control. Indeed, the very notion of strategic restraint was anathema to many in the Administration, who argued that restraint contributes to the emergence of new security threats by appeasing challengers and leaving big problems to fester. This antipathy toward restraint became all the more pronounced after 9/11, on the argument that "America was attacked not because it was too strong but because it was too weak."

But the Bush Administration was also sensitive to the view of many critics, not least those in Moscow, where it was seeking to build a partnership, that its "new strategic framework" would damage strategic stability. Accordingly, it elaborated a "strategy for stability" aimed at persuading doubters of the stabilizing benefits of political change in the U.S.-Russian relationship and of denying proliferators the strategic leverage they might seek. In the words of the White House, "We intend to continue working with friends and allies to create a new framework for security and stability that reflects the new strategic environment."[7] This "strategy for stability" emphasized persuasion and dialogue—with Moscow and others. Accordingly, the Administration undertook a major high-level diplomatic effort in the spring and summer of 2001 to make the case around the world that the "new strategic framework" would contribute to stability and not undermine it.

But implementation of this "strategy for stability" was quickly overshadowed by 9/11. Inside the Administration, a very different view of the strategic environment began to take shape. At its most senior levels, the Bush Administration began to talk about "a new balance of power" pitting the forces of international order against the anarchy of those at "the crossroads of tyranny and technology."

China's Place in the Bush Administration's Strategic Concepts

In the new strategic framework, China is conspicuous by its absence. In the strategy for stability, China's place was short-lived. The Bush Administration originally saw no need or opportunity to transform the political relationship with China in the way it did with Russia.

START and SORT were clearly focused on U.S. and Russian arsenals. The Administration thought very little about missile defense or the CTBT as they related to China. China was relevant to this early Bush Administration vision of the strategic environment to the extent that it was deemed a part of the "historic opportunity." Thinking in the Pentagon seemed headed in a different direction, however, as the Quadrennial Defense Review (QDR) of this period seemed to highlight China as a likely future peer competitor who must be dissuaded from choosing confrontation with America.

In contrast, in the "strategy for stability," China had an early place. As the Bush Administration gave its six-month notice of intended withdrawal from the Anti-Ballistic Missile Treaty in December 2001, it offered dialogues to both Moscow and Beijing aimed at sending the message that the new U.S. posture was good for strategic stability. In summer of 2001, the Administration publicly assured China that it sought only a limited missile defense against rogue states and that it did not seek a defense effective against China's nuclear force.[8] But the larger dialogue with Beijing did not get off to a quick start. It was about to begin just as 9/11 occurred. Moreover, the next steps were then held hostage by competing objectives, especially the Administration's effort to get China to stop proliferation behaviors inconsistent with international norms and U.S. preferences. Over time, China's place in this strategy evolved. The Bush Administration pursued a broad agenda of strategic cooperation with China after 9/11, aimed not just at counterterrorism and counterinsurgency in Afghanistan but also at stability and nonproliferation in various Asian subregions (all part of the "constructive agendas of cooperative action"). The acceptance of a leading Chinese role in the Six-Party Talks on the North Korean nuclear issue and the encouragement of China to accept a role as a "responsible stakeholder" in international stability were representative of the Bush Administration's effort to deepen strategic cooperation.

In sum, from the perspective of the Bush Administration, there appears to be no logic for arms control measures in the U.S.-PRC relationship. The ideas guiding its vision of strategic stability simply do not encompass problems in Sino-American strategic relations for which arms control tools might be helpful.

It is important to note, however, that this perspective might have changed had 9/11 and the wars in Afghanistan and Iraq not intervened. The reason is simply that the Administration might have developed further some of its own thinking on how to achieve its political objectives through management of the strategic military relationship. Its thinking is unfinished on two main points.

The first relates to a general theory of arms control. Arms control measures have been criticized by senior members of the Bush Administration as not possible between enemies and not needed between friends. The implication that the strategic landscape divides readily into enemies and friends does not square with the strategic vision reflected in the Administration's own QDRs (and indeed its National Security Strategy), which posit a broad set of enemies and friends but also allies and potential adversaries in a strategic landscape marked above all by uncertainty and unpredictability. The QDRs of 2002 and 2006 made a strong case for the importance of assuring allies and friends and for dissuading potential adversaries and other "rising powers at strategic crossroads." For allies needing assurance and for potential adversaries who might be dissuaded from competition, arms control has functions that simply do not fit into an overly simplified dichotomy between friends and enemies. Allies in East Asia and elsewhere worried about China's military rise and about the possibility of strategic nuclear competition between China and the United States would be reassured by some understanding between Beijing and Washington that mitigates those risks and lends predictability to their security environments.

The second main point relates to dissuasion and how to operationalize it. As the Bush Administration has conceived it, dissuasion is not deterrence. Deterrence relates to the existing intent of some adversary to act and the possibility of inducing the adversary not to act on that intent by threatening the adversary with unacceptable costs. Dissuasion relates to the formation of the intent in the first place. It depends on an adversary calculating that future competition cannot serve its interests because it will not gain an advantage and might lose some current standing. Dissuasion focuses on a choice not yet made but which might plausibly be made for some future competition.

In the China-U.S. nuclear relationship, the choice that China appears not to have made but might yet make is to abandon its posture of nuclear minimalism, whether to sprint to some short-term advantage in the region (that could then be exploited to its advantage in an effort to compel reunification with Taiwan) or to move to a nuclear posture more suited to its future role as a major global power. To dissuade China from choosing such a path, the United States must persuade China that it (the United States) will not exploit Chinese restraint to China's detriment—for example, by exploiting its own power advantages to protect

Taiwan in a bid for formal independence. The implication of this way of thinking about dissuasion is that potential adversaries, like allies and friends, need some form of assurance. Arms control might be useful as a tool of assurance in supporting a dissuasion strategy by promising restraint in exchange for restraint shown.

Looking to the Future: When and How Might "Not Yet" and "Not Ever" Become "Now?"

New leaders in one country or both countries may see the strategic landscape in ways that create new demands for arms control. In the United States, there is considerable uncertainty about what ideas will guide the thinking of the Administration that follows the current one and takes leadership of the executive branch in January 2009. Partisan friction over the theory of arms control masks broad consensus about the value of continued nuclear reductions and the value of strategic stability with China, which suggests some rising interest in how to use arms control toward those ends. In China, the political leadership seems committed to deepening its strategic partnership with the United States and is willing to explore new military-to-military confidence building measures, including in the nuclear domain, toward that end.

But there are many variables other than leadership intent. Four other variables are explored here.

The first is the status and direction of the effort to reduce the nuclear arsenals of the United States and Russia. In 2007, Washington and Moscow appear to have committed themselves to allow START I to lapse when its implementation is complete in 2009 and also to accelerate the SORT targets and to extend the commitment to reductions further into the future. If the intended reductions proceed, decision-makers in both capitals will become increasingly interested in the impact of their deeper reductions on China's nuclear posture. Will China attempt to capitalize on the new opportunity to gain numerical parity? Or will Beijing somehow join in the reductions process even from a starting point of lower numbers? Alternatively, the bilateral U.S.-Russian reductions process could taper off or be halted for some extended period, which would decrease interest in arms control with China but would not lessen interest in how its strategic posture might adapt to changing circumstances.

The second variable is the status of the U.S. project to field the New Triad envisioned in the 2001 Nuclear Posture Review (NPR).

That review envisions reducing U.S. reliance on nuclear weapons by reducing their numbers, while at the same time increasing reliance on nonnuclear strike capabilities and missile defenses to protect itself and its allies from attacks and coercion at the hands of nuclear-armed enemies. That project has moved in fits and starts during the Bush years, and it has become clear that some of the most important transformations in U.S. capabilities will be slower to come and more costly than the authors of the 2001 NPR might have hoped. Despite occasional U.S. protests to the contrary, Chinese experts see the United States as intent on creating the military operational capability to strike preemptively against China's strategic forces by nonnuclear means, to absorb any limited Chinese retaliation in its missile defense, and thus to be free to try to coerce China in times of crisis over Taiwan or elsewhere. These experts see these capabilities as coming rapidly into being, largely because the size and operational characteristics of China's nuclear forces leave them vulnerable to such preemption. U.S. experts have generally seen the threat to China's deterrent as coming into being only in the far longer term. In either case, further U.S. progress in fielding the mix of new offensive and defensive capabilities will intensify, sooner rather than later, the need for U.S. leaders to come to terms with the type of strategic military relationship with China that best serves U.S. interests and what restraint the United States should be prepared to offer—if any—in the development of those capabilities in order to achieve its political objectives.

The third variable is the status of China's own efforts to modernize its strategic force. The 2006 Defense White Paper summarizes its objectives as follows:

> The Second Artillery Force aims at progressively improving its force structure of having both nuclear and conventional missiles, and raising its capabilities in strategic deterrence and conventional strike under conditions of informationization.... The Second Artillery Force is striving to build a streamlined and effective strategic force with both nuclear and conventional capabilities. It is quickening its steps to raise the informationization level of its weaponry and equipment systems, build an agile and efficient operational command and control system, and increase its capabilities of land-based strategic nuclear counterstrikes and precision strikes with conventional missiles. It is improving the construction of its battlefield system, and associated logistics and equipment, and raising the cost-effectiveness of integrated support. It is deepening the reform of training, enhancing integrated training, using scientific and technological achievements to raise training quality. It

is strengthening the safety management and control mechanism of nuclear missiles, and improving the relevant rules and regulations and technical preventive measures as well as emergency steps for handling nuclear accidents.[9]

If past practice is any guide, the deployment of new operational capabilities will be slow and also to some extent undeclared. But the past may be a poor guide, because China's own strategic landscape is different from that of the past. China's leaders may be poised to deploy new capabilities at a pace and scale determined largely by operational improvements to U.S. forces. They may also be poised to deploy these capabilities more rapidly, with the hope that doing so might dissuade the United States from seeking to meet those deployments with major changes to its own force posture. Alternatively, China's leaders may be reluctant to deploy significant new operational capabilities out of concern for inflaming the "China threat school" (those who see China as a clear threat with rapidly advancing military capabilities and rising ambitions) in a way that produces a backlash that drives its East Asian neighbors closer into American arms. These different interests could work for or against arms control.

A final variable is the status of political relations. Will the "moment of historic opportunity" have been well seized, bringing with it the consolidation of major-power peace and restraint envisioned in the 2002 National Security Strategy? In the three-way relationship between the United States, China, and Russia, might relations between two of the powers have deepened at the expense of the third (various configurations are conceivable)? Might we remain in a period of uncertainty and drift? Might there be, from Washington's perspective, a "sell-out" by Beijing or Moscow, as one or the other, or both, "defect" from the US-led world order and act more assertively to counterbalance American influence? If peer adversarial relations return, arms control might play no role—or it might play its former cold war-era role. In contrast, in a deepening major-power peace, arms control might well be unnecessary—though it might be helpful in enhancing a sense of predictability in the new setting. In a period of drift and uncertainty, arms control might be seen as helpful to limit the damage done to political relations by intensifying strategic military competition.

These four variables could combine in the future to increase or decrease the interest of political leaders in both countries to explore arms control approaches to strategic problems in the bilateral relationship. But what problems might they address? Is there a strategic problem? From China's perspective, the answer is a clear "yes." From the perspective of the United States, the problem has not come into clear focus.

From China's perspective, the strategic problem is well demonstrated in the Bush Administration's Nuclear Posture Review and National Security Strategy (NSS). The NPR signals U.S. intent to field a New Triad of capabilities that will put at risk the viability of China's deterrent. The NSS signals U.S. intent to act proactively against "gathering threats," including with the use of preemptive military means. Every reassurance from U.S. leaders that missile defense is "not pointed at China" seems to reinforce the Chinese concern that the United States either does not understand the impact of its new doctrines and capabilities on Chinese interests or is being devious in denying the intent to impact those interests. Accordingly, China's expert community tends to see the modernization of China's strategic posture as necessary to preserve a status quo of mutual vulnerability in the relationship in the face of U.S. efforts to undo this status quo. Some also perceive a dilemma for China here: taking steps to preserve the status quo will consolidate the view in the United States that China seeks to upset the status quo as it rises by exploiting its rising economic power to become a peer nuclear adversary to the United States.

Further, from China's perspective, this strategic problem is not simply a reflection of the thinking of any one administration that is perishable with the next presidential election. China's experts see the U.S. move to a hegemonic position as a natural result of the end of the cold war, its unfettered use of military power as a consequence of the loss of the Soviet counterbalancing influence, and the U.S. desire for improved nonnuclear strategic strike capabilities and also ballistic missile defense as already extant in the 1990s and likely to long outlive the Bush Administration.

From a U.S. perspective, the strategic problem does not have this clear focus. The fact that the Bush Administration's New Strategic Framework treats China as an afterthought is entirely consistent with a U.S. strategic community that worries a fair amount about the rogue state nuclear problem, far less about the U.S. nuclear relationship with Russia, and barely at all about the U.S. nuclear relationship with China. From a U.S. perspective, there are two primary potential problems in the strategic relationship.

The first potential problem is that strategic military relations may develop in ways that undermine political objectives. The political objectives seem clear enough: to deepen strategic partnership by engaging China as a "responsible stakeholder" while also dissuading it from seeking peer adversarial competitions. An intensification of strategic military competition in the offense/defense realm could work against both objectives. That intensification could well result from the twin tracks of strategic modernization being pursued by the United States and China. The United States seeks offense/defense transformation and accordingly continues to field missile defenses as well as improved strategic strike assets, especially conventional ones, and the technical systems for intelligence, surveillance, and reconnaissance that enable those assets to be effective. In parallel, China seeks to "increase," "improve," and "raise" its counterstrike capabilities and accordingly is diversifying its strategic delivery systems, improving its missile defense penetration capabilities, and increasing the number of warheads deliverable in a retaliatory strike (and thus, of course, in a first strike too). The further the two countries move down these pathways, the greater the risk that the force deployments will become interlinked and competitive. The United States will be more inclined to see China as an emerging nuclear threat. China will be inclined to see the United States as seeking to escape the nuclear balance of power in ways that will enable it to again wield nuclear threats as it did in the 1950s. To utilize the language of the Bush Administration, nuclear weapons would come out of the background and into the foreground of the China-U.S. political relationship and become a major currency there. This would be an unfortunate result for an Administration committed to "seizing the historic opportunity" to put major-power relations onto a new footing.

The second potential problem lies in the U.S.-Russian relationship. Russian experts are already worried about the potential for an intensification of China-U.S. strategic military competition.[10] They worry that this competition will induce the United States to develop and deploy the kind of offense and defense capabilities that will ultimately be threatening to the viability of Russia's deterrent. Indeed, some Russians speculate privately that New Triad "hawks" in the United States are trying to motivate a stiff Chinese response to developments in the U.S. posture for the very purpose of motivating U.S. defense planners to make the kinds of New Triad investments that ultimately will give the United States military leverage over Russia. Russia's re-embrace of nuclear weapons in its overall military posture is already well advanced and it is not difficult to conceive of a renewal of more intense efforts to counter the feared future strategic military advantages of the United States. In other words, the strategic problem here is that a failure to dampen incipient problems in the China-U.S. strategic relationship could intensify problems in the U.S.-Russian strategic relationship in a way that would accelerate Russia's return to nuclear competition and undermine lingering hopes for a renewal of strategic partnership based on common interests.

Let us return to the main question: what role might nuclear arms control play in the China-U.S. strategic relationship? Put differently, what is the restraint that might be desired in the strategic behaviors of the major powers? China desires that the United States be restrained in development of the entire New Triad (and, in addition, space superiority) and that the United States maintains its focus as promised on regional adversaries armed with WMD and not on China. The United States desires that China be restrained in deployment of modern nuclear strike systems—and also that it not assist regional powers in acquiring nuclear weapons, their delivery systems, or missile defense penetration aids. These are fundamentally restraints in intentions. As conceived, they are also mutually contingent in nature. That means, each may be prepared to be restrained in the manner desired by the other, but only on the condition that the other offers restraint of the forms it desires.

This suggests a possible role for arms control in the Sino-US relationship: elaboration of the mutual contingent character of restraint in the development of their strategic postures. What intention does each side have for the future strategic military relationship as, and after, current programs of modernization are implemented—the status quo, the status quo ante, or superiority? What is the restraint each might be prepared to offer? What are the conditions of that restraint?

The importance of finding answers to these questions will likely rise as changes occur in the four variables noted above. Reductions in the nuclear forces of the United States and Russia are likely to continue in the coming years, bringing heightened interest in what can be done to help motivate China not to build up as they build down. Force modernization by the United States and China will intensify the possibility of strategic competition of a kind that works against political objectives. The need for strategic partnership seems likely only to intensify as "the long war" unfolds in new dimensions and as common transnational problems in the economy, environment, and so on compel new forms of cooperation.

If China and the United States can find a basis for mutual restraint in the development of their strategic postures, how might this be made politically binding? One possibility is a formal agreement codifying U.S. respect for PRC redlines and vice versa. This seems quite unlikely, however, and for various reasons. One is the multidimensionality of the problem (various forms of offense and defense in East Asia and beyond). Another is that China is extremely reluctant to be drawn into an arms control process and treaty that might consolidate in American eyes a view of the China-U.S. nuclear relationship as adversarial and cold war-like. Another possible mechanism would be to bring China into a broad cap on deployed nuclear weapons encompassing also the United States and Russia. This might be more plausible if France and Britain were also parties—and such multilateral approaches have been of interest to China historically. But there seems little basis currently for thinking that the five original nuclear weapon states have a common vision of how restraint among them can best be expressed internationally.

If formal mechanisms seem unlikely, informal ones might seem more appealing. Toward this end, the Bush Administration or a likeminded successor could be more explicit about how China fits in the "new strategic framework," could say more about what it is prepared to do to assure China that developments in the U.S. strategic posture will not be tailored to China's disadvantage, and could be more explicit that it will not allow others in the U.S. government to interpret Chinese efforts to maintain the status quo ante as signaling a Chinese commitment to upset the status quo ante. A different administration, starting with a different view of what strategic stability requires globally, might find different routes to anticipate potential future buildups and mitigate the factors that could lead to them. Think of this as anticipatory threat reduction.

Future Prospects

There are many reasons to think that the prospects for informal arms control are fairly good. The leaders of both countries have endorsed nuclear dialogue as a way to help build confidence and consolidate desirable changes in the political relationship. In April 2006, Presidents Bush and Hu made a commitment to such dialogue as one of three military-to-military confidence building measures. Moreover, the two countries already exercise a great deal of restraint in the development of their strategic postures toward one another. The sources of competition are incipient; there is no arms race—yet. In addition, the progress in creating and implementing multilateral arms control regimes involving China and the United States has helped to create the foundation on which further bilateral restraint might be built.

But there are also reasons to think that the prospects are fairly poor. The promised strategic dialogue has proven difficult to start, thus repeating prior experience of both the Clinton and Bush Administrations. Yet, without dialogue, neither side can know what types of restraint the other desires or is prepared to offer. Moreover, in the United States, thinking about China as a strategic problem—one requiring the integrated application of the soft and hard tools of American power—remains significantly underdeveloped. Policy is driven by largely unresolved competing instincts about engaging China and preparing for the worst. It is important also to note that U.S. capacities for the development of new concepts and approaches to arms control have been significantly reduced after a long period of disinterest and indeed antipathy in high levels of government.

Conclusions

Arms control has not played a central role in the strategic military relationship between the United States and China. But it might yet. Sooner or later, as U.S. and Russian reductions proceed, China will have to stop saying "not yet." Sooner or later, the strategic problems inherent in the ongoing modernization of Chinese and U.S. strategic forces will gain sufficient visibility and generate sufficient concern to motivate interest in avoiding military results that damage political objectives. Recognition in the United States that there are potential problems in the strategic military relationship requiring serious attention ought to help motivate some new thinking about how to manage that relationship. Any mutual understanding of the sources of reciprocal restraint will itself be a version of informal arms control. To the extent leaders perceive that restraint as perishable, they will pose new questions about whether more formal mechanisms can lend certainty and predictability to the strategic relationship. This means that arms control is likely to be on the Sino-U.S. agenda in the future even if it has not been there before and is not there today.

Notes

1. The views expressed here are the personal views of the author and should not be attributed to his employer or any of its sponsors.

2. See Walter C. Clemens, Jr., "China," in *Encyclopedia of Arms Control and Disarmament*, ed. Richard Dean Burns (New York: Charles Scribner's Sons, 1993), 59–74.
3. For more on shifting U.S. priorities, see Avis Bohlen, "The Rise and Fall of Arms Control," *Survival* 45, no. 3 (2003), 7–34; and "Reshaping U.S. Nonproliferation Strategy, An Interview with Undersecretary of State Robert Joseph," *Arms Control Today* 36, no. 5 (June 2006), 18–22.
4. See Clemens, "China."
5. Chinese President Jiang Zemin, remarks to the Conference on Disarmament, March 26, 1999.
6. See Remarks by the President to Students and Faculty at National Defense University, May 1, 2001.
7. See "Administration Missile Defense Papers," White House, July 11, 2001.
8. See "U.S., China to Discuss Missile Defense," White House Press Release, September 4, 2001, which included the following: "Our consultations with China will make clear that the U.S. missile defense program does not threaten China but seeks to counter limited missile threats from rogue states and the danger of accidental or unauthorized launches. Only those foreign parties with hostile intent toward the United States have grounds to fear U.S. missile defense."
9. Information Office of the State Council, *China's National Defense in 2006* (Beijing, P.R.C., December 29, 2006).
10. Dmitri Trenin, *Russia's China Problem* (Moscow: Carnegie Center Moscow, 1999). See also Alexander Pikayev, "The Rise and Fall of Start II: The Russian View," Working Paper, Carnegie Endowment Nonproliferation Project, Washington, D.C., November 6, 1999.

14

Comparing Perspectives: Dangers to Avoid, Prospects to Develop

Christopher P. Twomey

The previous chapters present perspectives on strategic nuclear issues between the United States and China that at times differ widely, although some interesting areas of commonality do exist. Overall, it is clear that most analysts see some grounds for concern in the nuclear relationship itself. These worries are compounded when potential differences in national interest are considered on issues such as the status of Taiwan, normalization of Japan, evolution of the U.S.-Japan and U.S.-Korean alliances, and other U.S. partnerships in the region (Singapore, Philippines, etc.). This is a dangerous combination: instability in strategic affairs and potential conflicts of national interest. The latter is a challenging one to address, and this chapter does not attempt to do so. However, there are aspects of the strategic instability that can be addressed, and it is here that analysts and policymakers ought to focus their attention.

This final chapter will begin by summarizing the key findings of each chapter. Thereafter, it will step back to assess the key differences in perception among them and evaluate the implications of these differences.

Summary of the Volume

This author's introduction in the first chapter in section I began by highlighting the context of Sino-American strategic relations. Both sides are engaged in extensive modernization, which has raised the prospects of instability in their bilateral relationship due to windows of opportunity and vulnerability for the two sides. Underlying conflicts of interest can exacerbate threat perceptions, making the windows of vulnerability particularly dangerous. Finally, that chapter surveyed the overall changes in the nuclear arena in the twenty-first century, noting the dangers of proliferation, the rise of nuclear multipolarity, and the diversification of strategic weapons (offensive, defensive, conventional with strategic effects, etc.). All of these greatly complicate the contemporary system.

David Welch began the second chapter arguing for the importance of disciplined learning from history and suggesting that the Cuban missile crisis, properly understood, has important lessons for contemporary Sino-American relations. Most importantly, he warned, "We do not 'manage' nuclear crises so much as weather them."[1] Welch provided a rigorous framework for analyzing crises, noting the existence of distinct stages in any crises with unique opportunities for successful management. After applying this to the Cuban Missile Crisis, he described the lessons it holds for contemporary Sino-American nuclear relations.

The next six chapters of section II offered paired perspectives that compare national views on strategic context, national security priorities, and nuclear doctrines. The first of these chapters (chapter 3) presented an American perspective on the strategic context within which nuclear weapons issues exist, finding much grounds for optimism. Michael May began by surveying the overall balance of power between the United States and China before turning to a broad characterization of the nuclear balance between the two. He characterized the latter as primarily shaped by a Chinese decision to avoid an arms race with the United States. He argued that this relationship would be relatively stable in strategic terms by surveying the makeup of the forces, the geographic setting, the relevant alliance relationships, the domestic politics in China and the United States, and the nature of the overall economic relationship. He argued for a rather minimalist view of the utility of nuclear weapons, emphasizing deterrence as their primary function, if not the sole one. He also evaluated the potential for international regimes to change this core stability, but found little reason for concern there.

The parallel chapter from the Chinese perspective, authored by Major General (retd.) Pan Zhenqiang, began its assessment of the Chinese perceptions by evaluating the way nuclear weapons were conceived of during the cold war, noting the importance of bipolarity and the centrality of nuclear weapons in that era. General Pan charted the importance of the nuclear balance, deterrence, nonproliferation efforts, and arms control to the cold war, and argued that many of these had a mixed legacy from that period. Turning to the post–cold war era, Pan noted the importance of global changes, but also argued for a number of factors unique to the nuclear arena. He argued that nearly all world powers have increased the role of nuclear weapons in their security planning and discussed the new challenges posed by regional nuclear powers. He concluded with an appeal for renewed efforts at nuclear disarmament.

Moving from the general strategic context of nuclear issues to more focused national perspectives on the sources of national strategic policy, Michael Nacht's chapter surveyed the important changes facing the United States today, highlighting the dangers of proliferation, radical Islam, and the rise of China. He then surveyed the evolution of U.S. strategic policy from the Clinton Administration to date, and the relations between the United States and the other great powers. He concluded by arguing for the declining relevance of mutual assured destruction as a conceptual guide for policy today, with particular emphasis on the Sino-American relationship and an evaluation of recent American policy toward China, noting both positive and negative elements.

Jia Qingguo provided a comparative chapter on the sources of Chinese policy. He began his chapter by surveying the core elements of China's stated strategic policy, including, but not limited to, minimum deterrence, security assurances, and opposition to the missile defense system. However, he went on to note the existence of important debates within China over these core elements. While emphasizing that there is no shift in China's policy, he summarized the arguments held by some Chinese that China's arsenal size is too small and that its "no first use" policy is anachronistic. Jia argued that the final resolution of this debate will occur at some point in the future and will depend on interaction between China's policy and that of other players.

The final two chapters in this section focused on nuclear doctrines and postures. James Wirtz evaluated the Bush Administration's nuclear policy as it pertains to China. He focused on the leaked portions of the Nuclear Posture Review (NPR) conducted in 2001 and summarized the key changes that were proposed. However, as he detailed, many of the proposals in the NPR were not implemented.

Indeed, he characterized American modernization efforts as facing deep political challenges within the beltway in Washington. Further, and contrary to Chinese perceptions, Wirtz argued, "Chinese nuclear capabilities have only exerted a minor influence on U.S. strategic policy."[2] Nevertheless, he highlighted a number of potential dangers in the relationship that warrant careful attention lest they lead to unanticipated escalation or conflict.

Senior Colonel Yao Yunzhu authored the parallel chapter summarizing Chinese nuclear operational concepts. Her chapter began by emphasizing the consistency of Chinese declaratory nuclear policy, with core elements of no first use; maintenance of limited, retaliatory capabilities; and diplomatic endeavors to reduce the importance of nuclear weapons. She went on to explicitly describe Chinese policy using terminology familiar from Western academic debates on the subject: strategic deterrence rather than operational and tactical utility; retaliatory rather than denial deterrence; central rather than extended deterrence; general rather than immediate deterrence; defensive rather than offensive deterrence; and minimum rather than limited or maximum deterrence. Turning to the environment China finds itself in, she characterized the situation as improving despite a number of complicated challenges, such as Taiwan and missile defense. She expected a continuation of past policy so long as prevailing conditions exist.

Next, in section III, the book surveyed the two nations' perspectives on regional challenges as they pertain to strategic nuclear issues and potential policies that can help address both these regional threats and the other broader concerns within Sino-American strategic issues. Rear Admiral Yang Yi authored the first of these chapters. Admiral Yang assessed the dangers stemming from the North Korean proliferation problem. He focused his attention on the potential for Japan to nuclearize, arguing this is a likely concern given Tokyo's own history and concerns about the U.S. nuclear umbrella. He discussed Japanese technological prowess, highlighting its ability to cross the threshold quickly. Yang also discussed South Korea's potential to cross the nuclear threshold. He concluded by discussing a range of options to check the North Korean potential to nuclearize, arguing that a reinvigoration of the Six-Party Talks is the optimal solution.

Next, Dr. Shen Dingli addressed the Sino-Indian relationship, which he argued is in the process of improving. He noted that historic legacies have not been positive and recognized the link between China and the Indian nuclear tests. He noted, "They [India and China] cannot talk officially about their nuclear relationship, but to some extent each watches the nuclear policy of the other in shaping its own."[3] Nevertheless, he argued that many factors have led to an improvement in the relationship. Shen also surveyed a number of specific elements in the relationship, including India's bid for a UN Security Council seat, the Sino-Indian border dispute, the broad strategic partnership initiative, and the economic relationship. In each of these areas, he found grounds for an optimistic perspective regarding the future of the relationship. In the security realm, too, he saw reasons for a positive view, although that required an explicitly narrow set of assumptions. He highlighted a range of factors that may contribute to strategic stability between the two nations, although he also noted the presence of potential problems, given China's relationship with Pakistan.

Scott Snyder offered a final perspective on regional issues, addressing the most problematic issue in East Asia. In his survey of the recent history of the North Korean nuclear crisis, he began with a discussion of the crisis on the peninsula in the early 1990s and characterizes the 1994 Agreed Framework as one of tacit acceptance of North Korean nuclear capacity. He then summarized the events of the recent crisis and noted the recent moves toward addressing it. Snyder then turned toward consideration of several possible future scenarios for North Korea, both with and without nuclear weapons, and examined their effects on regional affairs. He argued that Sino-American cooperation through the Six-Party Talks has not only made a positive contribution to addressing the North Korean problem but also led to positive externalities in the relationship between the two great powers.

The final two chapters in the volume turn to consider the prospects for resolving some of the problematic issues raised in the earlier chapters. Gu Guoliang provided an overview of Chinese nonproliferation and arms control policies with regard to strategic weapons. He argued that this aspect of Chinese foreign policy has increased in recent years, in the wake of China's rise and the end of the cold war. Perhaps even more importantly, he argued that China has increasingly found a comfort level with international arms control agreements as a form of foreign policy, and he highlighted this through several examples. He argued that an active arms control policy will continue to remain at the heart of Chinese strategic policy and that it could strongly contribute to the enhancement of regional and global stability.

Brad Roberts presented a sharply contrasting view. He described the Bush Administration's substantial shift in thinking regarding nuclear affairs embodied in the "new strategic framework" that included an antipathy toward such formal arms control. He further noted that some elements of that view will persist in American views toward arms control in the future, regardless of future domestic political changes. Roberts argued that the core issue shaping the prospects for future arms control between China and the United States is what degree of restraint each side is willing to offer the other. However, he also highlighted several additional factors: leadership intent in each country following domestic political changes, the future of Russian-U.S. agreements on nuclear weapons, the status of American modernization under the rubric of the new strategic triad and China's own modernization and potential buildup of its forces, and finally the broader Sino-American relationship. The interaction among these will do much to shape the nuclear relationship between Beijing and Washington.

Comparing Perspectives and Evaluating their Implications

Spanning across these chapters, a number of interesting perspectives arise. At one level, both nations feel deeply threatened. For the United States, the threat of terrorism manifests in the nuclear arena through an emphasis on steps to check proliferation and reduce the benefits of proliferation by developing strategies aimed at facing the emerging nuclear powers. This proliferation emphasis pervades the chapters discussing American policies. Chinese authors, too, found grave threats in the strategic sphere. While occasionally mentioning terrorism, for China these threats lie more on the emerging multipolar nuclear environment and on the U.S. side's modernization and status as the leading global power. Disturbingly, this is a notable contrast from the way many American's view China's security situation, suggesting that this factor is likely to be an enduring source of tension between the two. More positively, both sets of threat perceptions push the two countries toward a common concern with proliferation, suggesting that this can be an important area for cooperation, as discussed below.

In the case of other differences, there is even less of a silver lining. There continues to be a wide difference in understanding the core utility of nuclear weapons: deterrence. Chinese authors universally express views that depend on an existential view of nuclear deterrence. Thus, even the prospect of a small number of weapons detonating against an adversary is viewed as being sufficient to deter its action.

Most Americans hold that (although there is debate on this point) successful deterrence require a much more substantial *probability* of a much larger *quantity* of retaliation. This is a dangerous difference in perception since it colors Chinese assessments of the sufficiency of the American arsenal. It may also lead the United States to downplay Chinese signals of intentions in a crisis.

Similarly, deep differences remain in how each side views recent changes in the other's arsenal. For instance, Chinese analysts frequently refer to leaked official documents, such as at the Nuclear Posture Review, to infer about American doctrine and intentions. These, and other documents from the Strategic Command, suggest to the Chinese that the United States has at heart an offensive nuclear doctrine, and that its nuclear arsenal is ever more important in America's overall security strategy. However, American analysts emphasize a much more diverse set of political inputs in the policy-making process and come to very different conclusions than do the Chinese.

On the other hand, American views of Chinese policy raise questions about the depth with which the "No First Use" policy is held and the likely future trajectory of Beijing's arsenal. Chinese analysts as a group have very different views on these points, although there are some debates apparent in the chapters above (see, in particular, the views held by Professor Jia compared to those held by Senior Colonel Yao).

Underlying these and other differences is a persistent difficulty in the basic terminology used in nuclear affairs. For instance, the Chinese term usually used to describe China's own deterrence policy means literally "to counter military intimidation." The closest analogue to the term "deterrence" itself contains a strong element of coercion or compellence.[4] While this linguistic issue is well understood by American Sinologists and some Chinese specialists in U.S. security policy, it still colors the language used between the two sides in ways that have a subtle, but negative, effect on deliberation between the two sides. This issue of phrasing undermines any discussion of the positive aspects of a situation characterized by a "secure second strike potential for both sides." While such concepts are familiar to American analysts, and even comfortable to many, to Chinese ears these concepts are tainted.

While the fundamental difference in terminology is apparent in the chapters of this volume, in other areas there is an increasingly shared vocabulary. The chapters by Yao and Jia in particular describe strategies using terminology that is easily understood from an American strategic perspective (even though there are still substantive differences between their views and those held by Americans).

Turning to issues of policy, again there is a diverse pattern of agreement and difference. In several of the chapters, there appears a confluence of views on the dangers of the North Korean nuclearization and regional proliferation. This issue had not been one of their shared views in recent years, and likely accounts for the positive successes of the Six-Party Talks, such as they are. One question for the future will be about the extent to which this shared view can be used to lead to useful policy coordination between China and the United States on broader proliferation issues. In these chapters there is also a surprising degree of tolerance for the goals and approaches of the Proliferation Security Initiative. While there are certainly aspects of that program viewed with suspicion in Beijing, it is also clear that this is an area of potential cooperation between the two great powers.[5]

Finally, as discussed above, the United States' national missile defense program is viewed as deeply threatening in Beijing. While this comes across in several of the chapters on Chinese nuclear policy, there is a notable shift away from this aspect being viewed in primarily bilateral terms. That shift is an important one and bodes well for Sino-American relations narrowly, but it also increases the complexity of regional affairs: a number of concerns are raised regarding the potential use of missile defense systems by third parties, such as Japan and Taiwan. Clearly, these concerns are not trivial, but they are declining in importance in Sino-American relations.

The core theme that was the motivation for this volume highlighted the potential dangers of dyadic nuclear relations regardless of the broader degree of stability within the relationship. Even in the context of minimal competition for leadership—a circumstance that may, or may not, characterize Sino-American relations in the coming decade—strategic stability can be tenuous. There are clearly deep differences in the mutual understanding about each side's nuclear doctrine. Strategic concerns are sharply different, as are perceptions of the utility of arms control mechanisms to resolve them. On the other hand, there are important shared views about the dangers of proliferation, particularly over North Korea. Through evaluation of these similarities and differences, policymakers and analysts will come to a deeper understanding of this relationship, which is the most critical nuclear relationship in the twenty-first century. It is possible that future cooperation between the two sides on marginal issues can be further improved. Although this will not resolve the broader differences outlined above—on Taiwan, Japan, and the U.S.'s status in the region—it will reduce the prospect of misperception or inadvertent escalation. This narrow goal is perhaps the best that can be hoped for in the short and medium term.

Notes

1. See chapter 2.
2. See chapter 7.
3. See chapter 10.
4. For a useful description of this and related linguistic points, see Medeiros, Evan S. "Evolving Nuclear Doctrine," in *China's Nuclear Future*, ed. Paul J. Bolt and Albert S. Willner (Boulder, CO: Lynne Rienner, 2006).
5. For further discussion on both these points, see Christopher P. Twomey, "Explaining Chinese Foreign Policy toward North Korea: Navigating between the Scylla and Charybdis of Proliferation and Instability," *Journal of Contemporary China* 17, no. 55 (forthcoming, 2008).

CONTRIBUTORS

Christopher P. Twomey is assistant professor of National Security Affairs and codirector of the Center for Contemporary Conflict at the Naval Postgraduate School in Monterey, California. He writes on international security, strategic culture, perceptions and misperceptions, Asian security, and Chinese foreign policy. He previously coedited (with Susan Shirk) *Power and Prosperity: Economics and Security Linkages in Asia-Pacific* (Transaction/Rutgers, 1996) and has authored numerous book chapters. His articles have appeared in *Security Studies, Asian Survey, Journal of Contemporary China*, and *Current History*, among others.

David A. Welch is professor of political science and director of the Trudeau Centre for Peace and Conflict Studies at the University of Toronto. His research interests include international relations theory, international security, decision making, and ethics and international affairs.

Michael May is professor emeritus (research) in the Stanford University School of Engineering and a senior fellow with the Center for International Security and Cooperation of the Freeman-Spogli Institute for International Studies at Stanford University. He is also director emeritus of the Lawrence Livermore National Laboratory. He is a member of the Council on Foreign Relations and the Pacific Council on International Policy, and a fellow of the American Physical Society and the American Association for the Advancement of Science.

Major General (retd.) Pan Zhenqiang is deputy chairman of China's Foundation of International Studies. He is also director and professor of Research Institute for Strategy and Management, the Central University of Finance and Economics, Beijing, China; and executive councilor, China Reform forum. Maj. Gen. (retd.) Pan Zhenqiang is also former director of the Institute of Strategic Studies at the National Defense University of China.

Dr. Michael Nacht is the dean and professor of public policy at the Goldman School of Public Policy at the University of California, Berkeley. Nacht recently completed a three-year term as a member of the U.S. Department of Defense Threat Reduction Advisory Committee, for which he chaired panels on counterterrorism and counter proliferation of weapons of mass destruction, reporting to the deputy secretary of defense. He continues to consult with Los Alamos and Lawrence Livermore National Laboratories on national security and homeland defense.

Professor Jia Qingguo is professor and associate dean of the School of International Studies at Beijing University. He has published extensively on U.S.-China relations; relations between the Chinese mainland and Taiwan; Chinese foreign policy; as well as Chinese politics. He is a member of the editorial board of *Journal of Contemporary China* (USA); *Political Science* (New Zealand); *International Relations of the Asia-Pacific* (Japan); and *China Review* (Hong Kong). He is also vice president of the China Association for Asia-Pacific Studies, board member of the China Association of American Studies, and board member of the National Taiwan Studies Association.

James J. Wirtz is a professor of National Security Affairs, Naval Postgraduate School, Monterey California. During 2005–2007 he served as the president of the International Security and Arms Control Section of the American Political Science Association.

Dr. Yao Yunzhu is director of the Asia-Pacific Office at the Department of World Military Studies, Academy of Military Science, China. She holds a doctoral degree in strategic studies from the Academy of Military Science, and is member of the 10th National People's Congress. Dr. Yao's research interests include deterrence theory and Northeast Asian regional security affairs. She is a senior colonel in the People's Liberation Army.

Rear Admiral Yang Yi is deputy director general of the Institute of Strategic Studies at the National Defense University of China. He joined the Chinese Navy in 1968 and has spent his military career in various capacities, including director of Foreign Affairs Bureau of Navy, instructor of Surface Warfare Training Center of East Sea Fleet, and naval attaché of the Chinese Embassy in Washington, D.C.

Dr. Shen Dingli is a professor of international relations at Fudan University, is Executive Dean of International Studies and director of Center for American Studies at Fudan. He has a Ph.D. in physics and has consulted for the UN Secretary General on strategic planning. Dr. Shen works on China-US security and nuclear relationship, regional and international security, nonproliferation, as well as foreign and defense policy of China and the US. He publishes widely in China and abroad.

Scott Snyder is a senior associate in the International Relations program of The Asia Foundation and Pacific Forum CSIS, and is based in Washington, D.C. He spent four years in Seoul as Korea representative of The Asia Foundation during 2000–2004. Previously, he has served as a program officer in the Research and Studies Program of the U.S. Institute of Peace, and as acting director of The Asia Society's Contemporary Affairs Program. His publications include *Paved With Good Intentions: The NGO Experience in North Korea* (2003) (coedited with L. Gordon Flake) and *Negotiating on the Edge: North Korean Negotiating Behavior* (1999).

Dr. Gu Guoliang is the deputy director of the Institute of American Studies at the Chinese Academy of Social Science (CASS). From 1990 to 1995, he worked as counselor of the Chinese delegation to the UN Conference on Disarmament in Geneva. He founded and has been director of the Center for Arms Control and Nonproliferation Studies. He is also a professor at CASS and has been a visiting fellow with the Henry Stimson Center, the Monterey Institute of International Studies (United States), and Hong Kong University.

Brad Roberts is a member of the research staff at the Institute for Defense Analyses in Alexandria, Virginia. He is also an adjunct professor at George Washington University and a member of the executive board of the U.S. committee of the Council for Security Cooperation in the Asia Pacific. Dr. Roberts is widely published on issues of international security and weapons of mass destruction and has played a leading role in unofficial international dialogues on nuclear weapons issues.

Index

9/11 (attacks), 63, 73, 77, 93, 134, 146–147, 174, 189–190

Afghanistan, 67, 76–77, 79–80, 146, 148, 190
Aircraft, 24–25, 102, 114
  MiG interceptors, 24
  F-102A interceptors, 24
Al Qaeda, 67
Antiballistic missiles (ABM), 43
  See also: Missile defense
Anti-Ballistic Missile (ABM) Treaty, 59, 76–79, 93, 119, 187–188
Anti-Satellite (ASAT), 7, 10
Antisubmarine Warfare (ASW), 22
Anti-Submarine, 22, 26
Argentina, 66
Arms Control, 9, 45, 60–61, 65, 90, 119, 127, 132, 134–135, 145, 173–208
Arms Race, 3, 5–7, 43, 52, 58–62, 89, 93–94, 96, 106–107, 132, 173, 175, 181–182, 184, 186, 198, 202
Arsenal
  Conventional, 4–5, 193
  Nuclear, 4–6, 9, 33, 58–59, 66, 69, 74, 87–89, 91, 94–107, 112, 115, 118, 120–122, 128–131, 145, 157–158, 164, 181, 184, 186–192, 203, 207
  Strategic, 3, 5–7
Atomic (bomb), 57–58, 111, 128, 131, 153

Australia Group, 178

Balkans, 76
Ballistic missiles, 5–6, 10, 43, 59, 65, 76, 82–83, 87, 89, 93, 95, 107, 119, 177, 181, 187–189, 195
  DF-5 ballistic missiles, 43
  DF-4 ballistic missiles, 43
  See also: Intercontinental Ballistic Missiles (ICBM)
  See also: Liquid-fueled missiles
Ban Ki-moon, 165
Banco Delta Asia (BDA), 168
Baruch Plan, The, 58
Belarus, 76
Bilateral
  Agreements, 55, 176, 176, 183
  Relationship, 3, 81, 85, 108, 115, 137, 141–146, 149–150, 165–167, 185–188
  Security, 9, 60, 115, 134, 167–168, 194–199, 202, 208
  Stability, 8, 69
bin Laden, Osama, 74
Biological and Toxin Weapons Convention, 186
Bipolarity, 58, 63, 66, 116–117, 203
Blair, Prime Minister Tony, 80
Bolshakov, Georgi, 22, 24
Bombers, 5, 74
Bosnia, 76
Brazil, 66

Brooks, Amb. Linton, 98
  See also: Department of Energy
    (DOE)
  See also: Harvey, John
  See also: National Nuclear
    Security Administration
    (NNSA)
Bush, President George W., 32,
  65, 73, 75, 77–79, 84, 93–99,
  107, 119, 149, 165–166, 174,
  185–205

Castro, President Fidel, 26
Chechnya, 78–79, 91
Chemical Weapons Convention
  (CWC), 61, 177–178, 186
Chemical Weapons Convention
  Office (CWCO), 177
Cheney, Vice President Dick, 77
Civilian nuclear energy / reactors,
  145, 149
Clinton, President William (Bill),
  76–77, 79–82, 149, 152,
  154–155, 159, 174, 185,
  199, 203
Cold War, 4, 6, 8, 10, 16, 42,
  44, 47–51, 57–64, 73, 76,
  80–81, 94–95, 97–99, 103,
  107, 111, 115–117, 120–122,
  142, 145–146, 154, 170,
  173–175, 179, 185, 187,
  194–195, 198, 203, 205
Collective security, 61, 168
Command and Control (C2), 5, 16,
  18, 31, 95, 103, 167, 193
Comprehensive Test Ban Treaty
  (CTBT), 61, 76, 178, 181, 186,
  188, 190
Confidence and security-building
  measures (CSBMs), 32–33
Containment, 101, 174
Counterforce targeting, 115
Counterterrorism (CT), 80, 134, 190
Cuba / Cuban Missile Crisis, 2, 13,
  15–33, 49, 202

Dai Bingguo, 141
Defense Support Program, 6
Deng Xiaoping, Secretary General,
  CPC, 114–115, 119
Demilitarized Zone (DMZ), 155
Department of Energy (DOE), 159
  See also: Brooks, Amb. Linton
  See also: Harvey, John
  See also: National Nuclear
    Security Administration
    (NNSA)
Deterrence, 8–10, 17, 19–22, 24,
  27–31, 41, 44–46, 52, 55,
  59–62, 80, 87, 89–90, 94–96,
  102, 105, 111, 113–118,
  120–122, 145, 149, 157, 191,
  193, 202–204, 206–207
Dirty bomb, 67
Disarmament, 60–61, 65, 68–69,
  87, 89, 113, 127, 132, 134–135,
  145, 183, 186–187, 203
Dissuasion, 94, 191–192
Domino effect, 127–128, 155

East Turkestan Islamic/
  Independence Movement
  (ETIM), 146, 149
England, 53, 68, 89, 182
EP-3 incident, 16

"Few but effective" (jinggan
  youxiao), 112
First-use, 65, 82–83, 112,
  116
  See also: No First Use (NFU)
Fissile material, 145, 156, 158–161,
  181
"Five Principles of Peaceful
  Co-existence," 142
Force posture, 4, 194
France, 53, 68, 80, 89, 182,
  198
Freeman, Amb. Chas, 82
Full-scope safeguards (FSS), 146,
  149–150

Gandhi, Mahatma, 143
Germany, 42, 53, 68, 73–74, 80
Global Posture Review, 43
Global war on terror (GWOT), 73, 79, 93
Globalization, 48, 63, 180
Graphite reactor, 154
See also: Nuclear reactor
See also: Light Water reactor
Gross domestic product (GDP), 139, 181
Guam, 43
Gulf War, 104, 154

Haiti, 76
Harvey, John, 98–99, 103
See also: Brooks, Amb. Linton
See also: Department of Energy (DOE)
See also: National Nuclear Security Administration (NNSA)
Highly Enriched Uranium (HEU), 66, 183
Hu Jintao, President, 13, 198
Hu Xiaodi, Amb., 88
Human intelligence (HUMINT), 22–23
Hussein, Saddam, 77–78, 104, 154
Hydrogen bomb, 131

India, 6, 16, 49, 55, 66, 74, 80–81, 84, 107, 117–118, 121–122, 128, 137–150, 204–205
Information warfare (IW), 31
Intercontinental ballistic missiles (ICBM), 5–6, 25, 43, 83
DF-31 ICBM, 83
DF-31A road mobile ICBM, 83
Minuteman III land-based missiles, 5
See also: Ballistic Missiles
See also: Launch-on-Warning Doctrine

See also: Liquid-fueled missiles
See also: Maneuverable reentry vehicles (MaRV)
See also: Road-Mobile Missiles
International Atomic Energy Agency (IAEA), 150, 154–156, 159, 162, 167, 182, 186
Iran, 9, 54–55, 58, 66, 68, 74–75, 77, 79, 81, 90, 127, 183
Iraq, 32, 47, 49, 68, 74, 77–78, 80, 90, 93, 97, 104, 146–148, 154–155, 190
Islam, 49, 74, 80–81, 84–85, 127, 145–146, 148–149, 203
Israel, 75, 81, 138, 146

Japan, 3–4, 6, 8–9, 13, 42–43, 48–49, 54, 75–76, 80, 84–85, 106, 118, 120, 128–131, 139–141, 153, 155, 162–170, 182–183, 201, 204, 208, 209
Hiroshima, 44, 57, 131
Nagasaki, 44, 57
Jiang Zemin, President, 142, 187
Jihad, 74, 84
Joint military exercises, 137, 147
Junichiro Koizumi, Prime Minister, 139

Kashmir, 16
Kazakhstan, 76
Kennedy, John F., 17–18, 20, 24, 26, 31, 33
Kenya
Nairobi, 76
Khan, A. Q., 68, 81, 160
Khrushchev, Premier Nikita, 17–18, 22–26, 33
Korea, North aka Democratic Peoples Republic of Korea (DPRK), 3, 7, 9, 45–46, 49, 54, 75–77, 84–85, 90, 107–108, 117, 127, 129, 140, 153–170, 176, 204–205, 208

Korea, South aka Republic of Korea (ROK), 43, 48–49, 74, 80, 85, 107, 118, 128, 131, 140, 155, 165, 204
Korean Peninsula, 28–30, 66–67, 84, 90, 106, 107, 129, 131–133, 176, 201
Korean Peninsula Energy Development Organization (KEDO), 156
Korean War, 153, 170
Kosovo, The Republic of, 73
Kuwait, 104

Launch-on-Warning Doctrine, 5
Li Jijun, 87
Libya, 13, 68
Light-Water reactor, 150, 155–156, 158
See also: Nuclear reactor
See also: Graphite reactor
Line of actual control (LAC), 140
Liquid-fueled missiles, 5
See also: Ballistic missiles
See also: Intercontinental ballistic missiles (ICBM)
London Club, The, 68
Loss of face, 24, 31

Maneuverable reentry vehicles (MaRV), 79
Mao Zedong, Chairman, CPC, 42, 114–119
McNamara, Robert, 13, 15, 81
Military Modernization, 6, 63
Military-to-Military Contact (mil-to-mil), 146
Military spending, 4
Minimum deterrence, 80, 87, 90, 111, 116, 122, 149, 203
Mirror imaging, 17, 21
Misra, Special Representative R.K., 141
Missile Defense System / Program, 5–6, 9, 87, 89–90, 118–121, 132, 203, 208
See also: Antiballistic Missiles (ABM)
Missile silos, 7
Moscow Treaty, 4, 78, 94, 100, 107, 187–188
See also: Strategic Offensive Reductions Treaty (SORT)
Multilateral diplomacy, 7
Mutual Assured Destruction (MAD), 15–16, 33, 59, 81, 95, 189, 203
Mutual Balanced Force Reductions Talks, 60
Multiple Independently Targetable Reentry Vehicle (MIRV), 43

National Intelligence Estimate (NIE), 78
National Nuclear Security Administration (NNSA), 98
See also: Harvey, John
See also: Brooks, Amb. Linton
See also: Department of Energy (DOE)
National Security Strategy, 77, 174, 179, 188, 191, 194–195
Nehru, Prime Minister Jawaharlal, 142
New Strategic Framework, 188–189, 195, 198, 206
No First Use (NFU), 65, 82, 87–88, 91, 112, 123, 134, 144, 181–182, 187, 203–204, 207
See also: First-use
Nonnuclear Weapon States (NNWS), 59–60, 62, 65, 87–90, 112, 182
Non-State Actors, 67–68, 95, 167, 162
Nontraditional Security Threats, 63
"Normal Accident" Theory, 102–103
Normalization, 140, 155, 164, 168, 170, 201

Index

Norms, 19, 25, 46, 55, 63, 65, 163, 190
North Atlantic Treaty Organization (NATO), 58, 60–61, 79, 138
Nuclear Energy, 60, 79, 87, 89, 137, 149, 162, 182
Nuclear-Missile-Carrying Submarine Forces, 4
  Jl-2 submarine-launched ballistic Missiles, 83
  Nuclear-powered submarines carrying nuclear-armed ballistic missiles (SSBN), 5
  Submarine launched ballistic missiles, 5, 83
  Trident II D-5, 5
Nuclear Nonproliferation Regime, 41, 53–54, 60, 62, 66–67, 88, 90, 127, 134–135, 145–146, 155, 170, 173–174, 176–177, 179, 183, 186, 202
Nuclear Nonproliferation Treaty (NPT), 60–62, 65, 67–68, 106, 135, 140, 144, 146, 150, 155–156, 178, 186
Nuclear Posture Review (NPR), 6, 10, 44, 47, 52, 54, 65, 93–94, 192, 195, 203, 207
Nuclear reactor, 55, 150, 154–160, 158
  See also: Light-Water reactor
  See also: Graphite reactor
Nuclear Suppliers Group, 68, 137
Nuclear tests, 9, 97–98, 106–107, 127–128, 132, 140, 156, 159, 161–162, 164–170, 189, 204
Nuclear umbrella, 113, 115–116, 129, 163, 184, 204
Nuclear-Weapon-Free Zone / Nuclear Free Zone Treaty, 88, 134, 182
Nuclear Weapon States (NWS), 59–60, 62, 65, 87–90, 112, 182
Nunn-Lugar-Dominici Cooperative Threat Reduction Program, 79

"One China," 27, 29, 30, 137

Pakistan, 16, 49, 66, 68, 74, 81, 84, 107, 117–118, 128, 137–138, 140, 145–150, 166, 205
Paracels Islands, 13
  See also: Spratly Islands
  See also: South China Sea
Pentagon, 13, 43, 82, 93, 96, 190
People's Liberation Army (PLA), 4, 32, 82, 116
  See also: People's Liberation Army Navy (PLAN)
  See also: Second Artillery
People's Liberation Army Navy (PLAN), 13, 46, 147, 181
  See also: People's Liberation Army (PLA)
  See also: Second Artillery
Philippines, 32, 201
Photo intelligence (PHOTINT), 22–23
Plutonium, 131, 145, 155–156, 158–161
Pokran Nuclear Tests, 140
Positive security assurances, 89
Preemptive strike, 59, 132, 163
Proliferation optimists, 9, 15–16
Proliferation Security Initiative (PSI), 78, 163, 176, 208
Purchasing power parity (PPP), 139
Putin, President Vladimir, 79, 188

Quadrennial Defense Review (QDR), 43, 95, 97, 190–191

Rapprochement, 138, 142
Reactors, 55, 145, 150, 154–156, 159–160
Reagan, President Ronald, 94
Realism, 20, 22, 25, 27, 30, 52, 82, 100–101, 140–143, 148–149
Regimes, 41, 53, 67, 74, 90, 127, 145–146, 173–174, 176 179, 183, 199, 202

Reliable Replacement Warhead
    (RRW), 98, 100
Research and development (R&D),
    97, 132
Responsible stakeholder, 190, 196
Reunification, 7, 118, 180, 191
Revolution in Military Affairs
    (RMA), 31, 63, 184
Rice, former National Security
    Advisor Condoleezza, 77
Road-mobile missiles, 4, 83
Robust Nuclear Earth Penetrator
    (RNEP), 97
Roh Moo Hyun, President, 163
Rumsfeld, Secretary of Defense
    Donald, 77–78, 83
Russia, 5–7, 9, 10, 43, 46, 49, 52, 55,
    65, 69–70, 76, 78–79, 84, 89,
    91, 95–97, 107, 117–118, 122,
    134, 187–192, 194, 195–199,
    206

Safeguards, 13, 17, 25, 61, 88,
    102–103, 133, 146, 149–150,
    156–158, 179–182
Sagan, Scott, 102
Satellites, 4–7, 10–11, 130
Second Artillery, 114, 193
    See also: People's Liberation Army
        (PLA)
    See also: People's Liberation Army
        Navy (PLAN)
Second Strike, 15, 112, 115–117,
    120, 122, 207
Senkaku/Diaoyutai Islands, 13
Severe Acute Respiratory Syndrome
    (SARS), 137, 142
Sha Zukang, 87, 89, 90
Shanghai Cooperation
    Organization (SCO), 146, 183
Signaling / Signals, 16, 19, 21–23,
    26, 28–29, 142, 195, 198,
    207
Signals intelligence (SIGINT), 22–23
Singapore, 83, 201

Singh, Prime Minister Manmohan,
    149
Single-Integrated Operations Plan
    (SIOP), 96
Six-Party Talks, 3, 49, 66, 84, 118,
    127, 132, 133, 154, 157, 167–
    170, 176, 182–183, 190, 204–
    205, 208
Sixteen Character Guideline, 116
South China Sea, 8, 32
    See also: Paracels Islands
    See also: Spratly Islands
Somalia, 76
South Africa, 66
Soviet Union, The (USSR), 16, 20,
    24, 42, 44, 46–49, 58–59,
    62–63, 66, 73–74, 76, 78, 81,
    122, 154, 173–174, 185–186
Space (Outer Space), 6, 10, 16, 65,
    182, 186, 197
Special Representatives, 137, 142
Spratly Islands, 13, 32
    See also: Paracels Islands
    See also: South China Sea
Stockpile Stewardship Program
    (SSP), 76, 98
Strategic Arms Limitation Talks
    (SALT), 59
Strategic Arms Reduction Treaty
    (START), 59, 186–188, 190,
    192
Strategic deterrence, 97, 100, 105,
    113–114, 193, 204
Strategic forces, 3, 7, 10, 43, 193,
    199
Strategic Offensive Reductions
    Treaty (SORT), 4, 78, 94, 100,
    107, 187–188
    See also: Moscow Treaty
Strategic partnership, 117, 138–139,
    141–142, 146, 150, 192,
    196–197, 205
Strategic stability, 8, 41–42, 46,
    48–55, 57, 59–62, 69, 132, 185,
    189–190, 192, 198, 205, 208

Strategic triad, 95–97, 206
Sudan, 76
Switzerland, 68

Tactical nuclear weapons, 65, 187
Taiwan Relations Act, 118
Taliban, 77
Tang Jiaoxun, 61
Tanzania, 76
Terrorism / Counter Terrorism, 4, 43, 67–68, 80, 85, 93, 117, 134, 145–146, 162, 174–175, 190, 206, 212
Three Principles of Non-Nuclearization, 128
Tibet, 138, 141–142
Transparency, 17, 20, 27
Turkey, 17, 22, 24

U-2 incident, 22–24, 26
Ukraine, 74, 76, 79, 133
United Nations, The, 60, 137, 155, 175, 179
United Nations Security Council Resolutions (UNSCR)
UNSCR 1540, 157, 163
UNSCR 984, 89, 112
UNSCR 1718, 162, 165
UNSCR 1695, 163, 165
Unilateral Declaration of Independence (UDI), 15, 26–27, 30–33
USS Cole, 76

Vajpayee, Atal Bihari, 141–143
Vietnam, 29, 31–32

Warsaw Pact, 58, 60–61
Wassenaar Arrangement, 178
Weapons of Mass Destruction (WMD), 63, 77–78, 80, 84, 108, 146, 163–164, 174–175, 179, 182, 197
White Papers, 88–89, 98, 112, 180, 183, 193
World Trade Center, The, 76, 93
World War, 16
World War One (WWI), 51
World War Two (WWII), 27, 42, 51, 129, 139

Xinjiang Uygur Autonomous Region, 175
Xiong Guangkai, General, 82

Yasukuni Shrine, 140

Zangger Committee, 68, 178
Zero sum, 28, 58
Zhou En-lai, Premier, 142
Zhu Chenghu, Major General, 82, 91
Zoelick, Secretary of State Robert, 77